bauhaus

BAUHAUS

bauhaus archiv   magdalena droste

bauhaus
1919–1933

benedikt taschen

Frontispiece: 'Bauhaus' sign on the
Dessau Bauhaus building, around 1930.

Published by the Bauhaus-Archiv Museum für Gestaltung,
Klingelhöferstr. 14, 1 Berlin 30
Responsible: Peter Hahn
Idea: Magdalena Droste

Cover design: Prof. Anton Stankowski, Stuttgart
Layout: Prof. Eckhard Neumann, Frankfurt/Main
Editor and production: Dr. Angelika Muthesius, Cologne
Biographies, bibliography and list of illustrations: Karsten Hintz, Berlin
English translation: Karen Williams, Cologne
Printed in Germany
ISBN 3-8228-0295-6

Contents

Preface

Seventy years after its foundation in Weimar, the Bauhaus has become a concept, indeed a catchphrase all over the world. The respect which it commands is associated above all with the design it pioneered, one which we now describe – with inadmissible simplism – as 'Bauhaus style'. The teachers at the Bauhaus acquired legendary fame and included the leading artists of the times, among them Wassily Kandinsky, Lyonel Feininger, Paul Klee and Oskar Schlemmer. The teaching strategies developed at the Bauhaus, in particular by Johannes Itten, Josef Albers and Lászlo Moholy-Nagy, were adopted internationally into the curriculums of art and design institutes and are still flourishing today. On the other hand, the avant-garde Bauhaus architecture developed in the twenties in the works of Walter Gropius and Ludwig Mies van der Rohe, with its monotone box-like constructions and soulless housing estates, is today not infrequently blamed for the ugliness of our cities and the violation of our countryside.
Simplifications, prejudices and misconceptions abound in reactions to the Bauhaus, a problem with which the Bauhaus itself had to contend even during the brief fourteen years of its existence. 'Bauhaus' became an abbreviation for the radical modernization of life and its positive and negative side-effects. The name stood for an entire programme, and the development and changing fortunes of the school were followed with widespread interest by supporters and critics alike.
The development of the Bauhaus unfolded more or less in tandem with the history of the first German Republic. Walter Gropius founded the Bauhaus in 1919 in Weimar, where the National Assembly had met to draw up a democratic constitution. Ludwig Mies van der Rohe, the last director of the Bauhaus, dissolved the school in Berlin in 1933, under heavy pressure from the National Socialists who had seized power just a few months before.
The suppression of the institution was not, however, enough to contain the influence of the ideas it had stood for, particularly since some of the most important Bauhaus teachers subsequently rose to prominence outside Germany, and above all in the United States of America. Thus Walter Gropius and Marcel Breuer became architects and architecture teachers at Harvard University, and likewise Ludwig Mies van der Rohe in Chicago; Josef Albers continued his teaching career at Black Mountain College, while Lászlo Moholy-Nagy founded the 'New Bauhaus' in Chicago in 1937. Other Bauhaus members worked in various parts of Europe, the Soviet Union and the Middle East. Others again remained – more or less quietly – in Nazi Germany.
The attention which the Bauhaus continued to attract even after its official closure was a tribute to its achievements in the few years between 1919-1933. The developments of this period require detailed, differentiated examination, for the effects of the Bauhaus were felt in the most varying areas of design. The Bauhaus developed – not without contradictions –

from the Expressionist flavour of the early Weimar years, via the Constructivist orientation of the Dessau years, to the increasingly architectural emphasis of the late Dessau and Berlin Bauhaus, and thereby from Walter Gropius via Hannes Meyer to Mies van der Rohe. Both the historical development of the Bauhaus and its spheres of work and activity are today documented in a large number of publications and exhibition catalogues exploiting important sources from a wide range of viewpoints, including design, architecture, educational theory and art. While histories of the Bauhaus written even as late as the sixties and seventies tended to be based extensively on Gropius' personal recollections, the last few years have seen an increasing number of more critical studies. There has nevertheless been no comprehensive history until now which takes into account the results of more recent research.
Magdalena Droste, for many years a member of the academic staff of the Bauhaus Archiv/Museum of Design, has undertaken to fill this gap. The present book, addressed to both general and specialist publics, traces the history of the Bauhaus from the revised perspective of recent years. It offers a clear and concise description of the structure and development of the Bauhaus from its origins to its final demise. Nor does it ignore the conflicts and contradictions which dogged both the aesthetics and the social aims of the Bauhaus.
The choice of illustrations played a particularly important role in the conception of this book. The large majority have been taken from the collection of the Bauhaus Archiv which has been compiled over the past thirty years. The Archiv's extensive resources have made it possible to illustrate areas previously somewhat neglected and thus to highlight the richness of Bauhaus design and teaching.
The impact of the Bauhaus has in no way subsided; a final summary of its effects is not yet due. This book, and its committed and differentiated approach, injects an exciting new stimulus into the continuing Bauhaus discussion.

Peter Hahn
Director
Bauhaus Archiv, Berlin

On the Origins of the Bauhaus

Facing, previous page: Fagus factory in Alfeld by Walter Gropius and Adolf Meyer. Begun in 1911.

The historical origins of the Bauhaus can be traced well back into the 19th century. They begin with the devastating consequences of the Industrial Revolution for the living conditions and manufactured products of the artisan and working classes, first in England and later in Germany. Increasing industrialization led to social restructuring and the proletarianization of broad sections of the population; at the same time, it meant rationalized and cheaper goods production. In the 19th century, England rose to the position of leading industrial nation in Europe. At the World Fairs, held regularly from 1851 onwards and offering each country a nationalistic opportunity to show off its latest technical and cultural achievements, England remained undisputed champion well into the nineties. The author John Ruskin was among the first to criticize the inhumanity of conditions in England, which he wanted to see improved by means of social reform and the rejection of machine manufacturing. He described his ideal – a revival of medieval methods of working – in his book 'The Stones of Venice' (1851-53).

His most important pupil and admirer was the highly-versatile William Morris, who was to translate Ruskin's ideas into reality with great success. He shared with Ruskin a 'hatred of modern civilization'[1] and its products; he felt it was necessary to reinvent every chair, table and bed, every spoon, jug and glass. Morris founded workshops which proved so influential that, by the eighties, their style – reflecting Gothic and oriental inspiration – has earned its own name: Arts and Crafts (ill., p.10).

Since the fifties, the English had also been reforming the traditional paths of training both as followed by craftsmen and as enshrined in art academies. But while the workshop movement started by Morris represented a practical kind of social Utopia, the economic interests underlying these educational reforms were very much down-to-earth: England wanted to maintain her leading position in the field of handicrafts.

The following few years saw the founding of numerous artisans' guilds, many seeking to combine their economic purpose with a community life-style.

When Morris realised that his reformative ideas were having only limited success and were failing to reach the broad mass of the population, he embraced Socialism and became one of the most important voices in the Socialist movement in England in the eighties and nineties.

Culture by and for the people has been the rallying cry of virtually every new cultural movement since time began, and was to accompany the founding of the Bauhaus, too.

Countries on the Continent had been attempting since the seventies to copy England's success in the field of industrial production. The key to a revitalization of the art industry was seen to lie in the revision of educational and training policies.

The Austrian Museum of Arts and Crafts was opened in Vienna. A similar museum was founded in Berlin in 1871. Its patroness and energetic champion was the Empress Augusta, anglophile wife of Wilhelm I, who wanted to boost the low morale of the German art industry. These museums, in which handicraft products were collected for study purposes, were affiliated with schools. But it was not until the nineties that a second wave of reform reached Germany via Belgium from England. This marked the arrival of Jugendstil, the German form of Art Nouveau which was to dominate Europe for the next ten to fifteen years.

In 1896 the Prussian Government sent 'cultural spy' Hermann Muthesius to England on a six-year mission to study the secrets of English success. Upon his recommendation, workshops were introduced at all Prussian handicraft schools and modern artists appointed as teachers. Peter Behrens,

Late medieval influences and two-dimensional decorative ornamentation on a floral theme characterize these two initials – the opening characters of a page or chapter – by William Morris from the years 1896 and 1871.

The Red House, which used simple forms from the late Middle Ages, was built in 1859 by the English architect Philip Webb for William Morris and his family.

Hans Poelzig and Bruno Paul respectively reformed the art academies in Düsseldorf, Breslau and Berlin. Otto Pankok introduced workshops at the Stuttgart School of Arts and Crafts while, in Weimar, Henry van de Velde headed one of the most successful modern art colleges of the day (ills. p.12 and 13). Admissions of women were increased in response to the demand for more trained personnel in industry.

Following the English example, small private workshops sprang up all over Germany making household goods, furniture and metal utensils. Among the most important of these were the Dresdner Werkstätten für Handwerkskunst (Dresden Workshops for Artist Craftsmanship), which later merged with the Münchner Werkstätten to form the Deutsche Werkstätten. But where the Arts and Crafts workshops in England had rejected methods of machine production, Germany embraced them with open arms. Richard Riemerschmid designed a range of 'machine furniture' and a little later Bruno Paul developed his own 'standard furniture programme'. Stylistically, too, the German products of the turn of the century had nothing left in common with the English products of the Arts and Crafts movement, which were still firmly entrenched in the 19th century.

In the course of the nineties Germany overtook England as the leading industrial nation and maintained her new position until the outbreak of the First World War in 1914.

Within a highly nationalistic climate, the search began for a stylistic language which would complement Germany's worldwide industrial reputation. The combination of economic, national and cultural considerations led, in 1907, to the founding in Munich of the German Werkbund, an association which was to represent the most successful and significant marriage of art and industry before the First World War.

Henry van de Velde was the builder and first head of the Grand-Ducal Saxon School of Arts and Crafts founded in 1907. These same buildings were later to house the Bauhaus workshops.

Opposite page: The Grand-Ducal Saxon Academy of Fine Art, also built to a design by van de Velde, faces the School of Arts and Crafts. The Bauhaus had administrative offices and studios here from 1919.
Below: Henry van de Velde in his studio in the Weimar Academy of Fine Art.

The German Werkbund was composed of twelve representatives of leading handicraft companies and artists, whose aim was the 'cooperation of art, industry and crafts in the ennoblement of commercial activity by means of education, propaganda and a united stand on pertinent questions'[2]. 'Quality work' was one of the Werkbund's highest aims and favourite catchphrases in its efforts to safeguard Germany's position as a major industrial power. Its impressive list of founder artists and architects included Richard Riemerschmid, Joseph Maria Olbrich, Josef Hoffmann, Bruno Paul, Fritz Schumacher, Wilhelm Kreis, Peter Behrens, Theodor Fischer, Paul Schultze-Naumburg and, today less familiar, Adelbert Niemeyer, Max Läuger and J.J. Scharvogel.
The Werkstätten mentioned above were no longer alone in producing artist-designed goods; the companies participating in the Werkbund now also employed artists. The Bahlsen biscuit factory in Hanover commissioned artists to design its entire production range – biscuit tins, posters, trade fair stands and architecture. Employed by the AEG electricity company, Peter Behrens created a uniform house style which hallmarked every company product from teapot to turbine factory (ills. p. 14 and 15). The Werkbund held its own exhibitions, organized touring exhibitions, published yearbooks and worked with art schools. Walter Gropius became a member of the Werkbund in 1912, having made a name for himself with a new factory, the Fagus shoe-last works in Alfeld near Hanover (ill., p. 8) which he designed together with his partner Adolf Meyer. The Fagus factory subsequently went down in history as the first building featuring a

A 'cathedral of work' was how Peter Behrens' AEG turbine factory in Berlin, one of the first modern industrial buildings, was described. Behrens' building is dignified through its emphasis upon the structural functions of load and support and its temple-like façade. This architectural monumentalization reinforced the image of industry as a growing economic power.

curtain wall; from a skeletal frame, the architects hung a glass façade which even extended to transparent corners. This glass-and-brick construction looked forward to the developments of the twenties and earned the 28-year-old Gropius his first widespread recognition as an architect. Not long afterwards, the Cologne Werkbund exhibition offered him a further opportunity to design a model factory and an office building. In emphasizing and disguising many of their structural elements, he sought to create symbols of the spirit and will of the age.[3]

The years leading up to the First World War saw not only a blossoming of the economy but also, for the first time under Wilhelm II, the organization of countless counter-movements devoted to the reform of life and civilization and attracting support from all classes and generations. At the same time, the Werkbund and the Jugendstil artists were trying to reconcile 'art and the machine'. For the first time youth was taken seriously as a generation in its own right, instead of being treated as an intermediate stage on the road to adulthood. There were later to be numerous links between such reform movements and the Bauhaus. The education system saw the spread of *Reformpädagogik,* a modern philosophy of education which called for the introduction of activity-based teaching and comprehensive schools. Numerous private schools were founded, many still existing today. The young middle-classes organised themselves into the 'Wandervogel' movement. They discussed and practised vegetarianism, naturism and anti-alcoholism. Various agricultural communes and cooperatives were set up, albeit often soon to founder. The 'Eden' fruit-growing colony was one of the

few exceptions. Even Gropius was to dream of his own 'estate' during the early years of the Bauhaus.
Culture-conservationists such as Paul Anton de Lagarde and Julius Langbehn enjoyed extraordinary success. Nietzsche's pessimistic view of the world attracted ever-more supporters among both middle classes and artists. There emerged a number of movements dedicated to the conservation of culture and civilization: the aims of the 'Dürerbund' (started in 1902) included popular education, the fostering of the arts and the preservation of local traditions. The architect Paul Schultze-Naumburg founded an 'Association for the Preservation of Local History and Culture'; the magazine 'Kunstwart' reflected more conservative educationist thinking. Strongly anti-Semitic, nationalistic and Teutonic-Christian attitudes developed side by side.
The emancipation of women also continued apace. The big cities were often the starting-point for 'bourgeois escape movements' such as that of the painter Fidus and his circle in Berlin before the War. The outbreak of the First World War was rapturously welcomed in Germany with almost unani-

Behrens designed almost the entire AEG product range in the spirit of the Werkbund.
Above: A poster for light bulbs from 1907.
Left: A table fan from a later production series, based on a modified version of Behrens' original design.

mous enthusiasm. Volunteers rushed to sign up, among them avant-garde artists such as Otto Dix, Oskar Kokoschka, Franz Marc, Max Beckmann and August Macke. While the intellectuals hoped for spiritual renewal, often in the spirit of Nietzsche, broad sections of the population shared the view of their Kaiser, Wilhelm II, that Germany would now have the chance to prove her world superiority once and for all. The Werkbund spoke of the 'triumph of German form'.

Doubts about the point of the War did not set in till 1916/17. Architects and artists published petitions and manifestos. There were early signs of the intellectual reorientation whose centre was to be the 'Arbeitsrat für Kunst' ('Art Soviet') founded in November 1918, shortly after the November Revolution, by a group of artists around architect Bruno Taut (ills., p.16 and 17).

Gropius, too, had spoken in 1917 of the 'necessity of an intellectual change of front', and he went to Berlin to participate in the radical developments there taking place. He wrote: 'The atmosphere here is highly charged, and we artists must strike while the iron is hot. I consider the Werkbund dead and buried; it no longer has a future.'[4]

Gropius had been involved since 1915 in correspondence regarding the directorship of the Weimar School of Arts and Crafts founded and run by Henry van de Velde. In 1914, even before war broke out, anti-foreigner resentment had led van de Velde (ill, p.13) to resign his position as director and to recommend Gropius, Hermann Obrist and August Endell as his possible successors. In the event van de Velde's school was closed in 1915. However, Weimar also had an Academy of Fine Art; its director, Fritz Mackensen, wanted to introduce an architecture course and thought Gropius might run it. The job description also included representing the handicrafts industry and the handicraft interests of the Grand Duchy of Thuringia. While still a soldier at the front, Gropius formulated his 'Proposals for the establishment of an educational institution to provide artistic advisory services to industry, trade and craft', which he sent to the Grand-Ducal Saxon Ministry of State in January 1916. In line with the ideas of the Werkbund, Gropius called for close cooperation between the industrialist and engineer on the one hand and the artist on the other; at the same time, however, he now cited the ideal of the medieval stonemasons' lodge where craftsmen worked in 'the same spirit', in the 'oneness of a common idea'.

The Chamberlain's office issued a statement turning down Gropius' proposals. It was felt that insufficient importance had been assigned to handicrafts. Rather than an architect, it would be better to appoint an acknowledged arts and crafts expert to guarantee the small and medium-sized Thuringian industries (pottery, textiles, basket-making, furniture) a better chance of commercial success.

'Arbeitsrat für Kunst' brochure, 1919.

Gropius remained in contact with the Academy of Fine Art, however. In 1917 its teaching staff called for the introduction of a department of architecture and handicrafts – just as Mackensen had done two years earlier. Having heard nothing about a possible appointment by January 1919, Gropius approached the Weimar authorities directly. At the same time he held talks with the teaching faculty, with the result that they unanimously called for his appointment as their new director. The Chamberlain's office and the provisional government of the then Free State of Saxe-Weimar now also gave him their backing.

In February, before finally accepting the job, Gropius submitted a cost estimate and aired his plans: 'The present conditions are unusually favourable; its closure means the School of Arts and Crafts can be fully redesigned, while a large number of teaching posts at the Academy of Fine Art are free. This opportunity to restructure a major institution of art education

Berlin 'Arbeitsrat für Kunst' pamphlet from 1919, with woodcut probably by Max Pechstein. Artists and intellectuals came together in 1918 to form the 'Arbeitsrat für Kunst' whose aim – inspired by the workers and soldiers' soviets set up during the revolutionary period – was to create a new culture. In the 'Stimmen' (left), 28 statements on the first Art Soviet programme were published.

using modern ideas without making radical incursions into its existing fabric is perhaps unique within Germany today.'[5]

At the end of March the government approved Gropius' request to head both schools under the single title of 'Staatliches Bauhaus in Weimar'. The names of the two original schools were invoked in a lengthy subtitle: 'United former Grand-Ducal Saxon Academy of Fine Art and former Grand-Ducal Saxon School of Arts and Crafts'.

On 12 April Gropius was at last appointed director of the new school – new in both name and nature. An act of administration had thus created the most contentious and modern art school of its day. Its foundation took place in the period of revolutionary unrest following the War – a period in which it was frequently unclear whether administrative authority for the school lay with the old Chamberlain's office or the new soviet government. Had it been delayed until the conservative forces had regrouped, its foundation is unlikely to have been approved.

In a Bauhaus Manifesto (ills., p.18 and 19) which he published throughout Germany, Gropius set out the programme and the aims of the new school: artists and craftsmen were together to create the 'building of the future'. The discussion of the 'modern ideas' behind art school reforms had been launched by Wilhelm von Bode, General Director of the Berlin State Museums, in an article of 1916. He argued that fine art academies, schools of arts and crafts and art schools should be united under a single roof. This would reduce the surplus of unemployed artists – the 'artist proletariat' as it was then called. Many artists, in particular architects, seized upon these new ideas, with Theodor Fischer writing 'In support of German architecture' in 1917 and architect Fritz Schumacher issuing his 'Reform of technical art education' in 1918. Richard Riemerschmid published his 'Aspects of art education' and architects Otto Bartning and Bruno Taut included 'An architectural Programme' in the 'Arbeitsrat' brochure.

Das Endziel aller bildnerischen Tätigkeit ist der Bau! Ihn zu schmücken war einst die vornehmste Aufgabe der bildenden Künste. sie waren unablösliche Bestandteile der großen Baukunst. Heute stehen sie in selbstgenügsamer Eigenheit. aus der sie erst wieder erlöst werden können durch bewußtes Mit- und Ineinanderwirken aller Werkleute untereinander. Architekten. Maler und Bildhauer müssen die vielgliedrige Gestalt des Baues in seiner Gesamtheit und in seinen Teilen wieder kennen und begreifen lernen. dann werden sich von selbst ihre Werke wieder mit architektonischem Geiste füllen. den sie in der Salonkunst verloren.

Die alten Kunstschulen vermochten diese Einheit nicht zu erzeugen. wie sollten sie auch. da Kunst nicht lehrbar ist. Sie müssen wieder in der Werkstatt aufgehen. Diese nur zeichnende und malende Welt der Musterzeichner und Kunstgewerbler muß endlich wieder eine bauende werden. Wenn der junge Mensch. der Liebe zur bildnerischen Tätigkeit in sich verspürt. wieder wie einst seine Bahn damit beginnt. ein Handwerk zu erlernen. so bleibt der unproduktive „Künstler" künftig nicht mehr zu unvollkommener Kunstübung verdammt. denn seine Fertigkeit bleibt nun dem Handwerk erhalten. wo er Vortreffliches zu leisten vermag.

Architekten. Bildhauer. Maler. wir alle müssen zum Handwerk ~~zurück~~! Denn es gibt keine „Kunst von Beruf". Es gibt keinen Wesensunterschied zwischen dem Künstler und dem Handwerker. Der Künstler ist eine Steigerung des Handwerkers. Gnade des Himmels läßt in seltenen Lichtmomenten. die jenseits seines Wollens stehen. unbewußt Kunst aus dem Werk seiner Hand erblühen. die Grundlage des Werkmäßigen aber ist unerläßlich für jeden Künstler. Dort ist der Urquell des schöpferischen Gestaltens.

Bilden wir also eine neue Zunft der Handwerker ohne die klassentrennende Anmaßung. die eine hochmütige Mauer zwischen Handwerkern und Künstlern errichten wollte! Wollen. erdenken. erschaffen wir gemeinsam den neuen Bau der Zukunft. der alles in einer Gestalt sein wird: Architektur und Plastik und Malerei. der aus Millionen Händen der Handwerker einst gen Himmel steigen wird als kristallenes Sinnbild eines neuen kommenden Glaubens.

WALTER GROPIUS.

Walter Gropius: Bauhaus Manifesto and Programme with opening woodcut by Lyonel Feininger, 1919.

The writings of Taut and Bartning in particular were of decisive importance for Gropius. In his programme Taut was the first to call for houses for the people and the involvement of every branch of art in architecture. He further demanded experimental buildings and exhibitions for the people. Taut believed, for example: 'There are no barriers between handicrafts and sculpture or painting; they are all one: building.' Gropius wrote: 'Let us together create the new building of the future, which will be everything in one form. Architecture and sculpture and painting.'

Perhaps even more important for Gropius' Bauhaus programme were the reform proposals put forward by architect Otto Bartning, another member of the 'Arbeitsrat für Kunst'. In January 1919 he published a 'Teaching plan for architecture and the fine arts on the basis of handicrafts'. Handicrafts were thus declared the foundation of art education.

Gropius adopted Bartning's concept of a 'Council of Masters'. The Bauhaus hierarchy of apprentice – journeyman – master had also been previously formulated in Bartning's writings.

With the first Bauhaus programme Gropius translated the ideas for reform developed during the revolutionary and post-revolutionary periods into an educational curriculum. But the Bauhaus wanted to be more than just the amalgamation of an art academy and a school of arts and crafts; instead,

PROGRAMM

DES

STAATLICHEN BAUHAUSES IN WEIMAR

Das Staatliche Bauhaus in Weimar ist durch Vereinigung der ehemaligen Großherzoglich Sächsischen Hochschule für bildende Kunst mit der ehemaligen Großherzoglich Sächsischen Kunstgewerbeschule unter Neuangliederung einer Abteilung für Baukunst entstanden.

Ziele des Bauhauses.

Das Bauhaus erstrebt die Sammlung alles künstlerischen Schaffens zur Einheit, die Wiedervereinigung aller werkkünstlerischen Disziplinen — Bildhauerei, Malerei, Kunstgewerbe und Handwerk — zu einer neuen Baukunst als deren unablösliche Bestandteile. Das letzte, wenn auch ferne Ziel des Bauhauses ist das Einheitskunstwerk — der große Bau —, in dem es keine Grenze gibt zwischen monumentaler und dekorativer Kunst.

Das Bauhaus will Architekten, Maler und Bildhauer aller Grade je nach ihren Fähigkeiten zu tüchtigen Handwerkern oder selbständig schaffenden Künstlern erziehen und eine Arbeitsgemeinschaft führender und werdender Werkkünstler gründen, die Bauwerke in ihrer Gesamtheit — Rohbau, Ausbau, Ausschmückung und Einrichtung — aus gleich geartetem Geist heraus einheitlich zu gestalten weiß.

Grundsätze des Bauhauses.

Kunst entsteht oberhalb aller Methoden, sie ist an sich nicht lehrbar, wohl aber das Handwerk. Architekten, Maler, Bildhauer sind Handwerker im Ursinn des Wortes, deshalb wird als unerläßliche Grundlage für alles bildnerische Schaffen die gründliche handwerkliche Ausbildung aller ~~Studierenden~~ in Werkstätten und auf Probier- und Werkplätzen gefordert. ~~Die eigenen Werkstätten sollen allmählich ausgebaut, mit fremden Werkstätten Lehrverträge abgeschlossen~~ werden.

Die Schule ist die Dienerin der Werkstatt, sie wird eines Tages in ihr aufgehen. Deshalb nicht Lehrer und Schüler im Bauhaus, sondern Meister Gesellen und Lehrlinge.

Die Art der Lehre entspringt dem Wesen der Werkstatt:

Organisches Gestalten aus handwerklichem Können entwickelt.

Vermeidung alles Starren; Bevorzugung des Schöpferischen; Freiheit der Individualität, aber strenges Studium.

Zunftgemäße Meister- und Gesellenproben vor dem Meisterrat des Bauhauses oder vor fremden Meistern.

Mitarbeit der Studierenden an den Arbeiten der Meister.

Auftragsvermittlung auch an Studierende.

Gemeinsame Planung umfangreicher utopischer Bauentwürfe — Volks- und Kultbauten — mit weitgestecktem Ziel. Mitarbeit aller Meister und Studierenden — Architekten, Maler, Bildhauer — an diesen Entwürfen mit dem Ziel allmählichen Einklangs aller zum Bau gehörigen Glieder und Teile.

Ständige Fühlung mit Führern der Handwerke und Industrien im Lande.

Fühlung mit dem öffentlichen Leben, mit dem Volke durch Ausstellungen und andere Veranstaltungen.

Neue Versuche im Ausstellungswesen zur Lösung des Problems, Bild und Plastik im architektonischen Rahmen zu zeigen.

Pflege freundschaftlichen Verkehrs zwischen Meistern und Studierenden außerhalb der Arbeit; dabei Theater, Vorträge, Dichtkunst, Musik, Kostümfeste. Aufbau eines heiteren Zeremoniells bei diesen Zusammenkünften.

Umfang der Lehre.

Die Lehre im Bauhaus umfaßt alle praktischen und wissenschaftlichen Gebiete des bildnerischen Schaffens.

A. Baukunst,
B. Malerei,
C. Bildhauerei

einschließlich aller handwerklichen Zweiggebiete.

Die Studierenden werden sowol handwerklich (1) wie zeichnerisch-malerisch (2) und wissenschaftlich-theoretisch (3) ausgebildet.

1. Die handwerkliche Ausbildung — sei es in eigenen allmählich zu ergänzenden, oder fremden durch Lehrvertrag verpflichteten Werkstätten — erstreckt sich auf:
   a) Bildhauer, Steinmetzen, Stukkatöre, Holzbildhauer, Keramiker, Gipsgießer,
   b) Schmiede, Schlosser, Gießer, her,
   c) Tischler,
   d) Dekorationsmaler, Glasmaler, Mosaiker, Emallöre,
   e) Radierer, Holzschneider, Lithographen, Kunstdrucker, Ziselöre,
   f) Weber.

Die handwerkliche Ausbildung bildet das Fundament der Lehre im Bauhause. Jeder Studierende soll ein Handwerk erlernen.

2. Die zeichnerische und malerische Ausbildung erstreckt sich auf:
   a) Freies Skizzieren aus dem Gedächtnis und der Fantasie,
   b) Zeichnen und Malen nach Köpfen, Akten und Tieren,
   c) Zeichnen und Malen von Landschaften, Figuren, Pflanzen und Stilleben,
   d) Komponieren,
   e) Ausführen von Wandbildern, Tafelbildern und Bilderschreinen,
   f) Entwerfen von Ornamenten,
   g) Schriftzeichnen,
   h) Konstruktions- und Projektionszeichnen,
   i) Entwerfen von Außen-, Garten- und Innenarchitekturen,
   k) Entwerfen von Möbeln und Gebrauchsgegenständen.
3. Die wissenschaftlich-theoretische Ausbildung erstreckt sich auf:
   a) Kunstgeschichte — nicht im Sinne von Stilgeschichte vorgetragen, sondern zur lebendigen Erkenntnis historischer Arbeitsweisen und Techniken,
   b) Materialkunde,
   c) Anatomie — am lebenden Modell,
   d) physikalische und chemische Farbenlehre,
   e) rationelles Malverfahren,
   f) Grundbegriffe von Buchführung, Vertragsabschlüssen, Verdingungen,
   g) allgemein interessante Einzelvorträge aus allen Gebieten der Kunst und Wissenschaft.

Einteilung der Lehre.

Die Ausbildung ist in drei Lehrgänge eingeteilt:

I. Lehrgang für Lehrlinge,
II. „ „ Gesellen,
III. „ „ Jungmeister.

Die Einzelausbildung bleibt dem Ermessen der einzelnen Meister im Rahmen des allgemeinen Programms und des in jedem Semester neu aufzustellenden Arbeitsverteilungsplanes überlassen.

Um den Studierenden eine möglichst vielseitige, umfassende technische und künstlerische Ausbildung zuteil werden zu lassen, wird der Arbeitsverteilungsplan zeitlich so eingeteilt, daß jeder angehende Architekt, Maler oder Bildhauer auch an einem Teil der anderen Lehrgänge teilnehmen kann.

Aufnahme.

Aufgenommen wird jede unbescholtene Person ohne Rücksicht auf Alter und Geschlecht, deren Vorbildung vom Meisterrat des Bauhauses als ausreichend erachtet wird, und soweit es der Raum zuläßt. Das Lehrgeld beträgt jährlich 180 Mark (es soll mit steigendem Verdienst des Bauhauses allmählich ganz verschwinden). Außerdem ist eine einmalige Aufnahmegebühr von 20 Mark zu zahlen. Ausländer zahlen den doppelten Betrag. Anfragen sind an das Sekretariat des Staatlichen Bauhauses in Weimar zu richten.

APRIL 1919.

Die Leitung des
Staatlichen Bauhauses in Weimar:
Walter Gropius.

its teaching was dominated by the both symbolic and practical goal of *Bauen* – building.

For Gropius, in line with the ideas of the 'Arbeitsrat', building was a social, intellectual and symbolic activity. It reconciled previously separate disciplines and callings and united them in a common task. Building was to level class differences and bring layman and artist together. This new philosophy of building was encapsulated in Lyonel Feininger's woodcut of a cathedral which illustrated the cover of the four-page Bauhaus Manifesto: beams of light converge upon the cathedral's three spires, representing the three arts of painting, sculpture and architecture. The symbolism of the cathedral had become particularly topical following the appearance of Wilhelm Worringer's book 'Problems of Form in Gothic Art' in 1912. Important architecture critics such as Adolf Behne and Karl Scheffler also saw the cathedral as an allegory of the total work of art and a symbol of social unity[6]. Bruno Taut, so greatly respected and admired by Gropius, had also used the drawing of a Gothic cathedral spire to illustrate his book 'The City Crown' (1915-17). Nevertheless, Hans M. Wingler, author of the first comprehensive history of the Bauhaus, rightly acknowledges the originality of Gropius' own achievement: 'The synthesis of ideas consummated in the Bauhaus ... not simply a summary, but an eminently creative act'[7].

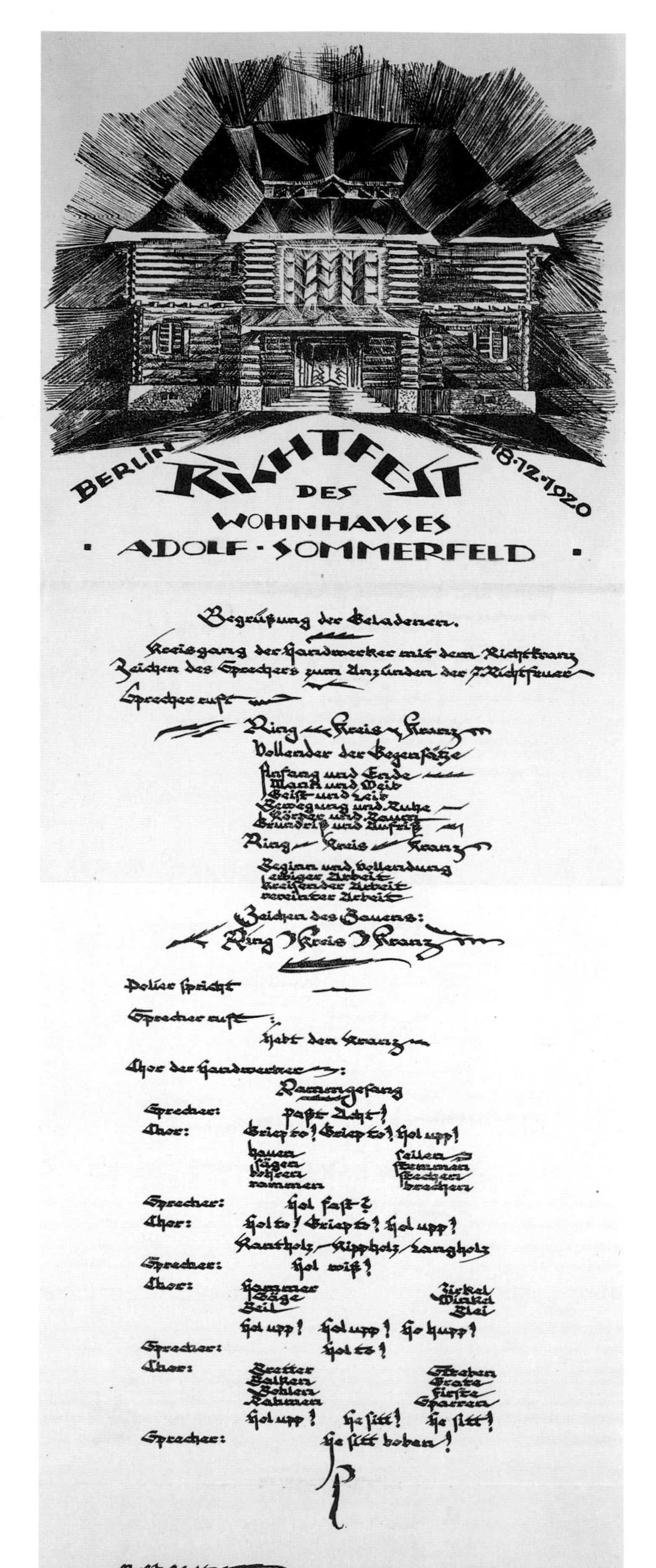

BERLIN RICHTFEST DES WOHNHAUSES 18.12.1920

· ADOLF · SOMMERFELD ·

Begrüßung der Geladenen.

Kreisgang der Handwerker mit dem Richtkranz

Zeichen des Sprechers zum Anzünden der 7 Richtfeuer

Sprecher ruft

Ring Kreis Kranz

Vollender der Gegensätze

Anfang und Ende
Mann und Weib
Geist und Leib
Bewegung und Ruhe
Körper und Raum
Grundriß und Aufriß

Ring Kreis Kranz

Beginn und Vollendung
ewiger Arbeit
kreisender Arbeit
vereinter Arbeit

Zeichen des Bauens:

Ring Kreis Kranz

Polier spricht

Sprecher ruft:

Hebt den Kranz

Chor der Handwerker:

Rammgesang

Sprecher: Paßt Acht!

Chor: Griep to! Griep to! Hol upp!

hauen, sägen, bohren, rammen
feilen, stemmen, stechen, brechen

Sprecher: Hol fast!

Chor: Hol to! Griep to! Hol upp!

Kantholz Kippholz Langholz

Sprecher: Hol wiß!

Chor: Hammer, Säge, Beil
Zirkel, Winkel, Blei

Hol upp! Hol upp! Ho hupp!

Sprecher: Hol to!

Chor: Bretter, Balken, Bohlen, Rahmen
Streben, Grate, Firste, Sparren

Hol upp! He sitt! He sitt!

Sprecher: He sitt boben!

Musik spielt

Weimar Bauhaus – Expressionist Bauhaus

The first Bauhaus seal, used from 1919 to 1922, was designed by Karl-Peter Röhl. It combines a number of Christian and other symbols, including a pyramid, Maltese cross, circle and star.

The Bauhaus Manifesto not only contained an emotive declaration of principle – 'The ultimate aim of all creative activity is the building!' – but also discussed Bauhaus goals, its teaching programme and admission requirements. Some 150 students had soon enrolled, almost half of them women. All were attracted by the modern programme and the avant-gardism of Feininger's woodcut on the title page (ill., p.18). Many arrived direct from active service, hoping for the chance to make a fresh start and give meaning to their lives. 'The call from Gropius was like a fanfare, rallying enthusiasts on all sides.'[8]

The Bauhaus was indeed the first art school reformed after the War to take up teaching in the new Republic. In many art schools it proved virtually impossible to implement any reforms at all; in others reform was delayed, as in Karlsruhe, or limited in scope. At first sight the Bauhaus programme resembled that taught in a number of art schools reformed before the War. Pupils were to study handicrafts, drawing and sciences. New, however, was the overall goal which Gropius set the school: the *jointly erected building* to which all would contribute through *craftsmanship.*

In place of the traditional professors, teaching was now given by Masters. Students were called apprentices and could progress to journeymen and finally young masters. Bauhaus affairs were decided by a Council of Masters, whose powers included the right to appoint new Masters.

Students were to be taught by both a Master of Form and Master of Craft. This, wrote Gropius in the Bauhaus Manifesto, would 'raze the arrogant wall between artist and artisan', and clear the way for the 'new building of the future.' Gropius hoped that the young people educated at the Bauhaus would carry its ideals into society at large. The school was never to abandon this dual ambition, and it remained an aspect of its special status and significance within the Weimar Republic. The early Bauhaus years were characterized by a powerful community spirit. An environment fit for 'new man' was to be planned, designed and built on the ruins of the old empire. All saw themselves as artists, but artists who would make their contribution to the 'cathedral of the future' through craftsmanship or teaching. This vision of a Utopian cathedral did not, however, prevent them from accepting practical commissions, e.g. for furniture, metal objects, carpets and interior decoration. Indeed, the reconciliation of these opposites gave the school its purpose and meaning. From contradictory forces arose a creative equilibrium whose stability was, in the following years, to be repeatedly tested, challenged and changed.

Teachers

In a letter dating from the earliest days of the Bauhaus, Gropius announced his intention of laying in Weimar 'the foundation stone of a Republic of Intellects'. The first step was to enlist the right personnel. 'It is naturally vital for everyone that we attract strong, lively personalities. We must not start with mediocrity; it is our duty to enlist powerful, famous personalities wherever possible, even if we do not yet fully understand them.'[9]

In the first year Gropius appointed to the Bauhaus three artists with very different backgrounds: the art theoretician and painter Johannes Itten (ill., p. 25), the painter Lyonel Feininger and the sculptor Gerhard Marcks.

Itten was undoubtedly the most influential of these three; he developed the *Vorkurs* (preliminary course) which was to become the core of the Bauhaus programme, and which forms the subject of a separate chapter in this book.

Gerhard Marcks, whom Gropius had known before the War, counted himself among the more conservative of the Bauhaus artists, but nevertheless fully backed Gropius' ideas at the beginning. As a sculptor he was

Facing, previous page: Programme for the topping-out ceremony at the Sommerfeld house on 18 December 1920; woodcut by Bauhaus student Martin Jahn.

Portrait of Walter Gropius, 1920.

Karl-Peter Röhl: Lithograph invitation to the Bauhaus opening celebrations in March 1919.

well-grounded in aspects of craftsmanship and had also already worked for a porcelain factory. He expressed his willingness to set up a pottery workshop. Feininger was one of the most well-known Expressionist painters of the time and the radicality of his pictures had made them the object of heated debate. He took charge of the printing workshop which, as one of the small number of workshops inherited from the earlier school, was still fully equipped.
In late 1919, both on the recommendation of Weimar resident and painter Johannes Molzahn and at Itten's request, Gropius contacted Georg Muche, another Expressionist painter who had achieved success at a young age in the Berlin gallery 'Der Sturm' founded by Herwarth Walden. He accepted a Bauhaus appointment and moved to Weimar in April 1920,

Timetable for the winter semester of 1921/22, painted by Lothar Schreyer. 'Werkstatt' (workshop) activities make up the large part of the day; there are also form classes by Itten and Klee. Other subjects include life drawing, technical drawing and lectures.

teaching in a number of workshops and in the *Vorkurs* from October 1920 onwards.

In 1920 the Council of Masters announced the appointments of Paul Klee and Oskar Schlemmer, both of whom took up their posts at the start of 1921. Lothar Schreyer, who joined the Bauhaus in 1921, had also found fame as a 'Sturm artist'. His task was to set up a theatre department. Although not included in the original curriculum, the theatre workshop was seen as an inseparable element of the Bauhaus whole, and in particular as a conceptual counterpart to 'building'. 'Building and theatre', 'work and play' were mutually to enrich each other. In 1922 the Council of Masters further appointed as Master Wassily Kandinsky, who had returned from Russia in 1921 and was the most important abstract artist of his day. Within three years Gropius had thus gathered at the Bauhaus a group of avant-garde artists who were officially employed for tasks which, at first sight, had nothing to do with their own speciality, painting.

They nevertheless saw the Bauhaus as an opportunity to help, through their teaching, to make art an automatic part of everyday life. Here they could turn spiritual reorientation into action. The artists bowed their heads before the overall Bauhaus concept and at the same time remained creative individuals within the whole.

Johannes Itten and his teaching

The most important personality during this first phase of the Bauhaus was the painter and art theoretician Johannes Itten. Itten had been running his own private art school in Vienna when Gropius was introduced to him by Gropius' first wife, Alma Mahler (later Werfel). Itten had originally trained as an elementary-school teacher and only took up painting later on. He studied in Stuttgart under Adolf Hoelzel, whose art and composition teachings exerted a profound influence upon him.

Itten must have made an immediate impression on Gropius, since the latter invited him to speak on 'Teachings of the Old Masters' at the opening of the

Johannes Itten in the Bauhaus robe he designed himself, 1920.

The Tempelherrenhaus in the park in Weimar, where Itten had his studio from 1919 to 1923. The 'Gothic building' designed by Goethe was badly damaged in the War; only the ruins can still be seen.

Bauhaus on 21 March 1919 in the Weimar National Theatre (ill., p. 23). On 1 June 1919 Itten attended the first meeting of the Council of Masters, where it was agreed he should start teaching on 1 October 1919. Itten's teaching will be the first to be discussed here since it soon became the backbone of Bauhaus education. Its influence was also to extend to activities in the workshops, where operations were only gradually getting under way.
The pedagogical principle on which Itten's teaching was based can be summarized in a pair of opposites: 'intuition and method', or 'subjective experience and objective recognition'. Itten often started his classes with gymnastic and breathing exercises to loosen up and relax his students, before seeking to create 'direction and order out of flow'[10]. The discovery of rhythm and the harmonious composition of different rhythms were among the recurring themes of his classes, which were divided into three main areas: studies of natural objects and materials, the analysis of Old Masters and life drawing.
The purpose of studying materials and natural objects was 'to bring clearly to light the essential and contradictory within each material'[11] and thus to

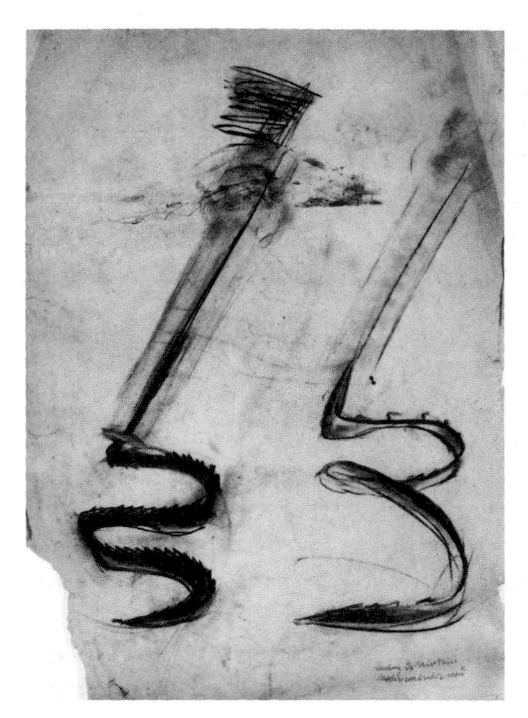

Klaus Rudolf Barthelmess: Two drawings after the materials study by M. Mirkin.

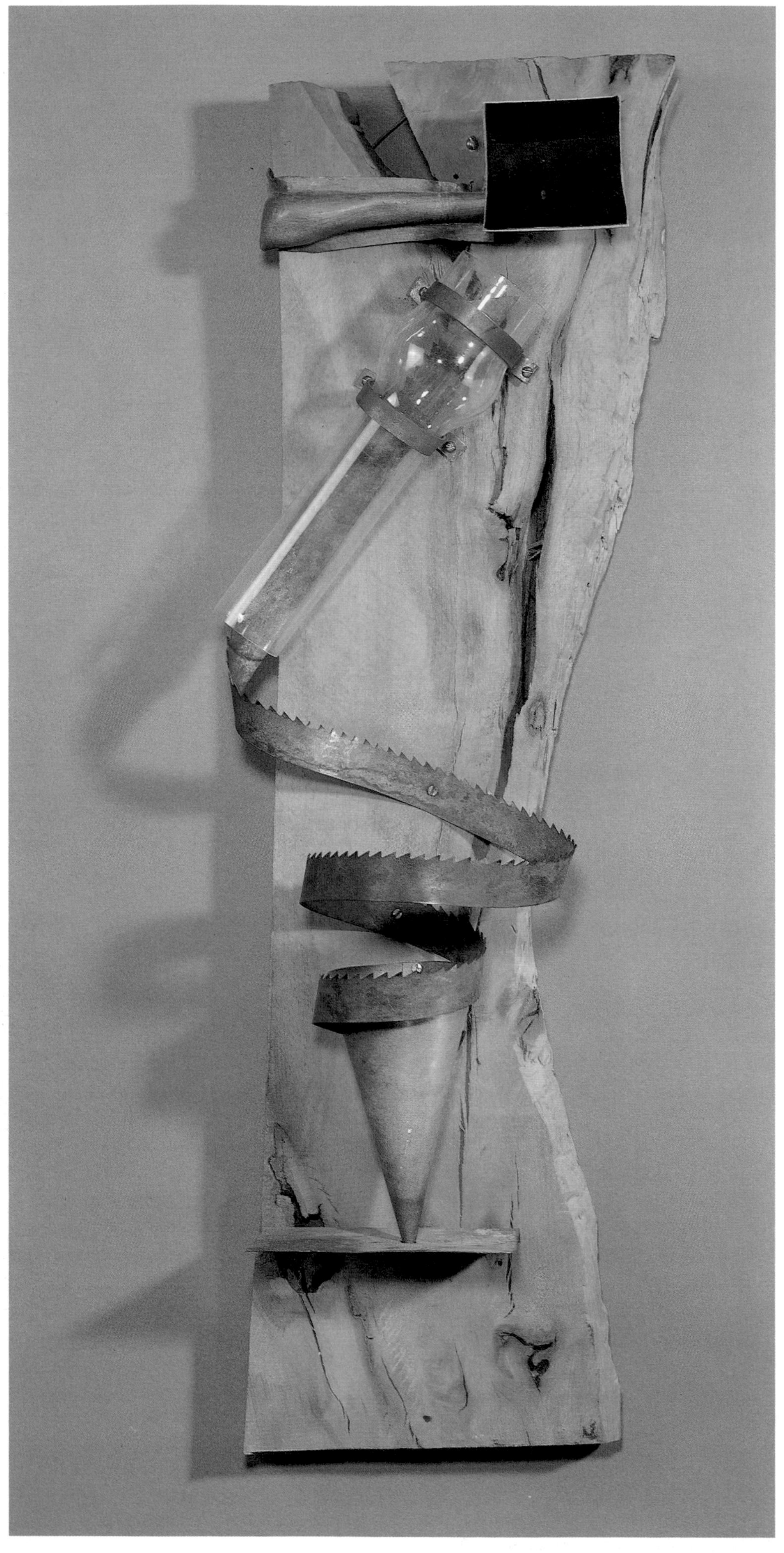

Study of contrasts using different materials by M. Mirkin. Reconstruction of his work of 1920. The Bauhaus catalogue of 1923 described the work as follows: 'Combined contrast effect, material contrast (glass, wood, iron), contrast of expressive forms (jagged-smooth); rhythmical contrast. Exercise to study similarity in expression using different means of expression simultaneously.'

develop and refine his pupils' feeling for materials. Students were given several days to complete their tasks. Many years later, Bauhaus student Alfred Arndt gave a particularly illuminating (and not unironic) description of one such exercise: 'The results were very different. The girls produced small, delicate objects about the size of a hand. Some of the chaps came in with great three-foot-high scraps. These were often real heaps of junk, covered in soot and rust. Others brought in single items, such as logs, stovepipes, wire, glass etc., and assembled them in the classroom. As always, Itten let the students decide which works were best. It was clear to all the students that Mirkin, a Pole, had won hands down. I can still see his "Horse" today. It was a wooden board, part smooth and part rough, which had a paraffin-lamp cylinder on top with a rusty saw through it, ending in a spiral. These sculptural studies were then drawn, with emphasis being placed on highlighting material contrasts and movement. Everyone was free to invent such plastic objects through drawing.'[12] Arndt later reconstructed the material study he describes here; two drawings of this same study also exist (ills., p. 26).

In parallel with such subjective studies Itten also taught theories of contrast, form and colour. Contrasts included, for example, rough-smooth, pointed-blunt, hard-soft, light-dark, large-small, top-bottom, heavy-light, round-square. Contrasts, too, taught a feeling for material and were a prepara-

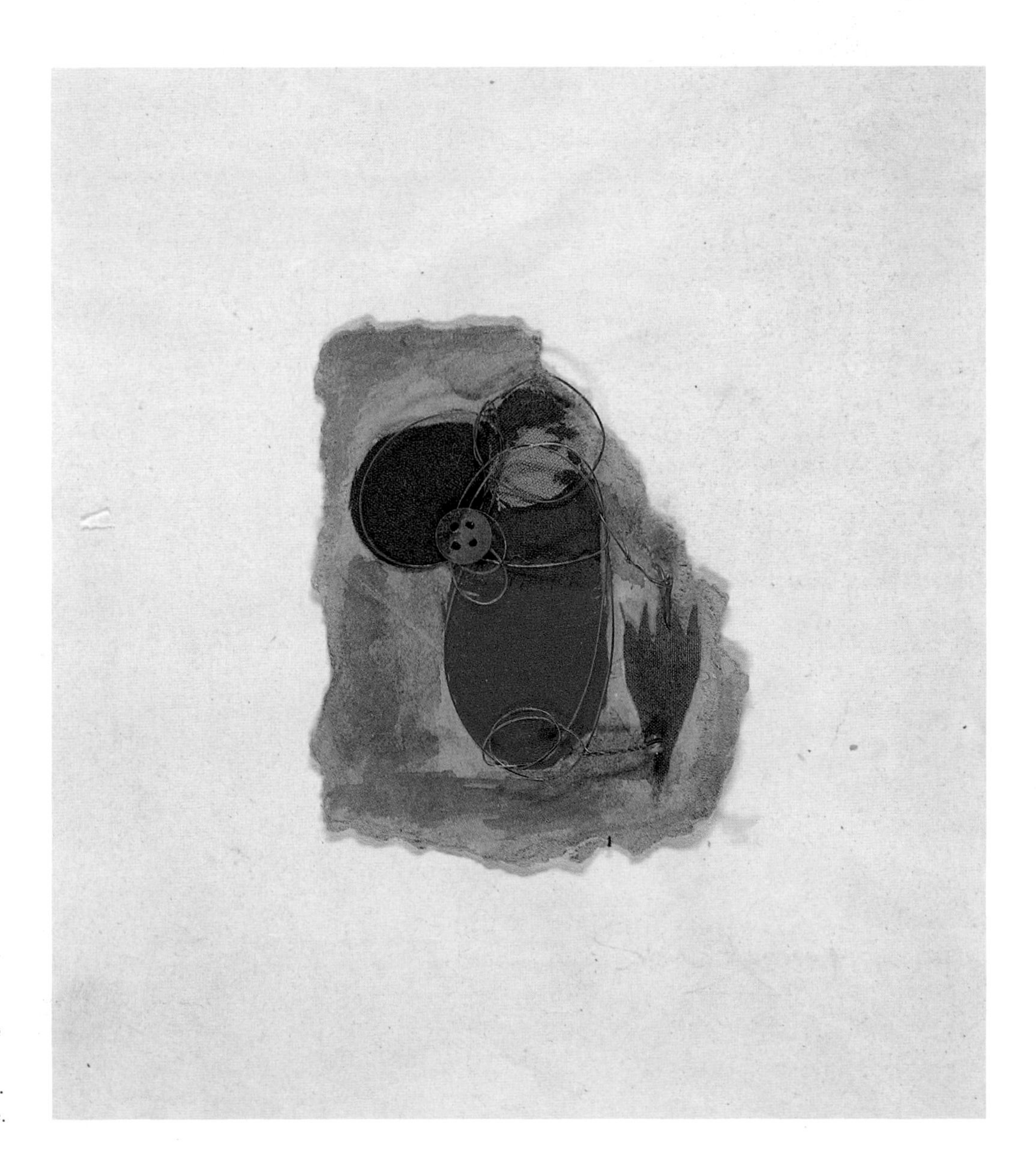

Like many material studies from Itten's *Vorkurs,* this 1921 work by Oskar Schepp is based on the contrast of several insubstantial materials such as cardboard, cloth, felt, wire and drawing pins. Schepp playfully uses these to compose a figure.

tion for workshop activities. Contrasts could be revealed in drawings of materials and natural objects, drawn with the help of form theories or illustrated as sculpture. Itten's theory of form took the elementary geometric shapes of circle, square and triangle and assigned to each a certain character (ills., p. 28 and 29). The circle was thus 'flowing' and 'central', the square 'calm' and the triangle 'diagonal'.
Primary colours and 'primary' forms were concepts which proved particularly influential in the following years at the Bauhaus. Paul Klee, who attended one of Itten's lessons, quickly adopted them into his own teaching. For Kandinsky, who had already published his own thoughts on colour theory in 1912 in 'Concerning the Spiritual in Art', they remained an indispensable part of his teaching, as will be seen below.
The principles and criteria central to the study of materials and natural

Cube composition by Else Mögelin, 1921. Itten later wrote of this exercise: 'In order to let students experience primary geometric forms in a three-dimensional manner, I had them model sculptural forms such as spheres, cylinders, cones and cubes.'

Rudolf Lutz: Plaster relief with square and rectangular form characters, 1920/21.

objects – contrast, form, rhythm – also formed the basis of the classes on 'Analysis of Old Masters' which Itten both instigated and taught.
Oskar Schlemmer provides a lively description of one such lesson: 'Itten gives "Analysis" in Weimar. Shows pictures which students then have to draw in terms of one or another essential – usually movement, line, curve. He then illustrates these in the example of a Gothic figure. Next he shows the weeping Mary Magdalene from the Grünewald Altar. The students attempt to extract some basic element from the very complicated composition. Itten looks at their efforts and explodes: If any of them had any artistic sensitivity at all, then when faced by such a powerful depiction of weeping, the weeping of the whole world, rather than trying to draw it they would simply sit down and burst into tears themselves. Then walks out slamming the door behind him!'[13]

Notes taken by Franz Singer on elementary forms and contrasts during Itten's *Vorkurs*.

Rudolf Lutz: Sculptural plaster study with various form characters, 1920/21.

The point was thus to experience works of art in their profoundness (ill., p. 30). When analyzing Old Masters, pupils could choose to concentrate upon the rhythm of a picture or its composition, its light-dark contrasts or its colours.
The same was true of the third major area of the Weimar curriculum, namely life drawing (ill., p. 51). Female models were used, although students often sat – clothed – for each other. These nude studies generally concentrate upon rhythm; true-to-life representations are the exception. What, therefore, was the particular value and significance of the preliminary course which Itten introduced at the Bauhaus?
The training traditionally given to first-year students at conventional art academies and schools of arts and crafts consisted only of drawing set objects such as plaster figures, ornaments and nudes. Students thus acquired most of their skills through copying. Itten, on the other hand, taught his students the fundamentals of colour and form theory, composition and design. The inspiration for what was then a new and modern style of teaching came both from the educational reform theories with which Itten was familiar and from the artists of the avant-garde.

The Isenheimer Altar by Mathias Grünewald, one of the most important works in the history of German painting, is a typical example of the medieval paintings that Itten frequently used in his 'Analysis of Old Masters'. The aim of such analysis was to experience and assimilate the tragic event depicted. Writing about his analyses in 1921, Itten said: 'Don't be discouraged if your version doesn't correspond to the original. The more completely the picture comes alive in you, the more complete will be your reproduction, which is a precise measure of your powers of experience. You experience the work of art, it is reborn in you.'

Gunta Stölzl: Thistle, drawn as part of Itten's *Vorkurs,* 1920. The thistle was a frequent subject in Itten's classes; its expressive form particularly suited his teaching purposes. In 1921 Itten wrote: 'I have a thistle before me. My motorial nerves experience a lacerated, spasmodic movement. My senses, touch and sight, record the sharp pointedness of its form movement and my spirit sees its essence. I experience a thistle.'

Itten's teaching was also aimed at the inner being; students were to find their own rhythm and develop a well-tuned personality.
Itten's influence on the early Bauhaus can hardly be overestimated. He not only organized and structured a preliminary course whose ideas are perpetuated, albeit modified over time, in many design courses today; he also, as we will see below, exerted a profound influence on activities in the workshops.
As a 'Master', Itten was greatly revered by his students. He wore a special Bauhaus-made outfit (ill., p. 25), as did many of his students; funnel-like trousers, wide at the top and narrow at the bottom, and a high-necked jacket fastened by a belt of the same material. Itten shaved his head, so that his 'head is half school-master, half priest ... His glasses shouldn't be forgotten, either.'[14]
Some 16 to 18 of his Vienna students followed him to Weimar to continue their studies; these 'Viennese' formed an influential group at the Bauhaus. The young painter Georg Muche (ill., p. 32), who joined the Bauhaus teaching staff in October 1920 to relieve Itten's workload, also attached himself to Itten's circle and became his friend and admirer. They later took it in turns to teach the preliminary course. Muche himself injected no new ideas into either practice or theory.

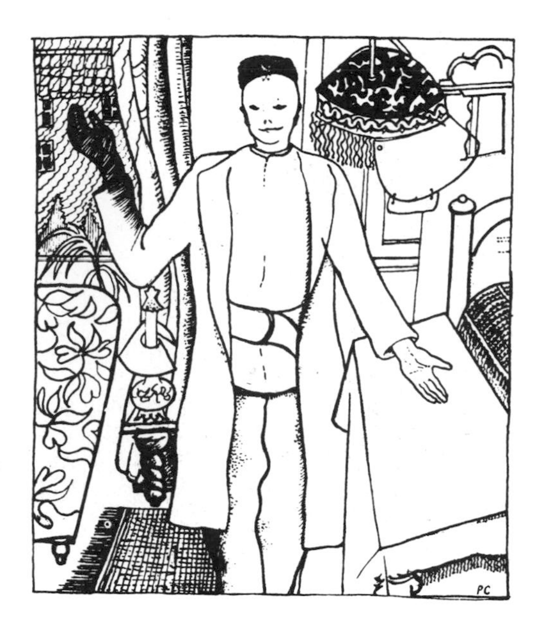

In 1921 Paul Citroen drew his friend Georg Muche 'in Bauhaus robes', as worn by Itten's devotees.

Johannes Itten: House of the White Man, 1920. Lithograph for the first Bauhaus Masters' portfolio.

Muche was at that time a disciple of Mazdaznan, a sect which had spread across Germany and with which Itten had been familiar since the 1910's. Mazdaznan prescribed a vegetarian diet, regular fasting, breathing exercises, sexual discipline and numerous health regulations, all of which Itten followed with increasing dedication. In 1920 Itten and Muche together attended a Mazdaznan congress in Leipzig, the sect's German stronghold, and subsequently started making converts at the Bauhaus. Their aim seems to have been the official introduction of Mazdaznan at the Bauhaus. For some time the Bauhaus canteen produced solely Mazdaznan fare, while Mazdaznan thought also began to filter into Bauhaus teaching. Itten made several contributions to art magazines on the subject. One essay – arguing that the white race represented the highest level of civilization – even reflected a primitive form of racism. This perhaps explains the origin of his lithograph, 'House of the White Man' (ill., p. 32). Bauhaus student Paul Citroen has left us the liveliest description of the Mazdaznan fellowship at the Bauhaus: 'Itten had something demonic about him. As a Master, he was either profoundly admired or, by his opponents (of whom there were many), equally profoundly hated. Whatever else, it was impossible to ignore him. For those of us within the Mazdaznan circle – a special community within the Bauhaus – Itten had a very special aura. You could almost call him a saint; his presence practically reduced us to whispers, and our respect for him was overwhelming. Should he treat us in a friendly and relaxed manner, we would be enraptured and inspired.'[15]
The Mazdaznan followers held 'gatherings of all kinds, lectures, exercises, religious services, consultations, meals – there was an incredibly active striving for the common aim of perfection ... Muche and his wife, closely involved in our circle, took an active part in everything...'

After Itten's departure from the Bauhaus in 1923, according to Citroen, 'our group was effectively redispersed within the main body of students. Mazdaznan no longer posed a problem at the Bauhaus.'
Itten was assisted not only by Georg Muche but also by Gertrud Grunow (ill., p. 33) who, at Itten's request, had taught at the Bauhaus since the end of 1919. Itten had met Grunow, a music teacher, a few months earlier and had been astonished by the similarities in their thinking.
Gertrud Grunow was initially employed as an assistant teacher. Her classes in 'Harmonization' were based on the belief that a universal equilibrium of colour, music, perception and form is anchored in each person, an equilibrium which can be rediscovered through physical and mental exercises. Like Itten, she believed that inner harmony was an essential precondition of human creativity. Grunow's most important teaching aid was a grand piano. Pupils were required to complete gymnastic and concentration exercises in individual lessons. Grunow advised her students on their choice of workshop and wrote a series of regular reports on the development of individual students.
Her pedagogical emphasis, like Itten's, lay on the inner self. It involved 'working into the unconscious and out of the unconsciousness and was thus uncontrollable'.[16]
One Bauhaus visitor described Grunow's classes thus: 'You close your eyes, and after a short period of inner reflection you receive an instruction, either to imagine a certain colour ball and to feel it by penetrating it with your hands, or to concentrate upon a note played at the piano. In less than no time almost everyone is fully in motion, each in their own individual way. These movements are not rhythmical à la Dalcroze; on the contrary, it is easy to distinguish the inhibited intellectuals from the relaxed types, the female nature from the male. The intellectualist, like an unredeemed soul, shuffles along with his hands in front of his eyes, while the redeemed soul moves with hands and legs in constant rhythm. One youth stands there reaching energetically into the air, arm over arm, as if brick-building. All the *men* have *pushing movements directed upwards,* while the *women* have *enveloping movements directed towards the ground.* To an observer, the expressive sign-language of the women's hands is astonishing, a yearning search accompanying the rhythm of their bodies ... What is the purpose of such exercises? They are paths to the discovery of natural elementary forms, and at the same time seek to create inner order in the individual, i.e. to encourage the regulating effect of external impressions upon the inner soul, so that the ordering powers of the intellect do not fall into temptation, that the ordering powers receive their inspiration from the soul within ... When seeking new forms, we must allow these *to be reborn in us from the totality of experience, from the oneness of nature and intellect.* Our path is first irrational and then increasingly rational.'[17] Recent years have seen repeated emphasis on the importance of Grunow's theories both for the Weimar Bauhaus and for Gropius himself.
When the Bauhaus constitution of January 1921 was reprinted in June 1922, one of its most important amendments concerned Grunow's harmonization classes. It now read: 'During the entire duration of study, *practical harmonization classes* on the common basis of sound, colour and form will be taught with the aim of creating a balance between the physical and mental properties of the individual.'[18]
In the Bauhaus brochure of 1923, Grunow's harmonization teaching is assigned a central significance. Gropius adopted a number of its ideas in his introductory essay. In his conclusion, he even took harmonization thinking as the basis for a definition of the nature of the new Bauhaus: 'A new statics of the horizontal is beginning to develop which seeks to counteract

Max Peiffer-Watenphul: Portrait of Gertrud Grunow, 1920.

Franz Singer: Chromatic circle from Gertrud Grunow's course. Every colour in this twelve-part circle, which includes silver and brown, is assigned to a part of the body and a musical note.

gravity through counterbalance. The symmetry of compositional elements ... diminishes as a logical consequence of the new teaching of equilibrium, which transforms the lifeless uniformity of mutually corresponding parts into an unsymmetrical but rhythmic balance.'[19]

The workshops

The workshops which Gropius had announced in the Bauhaus Manifesto could be set up only slowly. Gropius was constantly dogged by financial problems. It frequently proved difficult to find competent master craftsmen (only they were officially qualified to train apprentices). Much of the workshops' equipment had gone missing or been destroyed during the War. Only the bookbinding, graphic printing and weaving workshops were still functioning. The bookbinding workshop was privately owned by master book-binder Otto Dorfner, who was contracted to train Bauhaus apprentices. A similar solution was agreed for the weaving workshop, whose looms were the property of crafts teacher Helene Börner, a former teacher under van de Velde. She too was contracted to teach students, the Bauhaus purchasing her looms only later. Work in the joinery, stained-glass and Dornburg-based pottery workshops was only finally commenced at the end of 1920.

Gropius and the Council of Masters monitored the success and results of workshop training and regularly introduced reforms. Thus, for example, the original ruling allowing students to go straight into a workshop was quickly seen to have drawbacks – excessive consumption of materials with only poor results. In October 1920 the Council of Masters therefore resolved to make Itten's six-month preliminary course compulsory. Only those students who successfully passed this course (as decided by the Council of Masters at the end of the semester) could go on to join a workshop. 'The Bauhaus automatically spat out the untalented; they could stay for no longer than half a year.'[20] Working hours in the workshops were increased to six hours a day.

A course on form taught by Georg Muche and Itten was now made obligatory for students already working in the workshops. Technical drawing was also introduced, with Gropius teaching the theory and Adolf Meyer (longstanding partner in Gropius' private architecture practice) the practical side of the subject.

The aim of all these measures was to overlap and integrate theoretical form teaching with practical workshop training.

In October 1920 the Council of Masters also agreed a second far-reaching reform: every workshop was to be assigned its own permanent Master of Form. Apprentices – all of whom had to produce their own designs – would thus each have two mentors: a Master of Form and a Master of Craft. They had previously been free to choose their own Master of Form.

The bipolar teaching model was now fully established. Parallel tuition from an artist and a craftsman enabled the student to receive a more comprehensive education than a single Master could offer, and thus to produce polished designs to the highest standards of both craftsmanship and art. Gropius later wrote that 'it was necessary to work under two different teachers, since there were neither craftsmen with sufficient imagination to solve artistic problems nor artists with sufficient technical skills to take charge of workshop operations. A new generation first had to be trained who were able to combine both talents'.

In the early days Itten's influence was felt in almost every workshop. Together with Muche he was Master of Form of all except the graphic printing workshop, which was run by Feininger, and the pottery workshop headed by Marcks. In the next semester, however, Itten handed over the

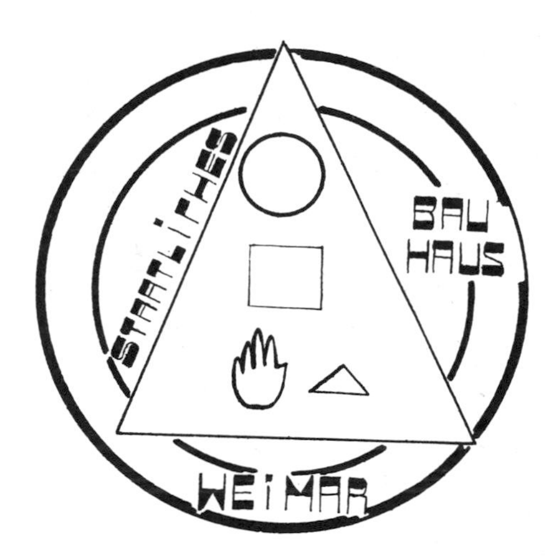

Student design for the Bauhaus seal from the year 1921.

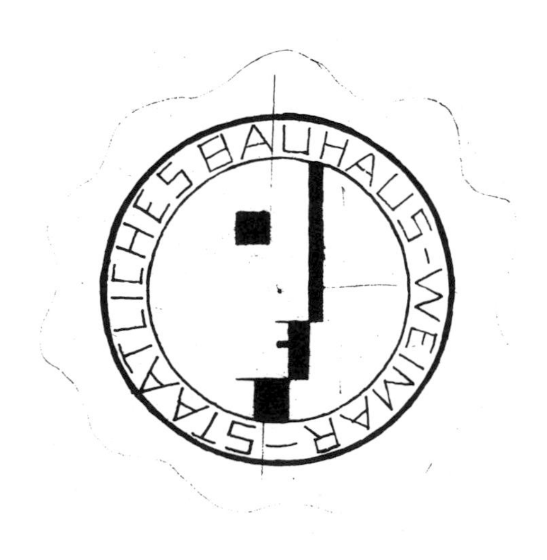

Oskar Schlemmer: Seal of the Weimar State Bauhaus, 1922.

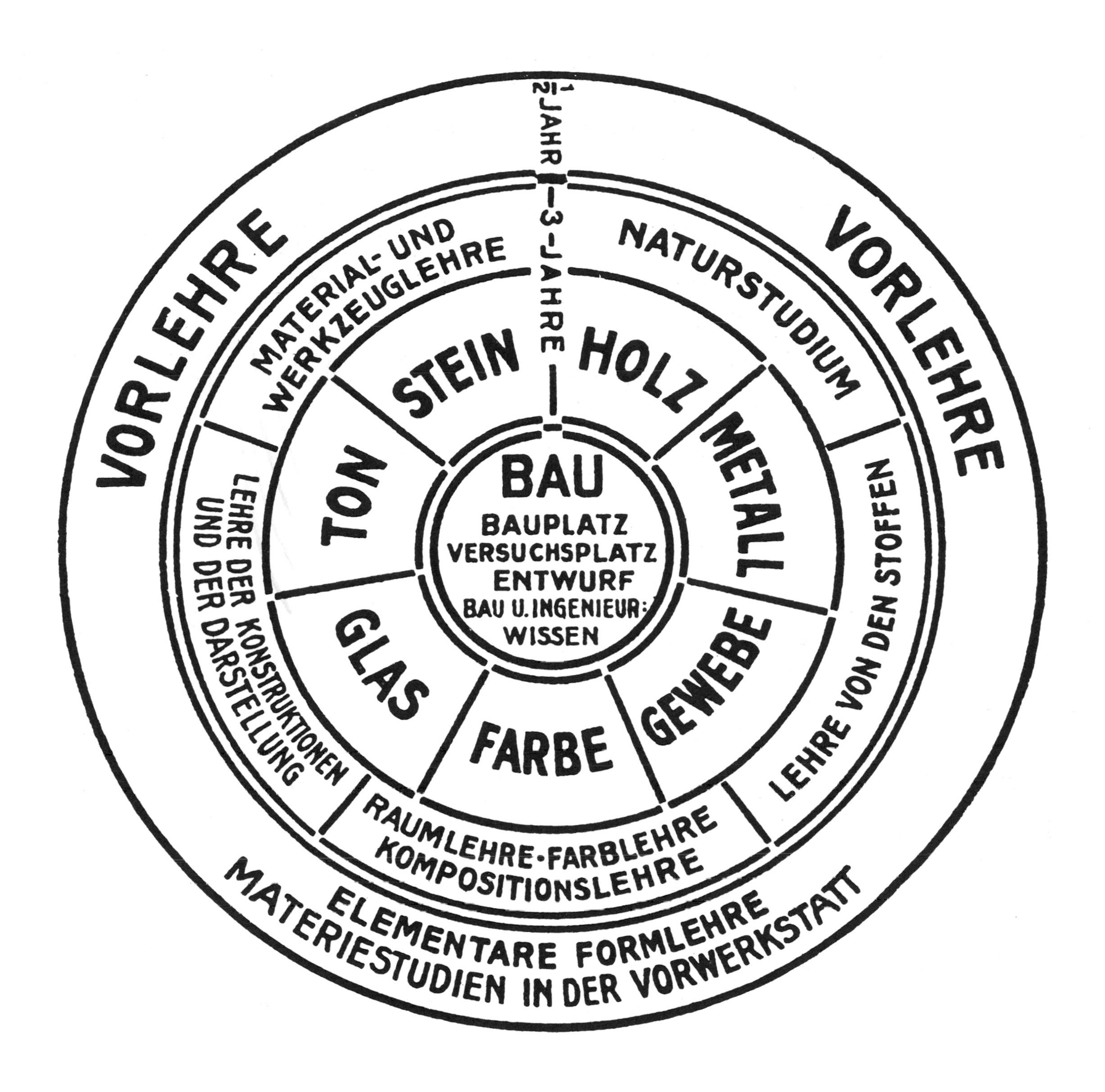

This diagram, which Gropius published in the Bauhaus statutes of 1922, illustrated the structure of the school curriculum. Training started with the six-month preliminary course ('Vorlehre'). The two middle rings represent the three-year period of workshop training together with form theory. The workshops are identified in terms of their materials; 'Holz' (wood) thus stands for the joinery and wood-carving workshops. In reality, form theory was taught less systematically than this diagram suggests. Building ('Bau') – the final, highest stage of education – was not yet offered. Compared to the programme of 1919 (ills., p.18 and 19), the handicraft basis of workshop training is here supplemented by theoretical classes addressing elementary questions of material and design.

Ida Kerkovius: Felt appliqué, 1921. This large work (206 x 164 cm) was made on a sewing machine and served as a wall-hanging for many years.

stone-sculpture workshop to Schlemmer; Muche took over the weaving, Klee the bookbinding and Gropius the joinery workshop. Only the metal, stained-glass and mural-painting workshops remained under Itten until October 1922, when reorganization lessened his influence.
Reports by the Masters of Form and Masters of Craft from the next few years give details about the numbers of apprentices and journeymen employed, about orders, commissions, visits to trade fairs and quantities of materials used. It was now obligatory to register as an apprentice with the Chamber of Handicrafts. The Bauhaus was already starting to buy its pupils' better designs for later commercial use.
The number of extra-curricular events was also increasing with each semester. For a time, writer and publisher Bruno Adler (another who had followed Itten from Vienna) lectured in art history, as did Wilhelm Koehler, director of the Weimar Landesmuseum and one of the most liberal museum directors of his day. There were even anatomy classes. Dora Wibiral, formerly a teacher at van de Velde's school, gave lettering classes, while the unknown painter Paul Dobe offered lessons in drawing from nature. These two last courses were soon dropped from the curriculum, however. Only now, after some two years of reform activity, were the outlines beginning to emerge of 'what Gropius had boldly sketched on paper'[21].

Otto Lindig: Tall lidded jug with decorative engraving, 1922. Height 50 cm. Lindig qualified as journeyman with this work. Composed of clearly distinct elements, the jug appears somewhat angular and is more sculpture than pottery.

Party – work – play

Itten taught under the motto 'Play becomes party – party becomes work – work becomes play'. The same link between work and play was in Gropius' mind when he wrote the Bauhaus Manifesto: 'Theatre, lectures, poetry, music, costume balls. Creation of festive ceremonies in these gatherings.' And indeed, the everyday life of the Weimar 'Bauhäusler' was punctuated by many such events. Gropius introduced Bauhaus evenings of literary readings with the intention of bringing together the local population and the youth of the Bauhaus. While the inhabitants of Weimar adopted a distanced, even oppositional stance to the Bauhaus and its pupils, many students were to remember these evenings for years to come. 'Erdmann played for us ... Theodor Däubler thundered his poems at us. Mrs. Lasker-Schüler held us spellbound with her staccato verses. A scholar read us Gilgamesh. The room was lit by a single candle which died away during the slow recitation of the lament.'[22] On other evenings, students themselves could read aloud. There were four important celebrations during the course of the year: the Lantern party (ill., p. 38), the summer

solstice party, the Kite festival (ill., p. 39) and finally the Christmas party, in which everyone joined in. It seems that the Lantern festival was first held on 21 June 1920 to mark the sixtieth birthday of Johannes Schlaf, poet and Weimar resident. It was subsequently combined with the celebrations held every year for Gropius' birthday on 18 May.
Gunta Stölzl, later head of the weaving workshop, remembers one of the earliest Christmas parties: 'Christmas was indescribably beautiful, something quite new, a "Festival of Love" in every detail. A beautiful tree, lights and apples, a long white table, big candles, beautifully laid, a big fir wreath, everything green. Under the tree everything white, on it countless presents. Gropius read the Christmas story, Emmy Heim sang. We were all given presents by Gropius, so kind and lovely and special to every Bauhäusler. Then a big meal. All in a spirit of celebration and a sense of the symbolism. Gropius served everyone their food in person. Like the washing of the feet.'[23] Some of the postcards accompanying these parties (ills., p. 38 and 39) were executed as lithographs in the graphic printing workshop, with pupils and Masters equally involved in their production.
It is today impossible to imagine the poverty and destitution which the Bauhaus students suffered in Weimar. Gropius organized gifts of clothing and free midday meals. Many were barely able to pay for their tuition. 'It was wonderful if you earned a Mark for a night's work as an extra at the theatre.'

Women at the Bauhaus

In the first two years the Council of Masters passed some major resolutions benefitting the large numbers of hopeful women students. In his first cost estimate for the Bauhaus, Gropius had reckoned with '50 ladies' and '100 gentlemen'; in practice, the Bauhaus took as many women as men, since the new Weimar Constitution guaranteed women unrestricted freedom of study. Academies could no longer – as they had been able to do before the War – refuse women entry, and many women seized the new opportunities now open to them.
In his first speech to the Bauhaus students Gropius made express reference to the women present. His notes referred to 'no special regard for ladies, all craftsmen in work', 'absolute equality of status, and therefore absolute equality of responsibility'.
As early as September 1920, however, Gropius was suggesting to the

Paul Klee: Postcard for the Lantern party, 1922.

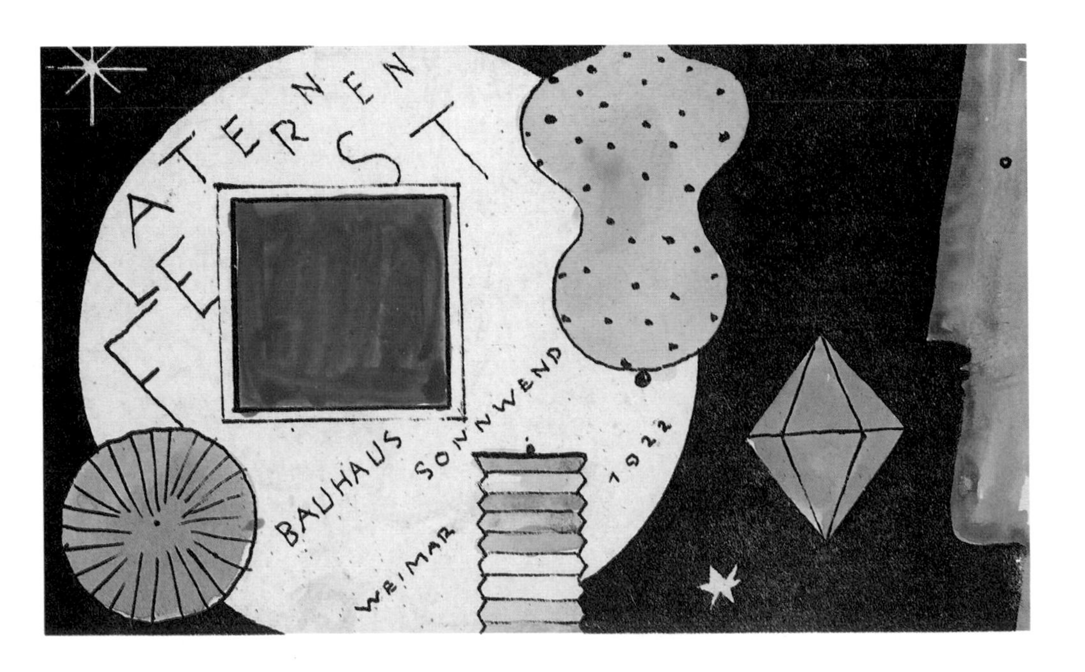

Oskar Schlemmer: Postcard for the Lantern party, 1922.

Lothar Schreyer: Watercolour postcard for the Kite festival, 1921.

Bauhäusler Rudolf Lutz in woman's costume with dadaist decoration, 1920 or 1921.

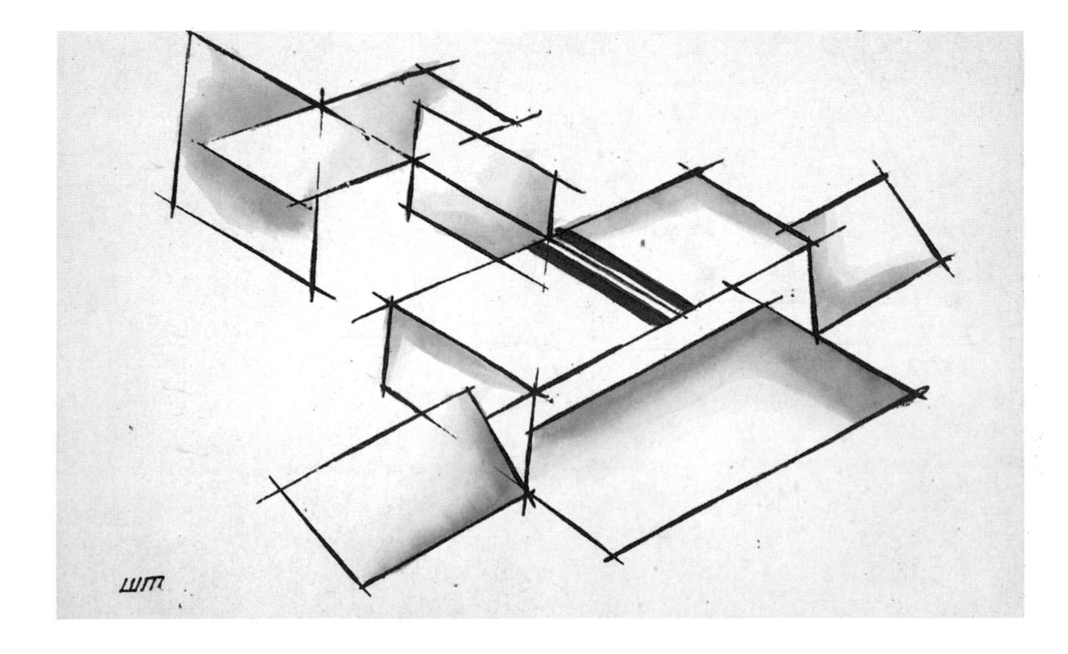

Wolfgang Molnár: Postcard for the Kite festival, 1922.

Four young women from the weaving workshop: Margret Leischner, Margret Dambeck, Liesel Henneberg, unknown.

Council of Masters that 'selection should be more rigorous right from the start, particularly in the case of the female sex, already over-represented in terms of numbers'. He further recommended that no 'unnecessary experiments' should be made, and that women should be sent direct from the *Vorkurs* to the weaving workshop (ills., p. 40 and 41), with pottery and bookbinding as possible alternatives. But the bookbinding workshop was dissolved in 1922 and Gropius and Marcks, head of the pottery workshop, had agreed in October 1923 to admit 'no women at all if possible into the workshop, both for their sakes and for the sake of the workshop'. A short while later, however, workforce shortages led to the admission to the workshop of two women who had not even completed the *Vorkurs*. No women at all were to be admitted to study architecture.
It may be noted that the Weimar Bauhaus presented a number of fundamental obstacles to the admission of women and that those who overcame the first hurdles were forcibly channelled into the weaving workshop. Much of the art then being produced by women was dismissed by men as 'feminine' or 'handicrafts'. The men were afraid of too strong an 'arty-crafty' tendency and saw the goal of the Bauhaus – architecture – endangered.

Architecture teaching and estate planning

'A new architecture', the 'great building' – these were the goals of Bauhaus education as formulated by Gropius in the Manifesto. Indeed, Gropius repeatedly sought to establish a department of architecture at the Weimar Bauhaus, but was met with almost insurmountable opposition from an adminstrative bureaucracy frequently disposed to thwart him. In autumn 1919 Gropius arranged for students interested in architecture to be able to spend an intermediate semester at the Weimar Baugewerkeschule, the architectural and civil engineering school run by Bauhaus sympathizer Paul Klopfer. Since the Ministry of the Interior refused to approve this arrangement, Gropius had the course, attended by some 15 students, take

In this design for a knotted carpet Gunta Stölzl combined a variety of very different structures, reflecting the influence of Itten's form theories on the weaving workshop. 1920-22.

Below: In 1925 Walter Hege photographed the two Bauhäusler Gertrud Arndt and Marianne Gugg (left) knotting carpets in the workshop. Their artificial poses recall those of angel musicians in medieval art.

place at the Bauhaus on a private basis. 'In the same year, some 10 guest students from the Bauhaus attended lectures at the Baugewerkeschule. At the Bauhaus itself, master builder Ernst Schumann taught projection and technical drawing.' In 'May 1920 a department of architecture was founded at the Bauhaus under the direction of Adolf Meyer, Walter Gropius' longest-standing colleague'[24], but the department was subsequently reclosed. There was thus never any systematic architecture teaching at the early Bauhaus.

The Bauhaus had, however, been offered a piece of land in 1920 on which Gropius planned to build an estate. 'We want to build and live in timber houses on this site', he wrote to architecture critic Adolf Behne on 2 June 1920. In the same year, Bauhaus student Walter Determann produced a plan of the entire estate and elevations, sectional views and ground-plans for the proposed timber houses (ills., p. 42 and 43).

Plans for the estate were developed further during the next few years. In 1923, the first large Bauhaus exhibition included models of estate and standardised 'type' housing.

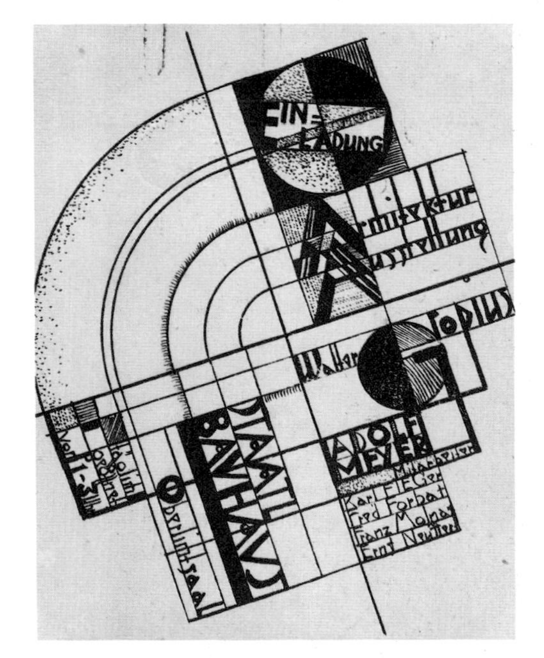

Gropius had pursued the idea of the housing estate as the ideal setting for a community living and working together since his involvement in the 'Arbeitsrat für Kunst'. In the early Weimar years he saw it as the only means of implementing reforms from top to bottom. 'The irony is that we are today unable to reform simply parts of the whole; we must confront life in the totalities in which it exists: housing estates, child education, gymnastics and much more.'[25] The proposed piece of land proved to be too steep for development and was eventually used as a vegetable garden for the Bauhaus canteen.

It was not until 1923 and the first large-scale Bauhaus exhibition that models of estate housing and standardized housing were shown. These, however, had been developed in Gropius' private architectural office. Meanwhile, the large housing estate still being planned in 1923 was represented at the exhibition by just one experimental house.

Gropius himself had been lecturing on spatial science since 1922. Closely related to the ideas of Johannes Itten and Gertrud Grunow was Gropius'

Anonymous: Invitation to an architecture exhibition of work by Walter Gropius and Adolf Meyer. In July 1922 Gropius and Meyer held an exhibition of their work since 1911, ranging from the Fagus factory and the Sommerfeld house to the Jena theatre. The design of the invitation is influenced by both Itten and Schlemmer.

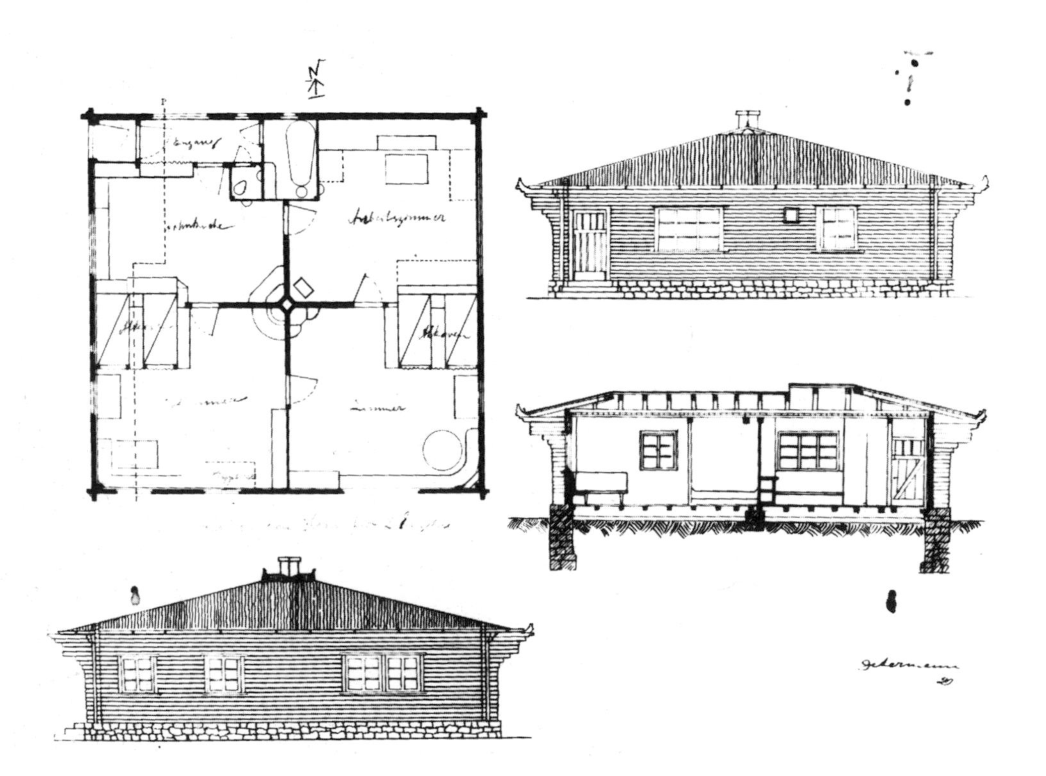

Walter Determann: Design for a timber house for the Bauhaus estate in Buchfart, near Weimar, 1920. The rather awkward ground-plan shows four rooms of almost equal size. The exterior design recalls the Sommerfeld house being planned contemporaneously by Gropius and Meyer.

BAUHAUS-SIEDELUNG.

Walter Gropius and Adolf Meyer: Sommerfeld house, Berlin 1920/21. The Sommerfeld house was the first large-scale joint project to be undertaken by the Bauhaus and the most attractive example of a building designed as a 'unified work of art'. As in the Gothic cathedral chosen to illustrate the Bauhaus Manifesto, the decorations both outside and inside are inseparable from the construction as a whole. The architecture reflects both Expressionist forms and the influence of the prairie houses designed by the American architect Frank Lloyd Wright.

Page 43: *Walter Determann:* Plan of a Bauhaus estate in Buchfart, near Weimar, 1920. Residential housing, workshops, communal facilities and a farm are laid out in a crystalline pattern. The estate was designed to house a residential, working and partly self-provisioning community.

concept of the 'future counterpoint of visual arts' which would also apply to architecture. Such a counterpoint had existed earlier in Gothic art, and in the art of Greece, Egypt and India, as proven by their use of quadrature and triangulature, according to which designs were derived from the basic dimensions of the triangle and square. Regular laws could be found governing spatial composition just as they existed for musical composition. In Gropius' own words: 'Confirmation everywhere. Itten, Grunow, Kandinsky, Ozenfant, Jeanneret.'[26]
In order to discover such laws, intuition had to be combined with mathematics, real with transcendental laws; a constant interchange was needed between the individual and the cosmos. These esoteric theories belonged to the major themes of the early Bauhaus. We will encounter them again in the teachings of Klee, Kandinsky and Schlemmer.
Joint work on the 'building' was one of the most important of the Bauhaus goals, but it proved difficult to implement in practice. Eventually, in 1920, a private commission gave Gropius an opportunity both to boost Bauhaus finances with subcontracted work and to attempt a first communal project. The building contractor Adolf Sommerfeld asked Gropius to build a villa which, for reasons of economy, was to be made of teak salvaged from the wreck of a battleship (ill., p. 44). The villa was sited near Asternplatz in the Dahlem district of Berlin.
Gropius and Adolf Meyer supplied the architectural design; the foreman

was Fréd Forbát, a student who had already completed his architectural training under Theodor Fischer in Munich. The interior decoration was executed by the most competent Bauhaus students. Dörte Helm produced an appliqué curtain (ill., p. 49), Marcel Breuer created the seating in the hall (ills., p. 45 and 47), Josef Albers supplied a coloured stained-glass window (ill., p. 47), the mural-painting workshop decorated the walls and Joost Schmidt carved the names of towns linked with the Sommerfeld company into the hard teak (ill., p. 45). Wooden wainscots, door reliefs, banisters and heating cladding were all decoratively carved. The laying of the foundation stone was celebrated in a precisely-planned ceremony, underlining the importance of this first co-operative effort which, while owing much to the Expressionist 'zigzag style', also employed the elementary forms of circle, square and triangle. For the topping-out ceremony, the men had to wear guild clothing and the women specially-designed headscarves to ensure a homogeneous, uniform picture.

Sommerfeld house, entrance hall. Wood-carvings on the stairs by Joost Schmidt, chair by Marcel Breuer. The reliefs by Joost Schmidt on the banisters are characterized by rhythmical, formal and directional contrasts derived from Itten's teaching (ill., p.29), albeit somewhat subdued by the material, hard teak.

The Gropius-Itten Conflict

The important first major Bauhaus contract, the building and furnishing of the Sommerfeld house, was also the occasion of conflict between Gropius and Itten. Disagreement continued to smoulder over the next few years: 'Master Itten recently pronounced that one must decide either to produce personal, individual work in complete opposition to the commercial outside world or to seek an understanding with industry.'[27]

Gropius opposed this view: 'The Bauhaus in its present form will stand or fall depending on whether it accepts or rejects the necessity of commissions'[28]; the Bauhaus was otherwise in danger of becoming an 'island of recluses'. Commissions – usually passed on to the Bauhaus from Gropius' own private practice – were central to Gropius' thinking even before the Bauhaus was founded. In his cost estimate for the Bauhaus, he wrote that 'the school earning its own living is out of the question'. But Gropius nevertheless constantly sought contact with potential customers and met with trade associations and industrialists. When Gropius commissioned the joinery workshop to provide the seating for the Jena Theatre which he and Adolf Meyer had renovated, Itten handed in his notice. He increasingly withdrew from his workshop duties and concentrated on the preliminary course. At the end of the semester, in April 1923, he left the Bauhaus and went to Herrliberg, the centre of the Mazdaznan sect, where he spent some years teaching and running workshops. Itten refused to accept commissions on principle. He considered the highest aim of Bauhaus education the awakening and development of the creative individual in harmony with himself and the world. Harmonious man was also the goal of the Mazdaznan philosophy to which he and Muche subscribed. For Itten's circle, remarked Schlemmer pointedly in December 1921, 'meditation and ritual' were 'more important than work'.[29]

Itten's resignation gradually cleared the way for a new philosophy of teaching centred not upon the individual personality but upon the creation of new products to suit industrial requirements. His departure also meant a smaller role for the handicrafts and handmade products which Itten had seen as serving individual development.

Itten's successors, Josef Albers and László Moholy-Nagy, were to retain the basic principles of Itten's *Vorkurs* teaching, although they dropped those aspects relating to individual personality development.

The Weimar Bauhaus between political fronts

The Bauhaus was a state school and was thus both financially and politically dependent upon the government of the day. Gropius had skillfully succeeded in founding the school in the confusion of the months immediately following the War but, as it expanded and developed over the next few years, the Weimar Bauhaus ran into political opposition and was finally dissolved in 1925.

As from 1 May 1920 the Bauhaus fell within the jurisdiction of the Ministry for Education and Justice of the State of Thuringia, which had been formed from several small Thuringian territories. The government was composed of Social Democrats (SPD), Independent Social Democrats (USPD) and German Democrats (DDP), all favourably disposed towards the Bauhaus. In summer 1920, a government majority in the Landtag regional parliament approved the first Bauhaus budget in the face of right-wing opposition.

Following the second Landtag elections (11 September 1921), a new government was formed by the left-wing SPD and USPD parties. A Ministry of Education was created under Minister Max Greil, for whom the Bauhaus represented an important step on the road towards broader educational reform. 'Activity schools' and 'comprehensive schools' were the most important of the new educational concepts being discussed at that time.

Josef Albers: Coloured stained-glass window for the stairwell, 1922.

Marcel Breuer: Table in the Sommerfeld house, 1922.

Joost Schmidt: Front door and heating cladding in the Sommerfeld house, 1921.

Gropius repeatedly placed the Bauhaus, with its pioneering teaching strategies, within the context of educational reform. However, the right-wing victory in the third Thuringian Landtag elections (10 February 1924) spelled the inevitable end of the Bauhaus in Weimar.

The first attacks against the Bauhaus were already being mounted just a few months after its foundation in 1919. These were sparked off by the appointment of Lyonel Feininger; the Bauhaus was accused of Expressionist favouritism.

Although the Left maintained a majority at regional level until the 1923 elections, Weimar itself was dominated by 'monarchial civil servants, discharged military, pensioners and Grand-Ducal officials who had been adopted into the new Government'[30]. The local press was similarly conservative in its outlook. Bauhaus opponents recorded their first success soon after the formation of the State of Thuringia, when the Landtag resolved to revive under a new name the former Academy of Fine Art which had merged with the School of Arts and Crafts to form the 'Bauhaus'. On 4 April 1921, almost two years to the day after the launch of the Bauhaus, the new 'State College of Fine Art' was founded – a clear victory for the conservative professors from the 'Old Weimar school of painting'.

The most dangerous opponents of the Bauhaus were chiefly located at the levels of local and regional politics. Gropius was untiring in his defence of

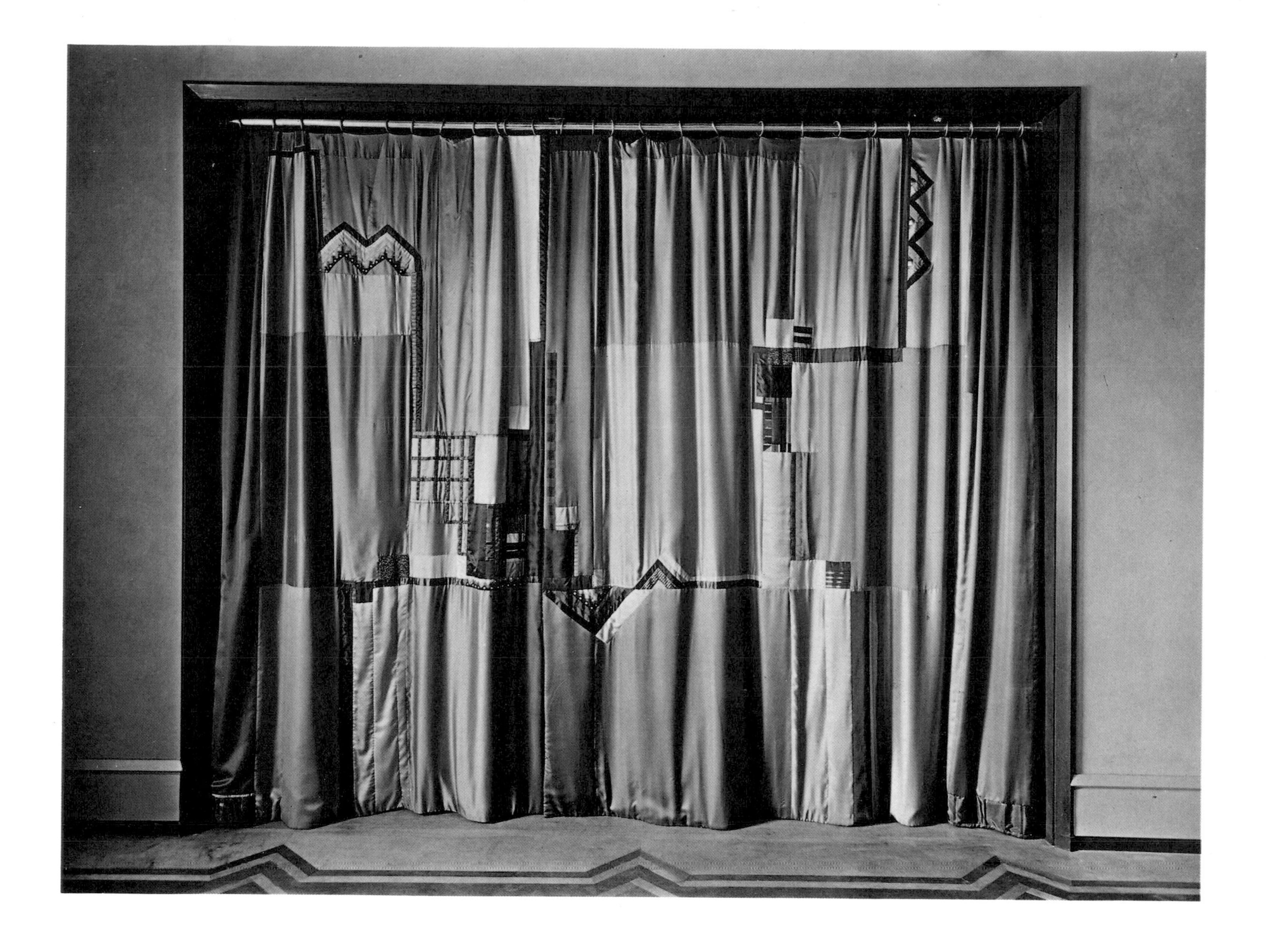

Dörte Helm: Curtain with appliqué work in the Sommerfeld house, 1920/21.

the Bauhaus and sought to disprove false accusations. His efforts sometimes led to legal actions which dragged on for years.
On lecture tours and, above all, via an inexhaustible stream of writings, Gropius sought to make allies and attract sympathizers. His membership of the Werkbund and the Federation of German Architects (and later the architect's association, 'Der Ring') proved useful.
'Ninety per cent of the tremendous efforts made by everyone involved in the Bauhaus undertaking' were spent, according to Gropius, 'on fighting opposition at local and national levels ... with only ten per cent left over for actual creative work'[31]. Gropius sought to keep the Bauhaus well clear of political controversies from the very beginning. He wanted a radical school, but not a political one. He had pursued similar principles as Bruno Taut's successor as head of the Berlin 'Arbeitsrat für Kunst'. The Council of Masters repeatedly advised the students to refrain from all political activity. In September 1921, Gropius turned down a lecture by Heinrich Vogeler to prevent the school being accused of Communist propagandism.
Viewed in its contemporary historical context, the attempt to make the Bauhaus unpolitical proved illusory. 'Its rejection of politics did not protect the Bauhaus against attack by political means'[32], concluded one historian. The first two years of the Bauhaus saw the school settle into its institutional role. In the workshops, all of which were fully equipped by mid-1921, the

new, tandem system of education was proving successful. Articles of apprenticeship were obligatory. Teaching was shared equally between Masters of Form and Masters of Craft. Itten's departure lifted the danger of sectarian isolation. The path was clear for establishing contacts with trade and industry and accepting commissions, and thus also for earning useful extra income.
In these two years the Bauhaus represented a melting-pot of highly contradictory ideas. At the beginning, German nationalists and anti-Jewish students tried to gain the upper hand. Messianic visionaries such as the preacher Louis Häusser were allowed to speak and Itten and Muche to canvass for their vegetarian Mazdaznan beliefs.
Anarchist, socialist, conservationist, life-reformist and esoteric schools of thought all found support at the Bauhaus.
Since the character and direction of the school were – at least in its first year – still relatively unclear, the Bauhaus attracted large numbers of students seeking a traditional painter's training. These included the later painter Max Peiffer-Watenphul (who produced one of most beautiful early Bauhaus carpets), painter Vincent Weber and painter Werner Gilles, who attended one of Gertrud Grunow's courses. The school was shaken by a succession of early exoduses; in 1919, 16 students, including several from the aristocracy, left en bloc following the attempt by one of their fellows, Gross, to found a national Bauhaus. Many students subsequently went off on grand tours of Italy.

Gertrud Arndt: Life drawing from Paul Klee's course, 1924.

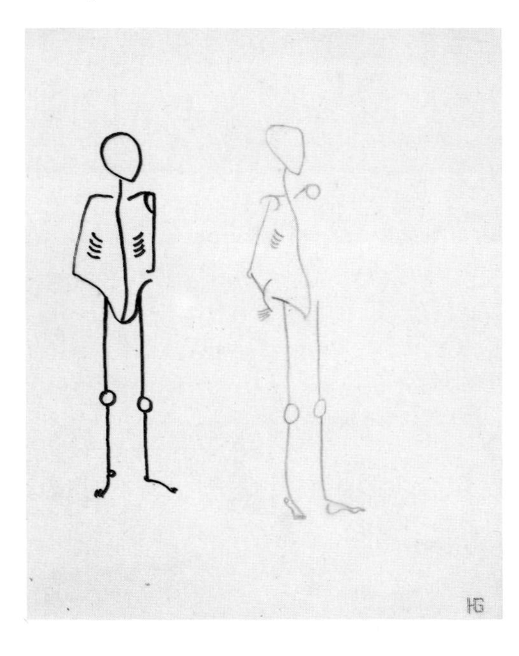

The fact that the school was nevertheless able to survive, and indeed flourish, was a tribute to the leadership qualities of its director, Walter Gropius.
Each Master could submit a written statement of his stance on important questions – in the case of the conflict of principles between Gropius and Itten, for example, and in the discussion of whether Masters should in fact be called 'Master' or 'Professor'. The students elected student representatives with seats and votes in the Bauhaus Council. The Bauhaus Council was a larger decision-making body set up in 1922 in which the Masters of Form were joined by the Masters of Crafts and journeymen and student representatives. These were allowed to participate in discussions on selections and expulsions and on the school's constitution. The students started publishing their own journal, 'Austausch' (Exchange), as early as 1919. There were regular internal competitions, such as for the Bauhaus seal in 1919 (ill, p. 22) and again in 1921 (ill., p. 34). Gropius informed students of new developments in specially-held assemblies. He thus created a strong sense of community spirit, co-operation and shared responsibility.
Gropius described his style of leadership in a letter to one disenchanted with the Bauhaus, Ferdinand Kramer: 'My sole aim is to leave everything in suspension, in flux, in order to avoid our community solidifying into a conventional academy. Our initial resources may be few, but our spirits are high, receptive and excited, and that seems to me to be the most important thing right now.'[33]
Insofar as they can be deduced from writings, letters, reports and works of art, the major themes underlying these first two Bauhaus years cannot be summarized under a single heading. They remained the concepts announced in the original Manifesto: *community, handicraft, architecture.* They were adopted and developed by pupils and teachers alike; elementary forms and primary colours were used as the first components of a counterpoint to visual art which was to form a common ground between artists and craftsmen and in whose rhythm the individual was to find his own identity and space as well as his relationship to the cosmic whole.
The accent was soon to shift in the next phase of the Bauhaus. Although

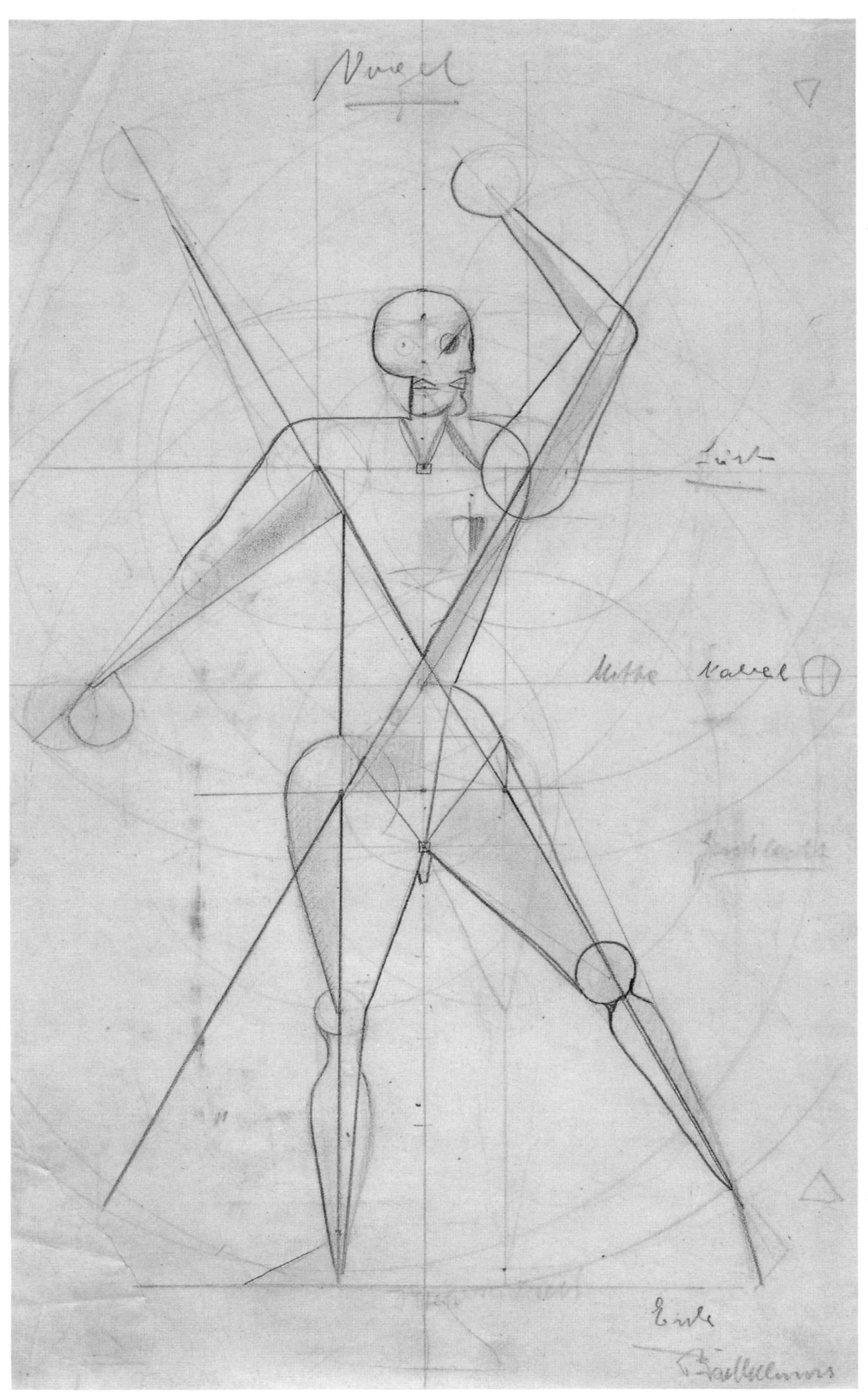

these basic principles remained important, the design discussion was now dominated by the concepts of *type* and *function* and the confrontation with *technology* and *industry.*

This first phase of the Bauhaus has been examined in broad terms and under the heading of 'Expressionism' for the reason that it was dominated by a preoccupation with the individual and his cosmic integration. Social concerns were less real. Following the loss of the War, many intellectuals and artists of the times were preoccupied with intellectual review and the search for a meaning to life. But Expressionism was being pronounced dead with increasing frequency and the Bauhaus, too, was seeking new orientation.

Left: *Klaus Barthelmess:* Life drawing from Schlemmer's course, around 1922.

Right: *Rudolf Lutz:* Life drawing from Itten's course, around 1921. A comparison of these three life drawings reveals the very different approaches adopted towards the human image at the early Bauhaus. The drawing from Klee's course (p.50) focusses simply upon the points of joint movement, while the drawing from Itten's course (above right) aims at capturing rhythm. The drawing from Schlemmer's course (above left) is concerned with idealizing the human form.

Art and Technology – A New Unity

De Stijl at the Bauhaus

The person most responsible for the final suppression of the Expressionist Bauhaus was Dutch artist Theo van Doesburg (ill., p. 57), one of the founders of De Stijl.

'Expressionist jam' was what he thought people were making at the Bauhaus. 'Everyone does what they feel like at the time, far removed from any strict discipline ... Where is there even an attempt to create a unified work of art, a unified configuration of space, form, colour?'[34] asked van Doesburg's artist colleague, Vilmos Huszár.

Van Doesburg founded the De Stijl group of artists together with Piet Mondrian in 1917. They believed art should reconcile the great polarities of life – 'Nature and the intellect, in other words the female and male principles, the negative and the positive, the static and the dynamic, the horizontal and the vertical'[35]. The right angle and the three primary colours, supplemented by black, white and grey, composed the basic elements of expression. With the means of artistic creation thus specified, it would be possible to overcome the 'supremacy of the individual' and create 'collectivist solutions'.

Van Doesburg had already visited the Bauhaus in December 1920 and had followed its activities with great interest. Although he was unimpressed by its products, he recognized the school's enormous potential and prepared an article for his 'De Stijl' journal for which he asked the Bauhaus to supply material.

In April 1921 van Doesburg moved to Weimar, where he hoped for a teaching appointment. In February 1922 he announced a new De Stijl course for young artists:

'Stijl Course I

At the request of a number of young artists, I have decided to start a Stijl course to meet the general need for a positive, contemporary form of expression. The aims of this course will be:

1 To explain the principles of the new, radical style of design developed by "De Stijl" in 1916 (Course A);
2 On the basis of these principles, which apply to all plastic art, to develop a total work of art (Course B).

Conditions of participation:
Participants must already be working in a similar direction. Students will be charged 10 Marks per hour towards photography, equipment, light and heating costs, etc.

Duration:
The course shall be composed of a theoretical part (Part A) and a practical part (Part B). The two parts complement each other. The entire course will last from 8 March to 8 July. 2 lessons a day. 1 theory lesson, 1 practical lesson.
Wednesday evening from 7 – 9 p. m.
Location:
Provisionally in Atelier Röhl, Burhfarterstr. 12 II
Applications:
Applications for the whole course can be made with Werner Gräff, Herderplatz 10, or with my wife.
Weimar, 20 February 1922

Theo van Doesburg'[36]

Gerrit Rietveld: Red-and-blue chair, 1917.

Opposite page: *Marcel Breuer:* Wood-slat chair, second version, 1923. Stained maple with horsehair fabric.

Facing, previous page: *Georg Muche* (idea) and *Adolf Meyer* (planning and execution): Experimental 'Haus Am Horn' in Weimar, 1923; photo 1988.

Doesburg used Dadaist means to attack the Bauhaus, while at the same time emphasizing his influence on the school. The 'State Bauhaus balance sheet', which appeared in 'Mécano' in 1923, concluded: 'outside square inside bourgeois'.

Opposite page: In 1924 Herbert Bayer was designing buildings for advertising purposes not so very far from those of the advertising world today. By including photography, film, sound, light and movement he turned advertising into a multimedia spectacle. In the newspaper kiosk illustrated here, Bayer uses pictures and illuminated signs. The kiosk is composed of planes in space like designs by De Stijl.

Weimar years. In his lectures, Gropius sought a 'common denominator' in architecture; in the workshops, elementary forms and primary colours became the starting-points for design. The ideas of the Bauhaus and van Doesburg were in many cases identical, but van Doesburg's criticism and the clear, constructive forms of De Stijl products served to precipitate and accelerate the Bauhaus' move towards a new style. At the same time Gropius sought to give activities in the workshops a new purpose and direction. Up till then, students had simply used the workshops to practise crafts on the basis of what they had learned in the *Vorkurs*. Specific tasks were lacking, however, since practical work on the 'joint building' remained the exception. The Bauhaus needed to 'create typical ... forms symbolizing the outside world', demanded Gropius in 1922. A short while later, he began tirelessly publicizing a new slogan: '...art and technology, a new unity...' Gropius thus put the Bauhaus onto a completely new footing – for the motto in 1919 had been 'Art and craft – a new unity'.

How had this change come about? In the years immediately following the War, the appreciation of the importance of handicrafts was born of economic necessity; in an impoverished Germany, weakened by a depleted workforce and reparations, the economy needed years to recover.

Gropius courted Thuringian artisan's associations intensively from the very beginning of his directorship, but was generally met with incomprehension. There was also a widespread fear of competition; ideally, the artisan's associations would have liked to see the Bauhaus closed down altogether. A number of contacts were established with industry, however, although many of these failed to bear lasting fruit.

On the other hand, Gropius had intended the school to be productive right from the start; this was to be yet another factor distinguishing the Bauhaus from other schools. A series of students who had received two years of artistic and handicraft training could now devote themselves to this goal. The most competent of these, those who had passed their apprentice's final qualifying examination, were employed and paid as journeymen.

A second important reason behind the orientation towards prototypical products was one of a financial nature. Gropius wanted the school to gradually free itself from state subsidies and thus now added production workshops to the existing teaching workshops. This provided the more senior, qualified journeymen with opportunities to earn money – without which they would not have remained at the Bauhaus. There were soon other political and financial pressures: in June 1922, a government loan to enable the school to equip its new production workshops carried the stipulation that the Bauhaus should organize a large exhibition in 1923. Gropius felt the date was premature but was forced to bow to political demands. He wanted material for the exhibition to be manufactured as part of the productive phase now beginning. Another urgent reason for greater production at the Bauhaus was the need to counteract the economic threat to Masters, journeymen and apprentices posed by the inflation which had been growing since September 1922.

A first attempt to improve Bauhaus finances without recourse to Thuringian state subsidies was a Bauhaus portfolio of graphic prints, planned since 1921. 'We decided to publish the portfolio in order to obtain greater funding for our work than the State of Thuringia can provide.'[41]

In 1922 Gropius also began investigating the possibility of founding a limited company to market Bauhaus products. This, too, was to free the Bauhaus from its dependence on the State.

The early change of direction thus purposefully planned and slowly implemented by Gropius represents a turning-point in the history of the

JOURNALE
ZEI-
ZEITUNGEN
ZEITUNGEN
Kurs
Sport
Radio
Handel
Berliner
Die junge Frau
Neueste
Technikum Ringen
WA 14

Bauhaus. The Bauhaus thereby chose as its goal a new field of activity – contemporary design for industrial production, a field with which almost no one had concerned themselves before. Indeed, Germany was not to start using the word 'design' until after 1945. For everyone seeking to come to terms with the 'age of the machine', the Bauhaus was soon to stand for the very opposite of handicraft, artisan activity.

The spirit of the new slogan was soon felt within the school itself. Gerhard Marcks and Lyonel Feininger, relatively conservative artists by Bauhaus standards, each reacted with caution: 'You know I only half support this idea (of an "industrial Bauhaus"). I think people are more important than successful cutlery manufacture, and people develop through crafts ...'[42]

Feininger wrote to his wife, Julia: 'One thing is sure – unless we can produce "results" to show the outside world and win over the "industrialists", the future of the Bauhaus looks very bleak indeed. We now have to aim at earnings – at sales and mass production! But that's anathema to all of us and a serious obstacle to the development process.'[43]

Work produced in the preliminary course taught by László Moholy-Nagy, around 1923.

Untroubled by such doubts, Gropius chose as Itten's successor an artist who fully supported the Bauhaus' new direction and who quickly became Gropius' most influential colleague: László Moholy-Nagy (ill, p. 61). The 28-year-old Hungarian had been living in Germany since 1920 and had made a name for himself in his first exhibition at the 'Sturm' gallery in Berlin. Although Moholy was officially employed as the new head of the *Vorkurs* and metal workshop, his enthusiasm and flair stimulated the entire Bauhaus. He was soon to introduce a modern style of house print which revolutionized the public face of the Bauhaus. Internally, he called for deliberate confrontation with the world of technology. 'Moholy wants the Masters of Craft to be active on a larger and livelier scale, and the people leaving the workshops to have better and broader skills, through the deliberate employment of machines.'[44]

Almost no other Master attracted such intense criticism: 'Moholy burst into the Bauhaus like a strong, eager dog and, with unfailing instinct, unearthed and attacked its unresolved, tradition-bound problems ... no one got more involved in things than he did.'[45]

Klee, however, spoke of his 'stereotype spirituality' and Hannes Meyer, later Bauhaus director, called him a 'painting journalist'.

Gropius took this new appointment as an opportunity to discuss and subsequently implement fundamental changes to the *Vorkurs.* Drawing, so important to Itten, was virtually dropped altogether. While hundreds of drawings have survived from Itten's lessons, the numbers from Moholy's classes can be counted on the fingers of just two hands. Moholy gave a sort of preparatory course in which students built three-dimensional objects, exercises in spatial equilibrium based on an asymmetrical balance of glass, plexiglass, wood and metal (ill., p. 60).

In the long term, however, it was the materials course – for which Gropius appointed the former elementary-school teacher and Bauhaus student Josef Albers – which was to prove the more important and influential. This part of the preliminary course was intended as a form of preparation – although by no means a replacement – for work in the workshops. Students visited factories and businesses, familiarized themselves with simple tools and learned to work with materials singly and in combinations. Although Albers took much of his material from Itten's *Vorkurs,* it was in a streamlined, rationalised form. When László Moholy-Nagy left the Bauhaus in 1928, Albers took over the whole *Vorkurs,* which he continued to expand and systemize.

The preliminary course, which until 1923 had only lasted six months, was now extended to one year. Klee and Kandinsky's courses in the theory of

In 1925 Lucia Moholy photographed her husband in the red workman's overalls that he often wore at the Bauhaus, and which matched his conception of the artist: the designer as technician.

form also fell within the scope of the preliminary course, which was supplemented as from the second semester by training in a workshop. Articles of apprenticeship were officially concluded in the second semester. These briefly-outlined reforms actually took place in several stages. They, too, indicate that the Bauhaus was never at any stage in its history a rigid system, but was always ready to respond flexibly to changing circumstance and the lessons of experience.
These reforms, and the appointment of Moholy-Nagy, marked the beginning of a new chapter in Bauhaus history.

Paul Klee: Woodland Berry, 1921/22. Watercolour.

Paul Klee's classes

When Paul Klee accepted the offer to teach at the Bauhaus he had no previous teaching experience. He had attended an academy only briefly and had acquired the vast part of his knowledge and skill by autodidactic means. His animated interest in new art school programmes had started in the days of the Munich Revolution. Not long afterwards, Oskar Schlemmer – then spokesman for the Stuttgart art students – had unsuccessfully sought to secure him an appointment at the Stuttgart academy.
Klee, the subject of three monographs published almost simultaneously in 1921, was still relatively unknown to the general public. He was well-respected in avant-garde circles, however, and had just achieved his first successes on the art market. Around 1920 he was considered one of the most important of the Expressionist artists. For Klee, whose art always reflected the spirit of the age, the obligation to teach was an additional reason to now change the technique, style and content of his art and at the same time to develop a method of art instruction appropriate to an introductory course on form. His course took place in part parallel to and in part

Franz Singer: Colour penetration of yellow and violet. Watercolour from Paul Klee's course, around 1922/23.

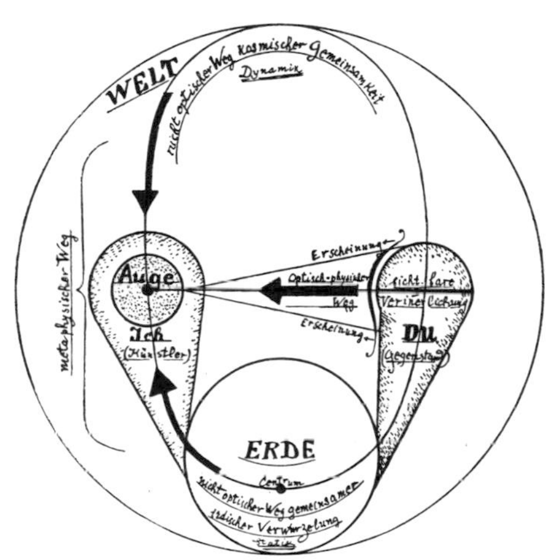

In his 1923 essay entitled 'Paths of Nature Study , which Klee illustrated with this diagram showing the relationship between artist, object and outside world, he wrote: 'All paths converge in the eye and, converted into form at their meeting-point, lead to the synthesis of outer sight and inner seeing. From this meeting-point, manual entities form which are totally different from the optical image of an object and yet, from the point of view of totality, do not contradict it.'

after the *Vorkurs.* Klee and Schlemmer took over the life drawing course from Itten, each teaching a semester in turn (ills., p. 50 and 51).
After just a few months of teaching, at the start of the winter semester of 1921/22, Klee's class became a 'pictorial form theory' course, whereby he chose as his starting-point the two-dimensional panel which was his most popular medium. He wrote down all the lectures he gave up to 2 April 1922, enabling us to form a good picture of his first course. In the winter semester of 1922/23 he expanded his subject matter to include colour theory.
In his early lessons, attended by some 30 students, Klee chiefly analysed his own paintings. One of these, as Marianne Heymann remembered, was Klee's recently-completed 'Woodland Berry' watercolor (ill., p. 62). While Klee's previous watercolors had been guided purely by emotion, he now sought 'to construct tonality strictly on two colours...And drawing strictly matches artistic form'[46]. 'Woodland Berry' is itself based upon a pair of colours taken from the spectrum, namely yellow and violet. Black and green are used solely to accent.

Gertrud Arndt: Studies from Klee's course, 1923/24. These exercises practised the simple handling of geometric forms such as the circle and triangle and their relationships to each other – part of the 'handling of the formal tools' that Klee sought to teach. On the left-hand sheet: 3 forms in one form, logical/part-constructive/touching, interpenetrating, fully-constructive and neighbouring. On the right-hand sheet: logical/superimposed.

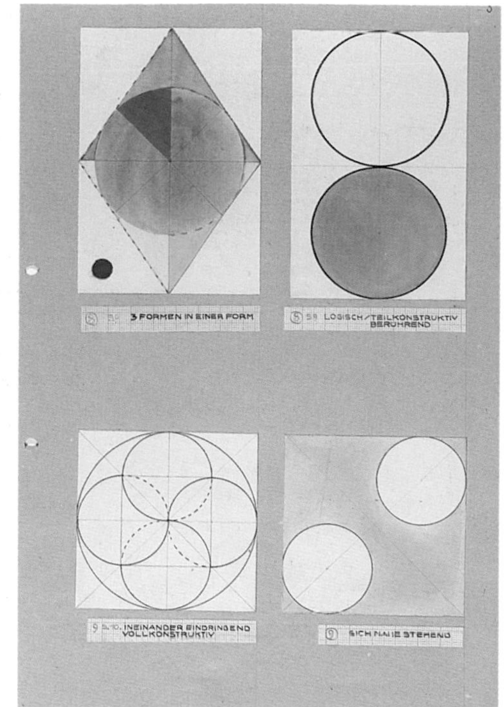

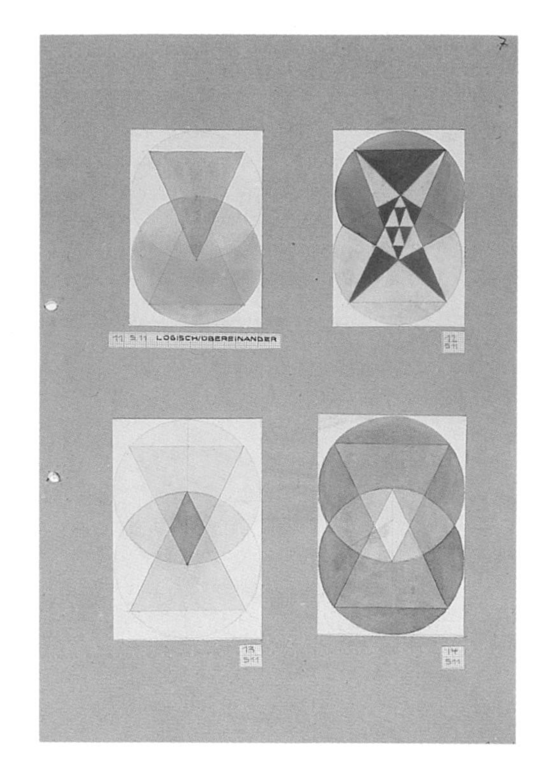

Gertrud Arndt: Exercises from Klee's course, 1924. Left: discriminate movement within the circle not tied to parallel and tied to parallel. Right: very rapid discriminate movements from point to point within each of the three elementary forms.

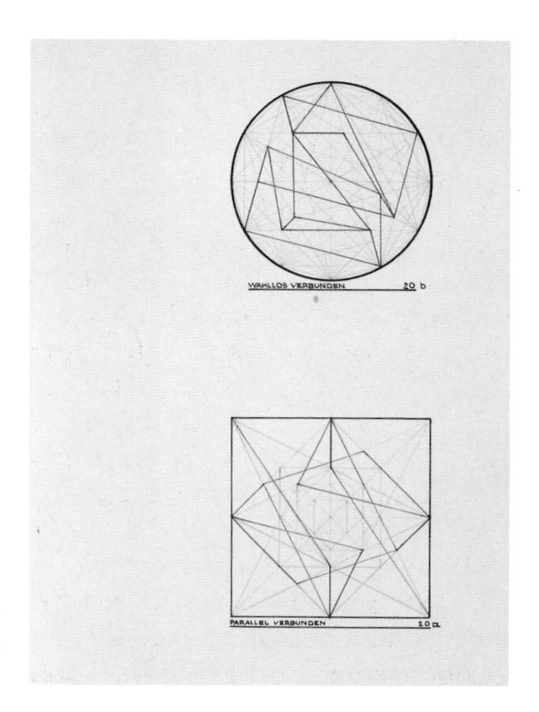

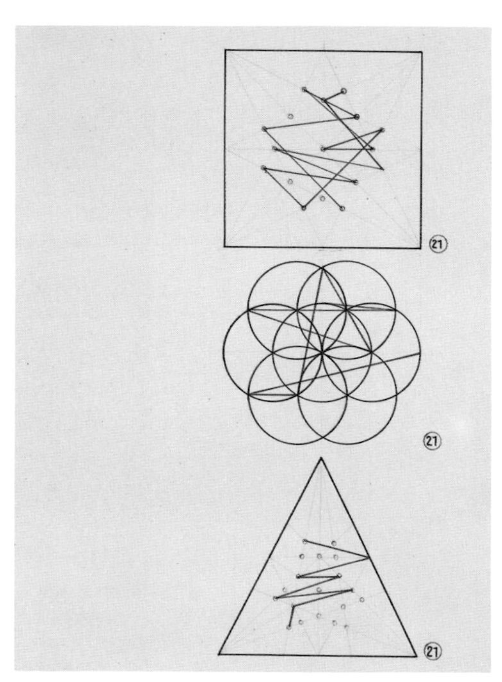

Colour-pair gradations, here explored half playfully and half systematically, were later the subject of systematic exercises by his students (ill., p. 63) as part of Klee's teaching on colour.
A history of the teachings on form which Klee refined into a definitive body of theory over the Weimar years has yet to be written. At the beginning, certainly, he borrowed much from Itten and Kandinsky. He attended Itten's classes and was familiar with Kandinsky's 'Concerning the Spiritual in Art' from 1912, an essay which had also inspired Itten.
Very like his two colleagues, Klee began his course by studying elementary forms, later introducing the primary colours (ill., p. 64). Many of the exercises known today start from such elementary forms. Their function was to encourage a feeling for the organization of planes and an appreciation of the infinite potential of design; using proportion, rotation, reflection etc., in

Timetable of the preliminary course for the summer semester of 1924. The timetable reveals that the preliminary course was dominated by Albers' materials course and Moholy's design classes, with Klee and Kandinsky teaching a total of only three lessons a week. The prelimary course also included life drawing, mathematics and physics, lectures and – provisionally – technical drawing as the introductory stage of an architecture course.

STUNDENPLAN FÜR VORLEHRE

VORMITTAG

	MONTAG	DIENSTAG	MITWOCH	DONNERSTAG	FREITAG	SAMSTAG
8-9		WERKARBEIT ALBERS REITHAUS				
9-10	GESTALTUNGS-STUDIEN MOHOLY REITHAUS					GESTALTUNGSSTUDIEN MOHOLY REITHAUS
10-11						
11-12						
12-1		GESTALTUNGSLEHRE FORM · KLEE · AKTSAAL			GESTALTUNGSLEHRE FARBE · KANDINSKY ·	

	MONTAG	DIENSTAG	MITWOCH	DONNERSTAG	FREITAG	SAMSTAG
2-3			WERKZEICHNEN GROPIUS · LANGE · MEYER RAUM 39			
3-4						
4-5	WISSENSCHAFTL · FÄCHER · MATH · PHYS · etc. AKTSAAL.	ZEICHNEN KLEE RAUM 39			ANALYTHISCH ZEICHNEN – KANDINSKY. R39	
5-6						VERSCHIEDENE VORTRÄGE
6-7						
7-8		ABENDAKT · KLEE OBLIGATORISCH FÜR VORKURS			ABENDAKT.	
8-9						

AN DEN GELB UMRANDETEN UNTERRICHTSSTUNDEN KÖNNEN ALLE GESELLEN UND LEHRLINGE TEILNEHMEN.

conjunction with exercises in colour theory, they offered an inexhaustible field of activity.

Like Itten and Grunow before him, and like Kandinsky and Schreyer his colleagues, Klee linked his theories to a system of cosmic unity which he illustrated in a diagram accompanying an essay on the study of Nature (ill., p. 63).

In his essay, he recommended the synthesis of the study of Nature and the study of the inner being, a synthesis which should be intensively practised. 'Through the experience he has gained via the different paths and translated into his work, the student reveals the level which his dialogue with natural objects has reached.' He passes through Nature to an understanding of the world, and is then able to 'freely create abstract forms'. Klee thus belatedly linked the two poles of his own autodidactic career and sought to make them bear fruit in his pupils through appropriate exercises. In this connection, for example, Gertrud Arndt drew snail shells, halves of apples and nudes (ill., p. 50). Tasks of this nature appear not to have proved successful, however; only a few have survived. At the Dessau Bauhaus they were abandoned altogether, and the drawing from nature which Klee had taught became part of Albers' *Vorkurs.*

Although, in his 'pictorial form theory' course, Klee 'systematically and comprehensively reflected the experience and knowledge he had gained through painting up to 1922'[47], his teaching featured many of the methods being explored in other courses, too. 'Synthesis' and 'analysis' were employed as central to Klee's theories of art.

Klee himself described his teaching thus: 'I see my role more and more clearly as time goes on, namely to communicate the understanding I have gained through the shaping of ideas (drawing and painting) regarding the organization of multiplicity into unity. This I communicate in part through synthesis (i.e. I let you see my work), in part through analysis (i.e. I dissect the works into their essential components).'[48] Klee was thus also concerned to distance himself from 'Itten's method of spontaneous initiation into artistic creation'[49], which had been the aim of the 'Analysis of Old Masters'.

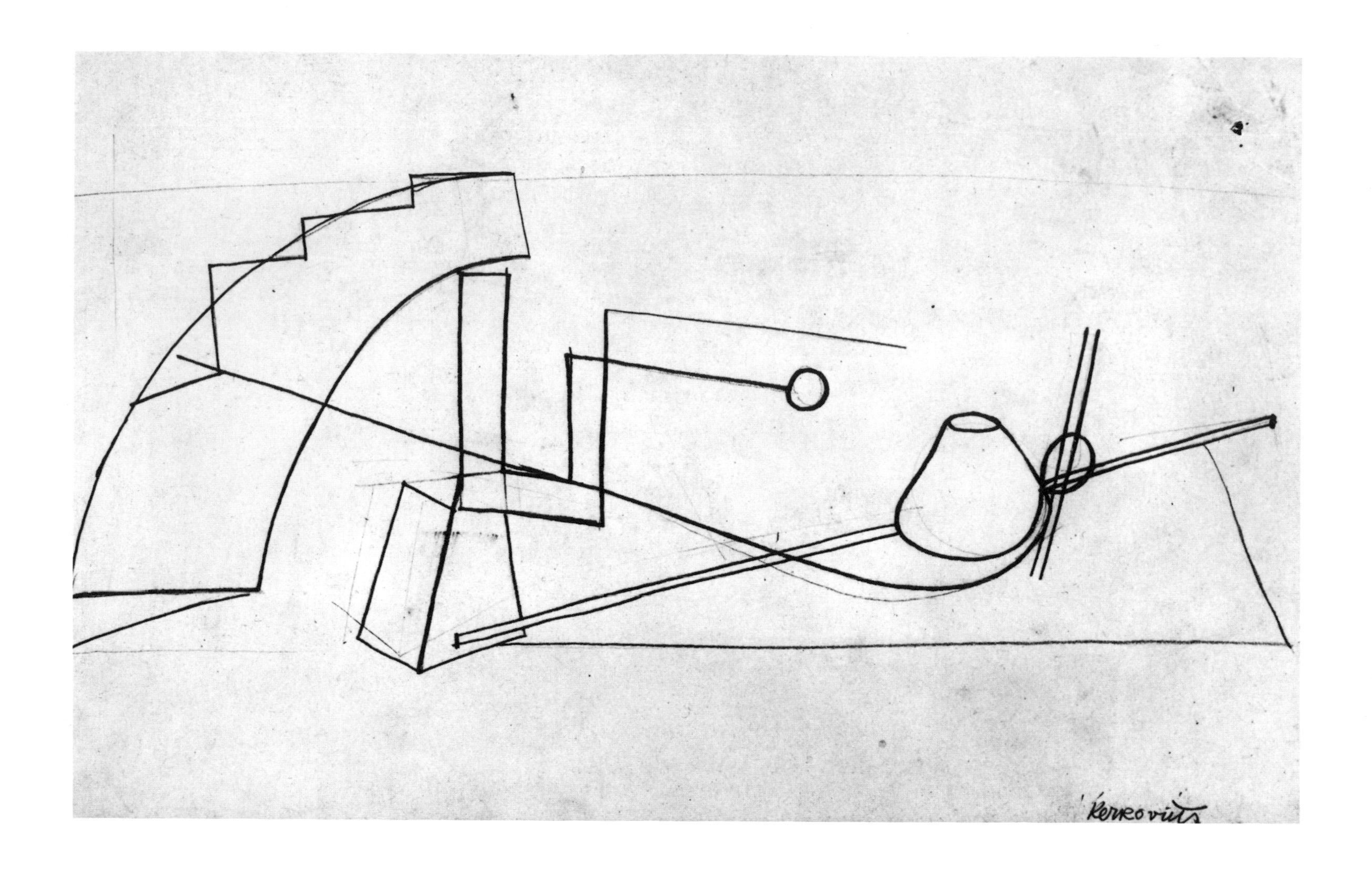

Wassily Kandinsky's classes

Kandinsky started work in the middle of 1922, taking over both the mural-painting workshop and – as part of the expanded form course – a course on colour. Kandinsky, like Klee, adopted a systematic approach to his teaching; he, too, took synthesis and analysis as his starting-points. While Klee associated synthesis with the individual picture, Kandinsky linked it to the concept of a 'Gesamtkunstwerk', a 'total work of art' combining several of the arts. He sought to realize such a synthesis in his stage designs for the theatre.

In 1912 Kandinsky had discussed the characters of certain colours and the different effects they produced in different forms in his book 'Concerning the Spiritual in Art'. It represented a first summary of his ideas, derived in part from other scientific disciplines. War and revolution prevented him from reaching a final conclusion, however.

In Russia, where he was a member of the Institute for Art and Culture (INChUK) after the Revolution, proposals Kandinsky put forward on artist education were rejected on the grounds that they were too subjective and insufficiently dedicated to social aims. This rejection was one of the reasons why Kandinsky left the country. His appointment to the Bauhaus came whilst he was living in Berlin. Everyone at the Bauhaus itself was familiar with Kandinsky's pre-War writings, and Klee was a personal acquaintance from his days as a member of the Munich-based 'Blauer Reiter' group.

Colour theory had played only a minor role in Itten's teaching, and Kandinsky's colour class was thus to fill an important gap in the timetable. Kandinsky's starting-points were the three primary colours, red, yellow and blue, and the elementary forms of circle, triangle and square.

Ida Kerkovius: Linear analysis of a still-life; drawing from Kandinsky's course, 1923.

Ludwig Hirschfeld-Mack: Identical elements on black and white backgrounds, around 1922. These compositions were designed to illustrate the differing spatial effects of colour. A dark object appears smaller than a light object of the same size.

In contrast to Paul Klee, however, Kandinsky was interested in the expressiveness of colour. In the early days of his Bauhaus teaching, he set the students in his mural-painting class and the co-organizer of his 'colour seminar', Ludwig Hirschfeld-Mack, to investigate. In one such exercise, the spatial impression created by white on black was illustrated and compared with the spatial effect created by black on grey (ill., p. 67). Starting from the question of the nature of colour and the relationship between colour and form, Kandinsky developed a series of classroom exercises which he regularly repeated. Analytic drawing formed another area of Kandinsky's teaching. Here students were required to copy the compositional tensions and essential lines of a still-life in a succession of steps (ill., p. 66) until they finally arrived at the skeletal outline of an abstract, internally harmonious painting. This process recalls Itten's 'Analysis of Old Masters'. But while Itten's aim was to train the inner being intuitively, Kandinsky was concerned with the execution of a logically-structured analysis.
Klee's instructions on drawing from nature were an attempt to translate what he had taught himself into a didactic method for others. Wassily Kandinsky's analytic drawing, which accounted for the larger part of his Weimar teaching, can be seen as a systemization of his intellectual confrontation with abstract painting in the years 1910-12. At that time, Kandinsky had wanted to depict objects in such as way that they were no more than 'memories' which provoked associations. Furthermore, formal elements (colour, organization on the plane) were to give the overall composition its power of expressiveness, since Kandinsky assigned specific effects to every shape and colour. He thus saw yellow as a typically earthy colour which reminded him of a sounding trumpet. Violet was sickly and sad. In

their analytical drawings, students thus retraced Kandinsky's own path from object to composition. In the 1926 Bauhaus book 'Point and Line to Plane', he published a first 'analysis of pictorial elements'.

The pottery workshop

Gerhard Marcks was, together with Itten and Feininger, one of the first three artists whom Gropius appointed to teach at the new Bauhaus. It is hard to explain what brought Gropius and Marcks together, since Marcks saw himself as 'national' and 'racial', often with anti-Semitic overtones. The programme of the 'Arbeitsrat für Kunst' and the first Bauhaus programme nevertheless met with his approval: 'We are essentially all striving for the same end: the fusion of all the fine arts into a masons' guild and a handicraft basis and training. But the rest I don't hold with.'[50]

The task of setting up a pottery workshop and training students was at first beset with enormous organizational and financial difficulties. Initial attempts to open the workshop in Weimar soon failed. In the course of 1920 negotiations were begun with Max Krehan, an unusually forward-looking master potter who ran his own workshop in Dornburg, some thirty kilometres outside Weimar, and who was prepared to collaborate with the Bauhaus. Five students committed themselves to working in Dornburg for the next two years. They lived in the stables of the local castle and grew vegetables on a garden plot. The minutes of a meeting of the Council of Masters on 20 September 1920 recorded: 'The external circumstances at Dornburg are very promising, and its boarding-school nature comes closest to Bauhaus intentions. The only danger is that the workshop will break away from the rest of the school if precautionary steps are not taken in good time'[51].

The Dornburgers indeed lived their own lives; '...the clay was dug from the woods, as was the potter's traditional right. The long Kasseler oven was charged with the carefully stacked, air-dry wares and the furnace stoked with three-foot logs through the stokehole. 24 hours pre-firing, 24 hours final firing, accompanied by schnapps and endless story-telling, at which the Krehan brothers excelled. The logs, which came from trees in the forest, naturally had to be chopped to size and split. It was pure "Nature" – all the more so with food in extremely short supply. But however hard the work, we took turns at life drawing and reading aloud on Saturday evenings, everything from Goethe to Strindberg.'[52]

Thanks to their physical separation, both the division of work and the cooperation between the Master of Form and Master of Craft can be followed here more clearly than in other workshops.

In Krehan's workshop, students learned the practical principles of turning, glazing and firing and worked on the so-called 'commercial firings' which brought in money. Marcks, who had already worked for ceramics companies, encouraged his students to experiment with pot shapes as well as teaching the history of ceramics.

The decision back at 'HQ' to supplement the teaching workshops with production workshops had a profound impact on each and every Weimar workshop.

In May 1923 the Bauhaus took over Krehan's workshop as a production workshop, and the technical and commercial sides of Master Marcks' workshop were now run by two different people. This division appeared to cause no great ill-feeling, however. Another change soon followed: at the beginning of 1924, journeyman Otto Lindig was made technical head of the Bauhaus pottery, while the commercial side was taken over by journeyman Theodor Bogler, who seems to have first completed an intensive course in commercial bookkeeping in the main Bauhaus offices.

Theodor Bogler: Mocca machine, 1923. Height 25.5 cm. The pot is composed of four parts stacked into a very compact form and already reflecting ideas on industrial form. A version of this pot was in fact manufactured by a porcelain factory later in the same year, but it proved too complicated for large-series production and therefore too expensive.

Opposite page: Tall lidded pot by Otto Lindig, 1922. Height 59 cm. In this pot Lindig abandons all reference to the traditional archetypes which had continued to appear in pottery until at least 1922. His search for new form led to this eccentric combination of approximated elementary forms and bodies, including cone, cylinder, spherical section and circle. The pot thereby becomes a sculpture which barely remains suitable for practical use. A very similar pot was produced in the metal workshop (ill., p.77).

Theodor Bogler: Combination teapot with lateral pipe handle, 1923. Height 10.5 cm. Bogler's combination teapot was produced in two sizes and several versions, with differing lids and handles (c.f. ill., opposite page). The name of this teapot reflected the idea that a limited number of simple, distinct parts could be variously combined to create different products. This matched Gropius' own views on industrial design as illustrated in his residential housing. But although the teapots were an expression of ideas on industrial form, they were not in fact composed of all the parts they suggest; the body was cast as a whole, with only the handle and spout being added later.

Gropius recognised the importance of mass-producing pottery goods at an early stage. On 5 April 1923 he wrote to Marcks: 'Yesterday I had a look at your many new pots. Almost all of them are unique, unrepeatable; it would be positively wrong not to look for ways of making the hard work that has gone into them accessible to large numbers of people (...) We must find ways of duplicating some of the articles with the help of machines.'[53] Marcks cautioned against this new philosophy, now influencing operations in all the other workshops, too. 'We must keep in mind the fact that the Bauhaus is meant to be a place of education (...) We believe practical production is the right path towards this goal. But production must never be allowed to become the goal itself. Otherwise the Bauhaus will just be another factory to add to the long list of those already existing.'[54]
Master Krehan also wanted to oppose the new development, but journeymen Bogler and Lindig had already opened successful negotiations with industry. In 1923, a set of storage containers designed for the kitchen of the Bauhaus experimental house were among the earliest earthenware goods to be industrially manufactured.
'The exhibition of 1923, the Bauhaus representations at the trade fairs in Leipzig and Frankfurt and successful participation in the 1924 Werkbund exhibition "Die Form" in Stuttgart brought encouraging feedback and growing orders for the pottery workshop, too. But with industry still hesitant, the workshop had to respond to the situation itself by expanding its capacity and rationalizing its production methods. As a result, output was

dominated by the castable pots by Lindig and Bogler, whose very form was designed to express the character of mass-production.'[55]
Lack of materials, shortage of space and the absence of a suitable oven were among the reasons which were ultimately to lead to the closure of the Bauhaus Dornburg workshop. Any hope of improving the situation was doomed by the critical financial situation in which the Weimar Bauhaus now found itself; the State was seeking to cut its funding by 50% in a cold-blooded move to starve the school to death.
The Bauhaus in Dessau was by no means happy with the fact that it had no new pottery workshop. László Moholy-Nagy, the most enthusiastic advocate of industrialization, described its absence in Dessau as 'doubly deplorable because the pottery workshop represents a vital component of the Bauhaus whole and because this is precisely the workshop universally recognized to have produced outstanding models and which has recently expanded its activities to include the production of porcelain as well as earthenware.' It was to be hoped 'that our nation's sizeable ceramics

Theodor Bogler: Combination teapot with eccentric lid and handle at rear, 1923. Height 12.7 cm.

Theodor Bogler: Combination teapot with transverse handle hooks and hoop handle, 1923. Height 12 cm.

industry will provide the means to reestablish a Bauhaus pottery workshop in Dessau'[56]. This hope was not, however, to be fulfilled.

The textile workshop

From the very start, the weaving workshops formed the territory of the many women who joined the Bauhaus, particularly in its early years. Since only some of these women could be rejected, but since they were clearly not to be allowed their fair share of the limited number of study places, the Council of Masters approved the setting up of a women's class. In doing so it revived an institution from the world of the academies and schools of arts and crafts. For many years such classes represented the only educational opportunity open to women, with textile techniques, decoration and decorative drawing their chief objects of study. In the course of 1920 the women's class turned into the textile class. Men were also allowed to join, but in practice remained the exception. In addition to weaving and knotting, the first 'Timetable of handicraft training in textile techniques', printed in July 1921 and almost certainly written by the former handicrafts teacher Helene Börner, included embroidery, decorative edging, crocheting, sewing and macramé. Weaving was originally planned as just one of many textile techniques to be learned. The aims of the original timetable soon shifted in favour of weaving, however, despite almost none of the many students having any practical experience. 'Everything technical – how the loom works, the different styles of weaving, how to thread – we had to learn by trial and error. For us poor self-taught students there was a lot of guesswork and not a few tears shed.'[57] The textile class became a weaving workshop. Oskar Schlemmer rhymed mockingly: 'Where there's wool you'll women find, weaving just to pass the time.' It was a fact that, since its revival in the wake of the Jugendstil movement, the art of weaving was practised almost exclusively by women. Men, like women, saw working with textiles as a 'natural' activity suited to women, and thereby perpetuated a division of labour according to sex which had been firmly entrenched since the 19th century, if not longer.

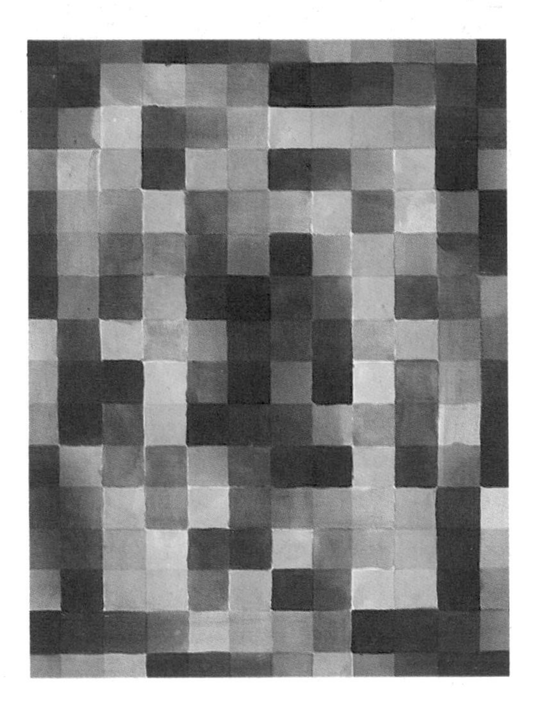

Gertrud Arndt: Design for a knotted carpet, 1924.

Viewed in the long term, Schlemmer's mockery was exposed as masculine arrogance. Weaving was in fact the most industrialized of all textile technologies and thus offered ideal preconditions for Bauhaus aims. Georg Muche took over from Itten as Master of Form in the weaving workshop in October 1920. He advised his students when deciding which designs to execute, but otherwise allowed the workshop a large degree of freedom. 'In the weaving workshop under Georg Muche, you could experiment very freely. It was up to the apprentice to decide whether to try a carpet or a pillow.'[58]

The weaving workshop worked particularly closely with the joinery workshop. The women produced furnishing materials and also contributed numerous carpets to the experimental Haus Am Horn.

As in the other workshops, teaching in the weaving workshop was complemented by a production workshop. Georg Muche threw himself into this task with particular zeal; at the end of October 1923 he produced his 'Proposals for the economic organization of the weaving workshop'. In March 1924 the workshop report noted that the restructuring of the production workshop was complete.

A number of people were often employed on commissions. Helene Börner, following the example of the metal workshop, liked to set her apprentices to work on such tasks. Exhibitions and trade fairs brought additional commissions.

Productive operations were, however, regularly hampered by materials and workforce shortages. The production department of the weaving

Lore Leudesdorff: Small slit gobelin, 1923. This work, the size of a side plate, may have been intended as a sample.

Georg Muche: Small Form Alphabet of the Weaving Workshop, 1922. Etching. Inspired by his role as head of the weaving workshop, Muche illustrated the turbulent and multifarious patterns created by the overlapping threads of the weavers in this 'Small Form Alphabet'.

workshop appears to have experienced problems similar to those facing the pottery workshop.
Women students had to gain part of their training outside the Bauhaus. In March 1922, two of the most talented, Gunta Stölzl and Benita Koch-Otte, attended a four-week dyeing course at the Krefeld dyeing college. Here they learned how to dye using both natural and chemical processes. Two years later they both attended the 'Manufacturer's Course' at the Krefeld silk weaving school, where they learned about weaves and materials. They then passed this knowledge on to the Bauhaus. Regular tuition was introduced only later.
But the lack of basic knowledge and system and the ignorance of tradition had its advantages, too. Students happily experimented with new methods and the Weimar years of the Bauhaus saw the creation of a large variety of woven and knotwork products with entirely new patterns and forms.
Inspiration for such stylistic innovations came above all from the teaching given by the artists. Almost every area of textile production up to 1921 was dominated by the influence of Itten. Pupils worked with the elementary forms of circle, triangle and square, often in combination with the primary colours. In Itten's *Vorkurs* they studied 'form characters', in elementary forms for example, and then translated these ideas into their knotwork and weaving. From Itten and – as of winter 1921 – from Klee, too, they learned

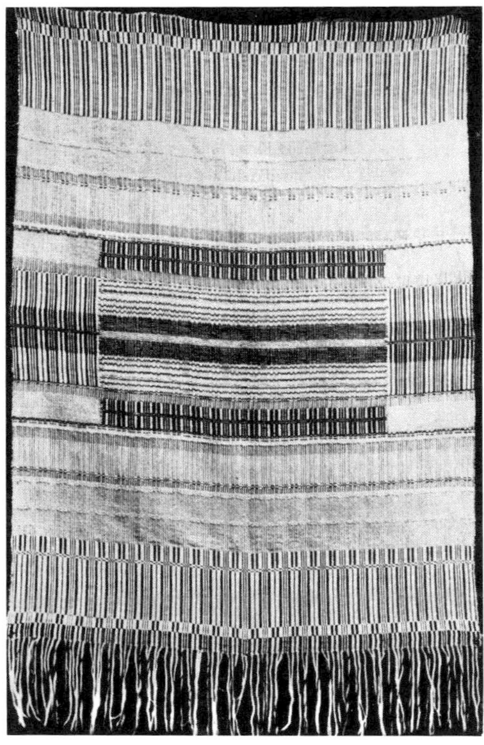

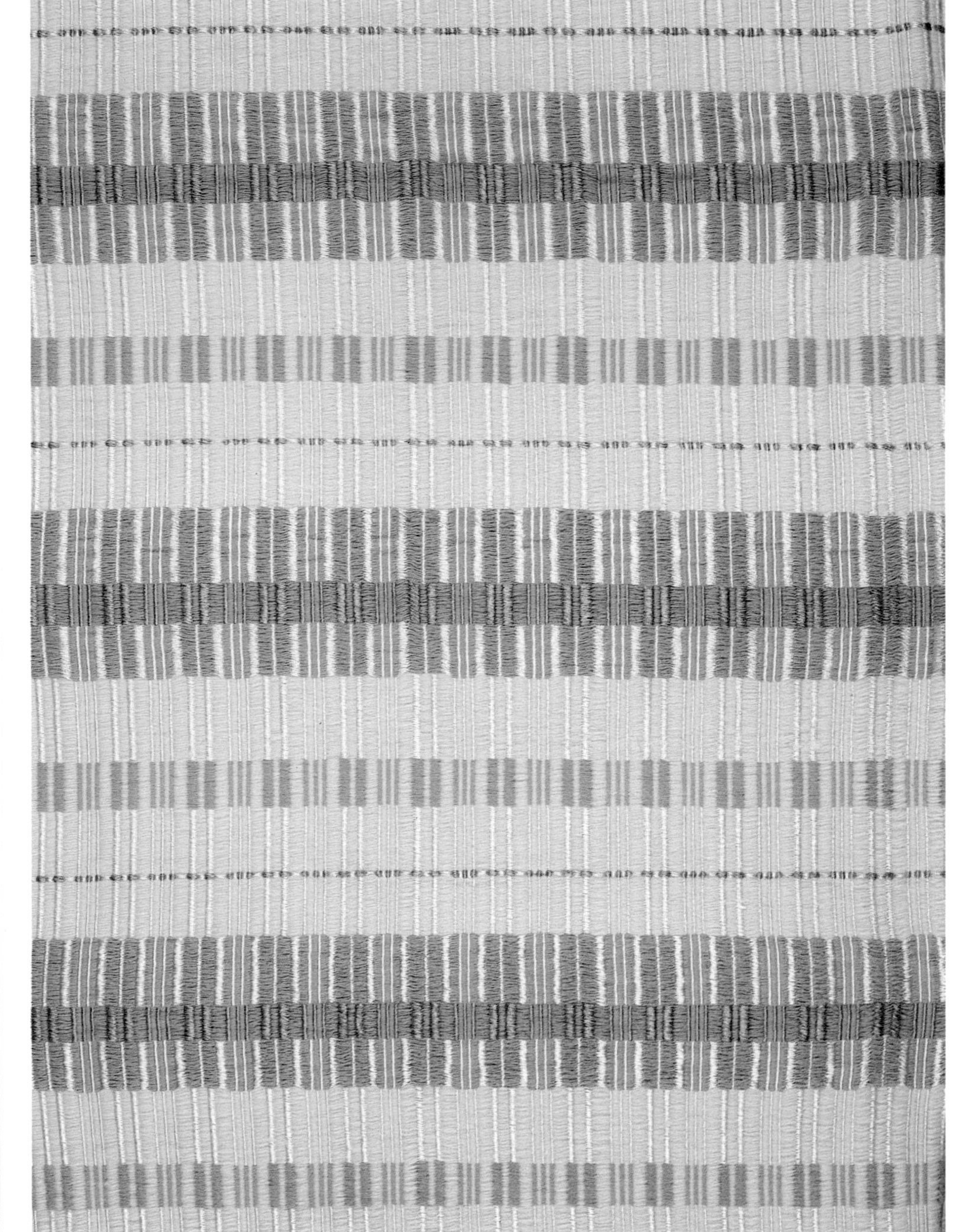

Left: This 'Blanket in White-Red-Green-Grey' of 1923 (120 x 170 cm) features vertical stripes of light-dark contrasts. Its symmetrical structure is interrupted in the centre by a group of horizontal stripes. This handmade blanket was intended as a prototype for machine mass-production.

Right: *Gunta Stölzl:* Blanket with fringe (section), 1923. Total size 118 x 100 cm. This piece was based on part of another carpet (above left). In addition to colour contrasts of white and green, Gunta Stölzl here also works with the material contrasts of wool (matt) and artificial silk (gloss). This blanket was reproduced several times.

that proportions could be used in the layering of simple striped patterns. The narrative tapestry – a medium which had blossomed during the Jugendstil period – was now replaced by constructive planar designs (ill., p. 74) in the spirit of a new abstract art. The teachings of Kandinsky and Moholy also played an influential role here. Wall hangings and carpets were now composed as non-concrete images.
The work produced was carefully documented: important single items were photographed, while the Bauhaus itself bought many of its students' works and thereby acquired the reproduction rights. An inventory was kept which listed the woven products to which the Bauhaus held the rights; by 1 April 1925 the list contained 183 items, including blankets, pillows, table-cloths, scarves, carpets, wall hangings, gobelins, runners, covers, foot-pillows, children's clothes, caps, blouse material, children's bedcovers, strips and sample lengths.

Otto Rittweger and Wolfgang Tümpel: Tea-infuser holder, 1924. Nickel.

The metal workshop

The metal workshop was not able to open its doors to students until 1920. It was headed by Master of Form Itten until the end of 1922, when he resigned in protest against Gropius' decision to encourage commission work.
In its first year, 1920, the metal workshop had no Master of Craft at all; Alfred Kopka, appointed in 1921, was soon dismissed on grounds of incompetence. In spring 1922 he was succeeded by gold and silversmith Christian Dell. Under Itten, the workshop concentrated mainly on every-day containers: pots, urns, candle-holders, teapots, boxes, tins. Many of these containers were based on the circle and the sphere and some even on the laws of the Golden Section. Other metal items still featured soft-organic forms reminiscent of Jugendstil.
When László Moholy-Nagy succeeded Johannes Itten in the summer semester of 1923, both style and direction quickly changed. Moholy welcomed the use of new materials and experiments were made with glass and

Opposite page, above: *Marianne Brandt:* Small tea-essence pot, 1924. Brass (silver-plated interior) and ebony, height 7.5 cm. Marianne Brandt combined elementary forms into objects of profound harmony.

Wolfgang Rössger and Friedrich Marby: Pot, 1924. Tombac and nickel. With its combination of sphere and cylinder, the pot is reminiscent of earthenware products of 1922 (ill., p.69). At least seven versions of this pot – with shorter neck and differently-positioned spouts and handles – were manufactured for commercial purposes in 1924.

Opposite page, below: Lucia Moholy took a great number of photographs of architecture and products from the period 1924 to 1928. The technical precision of her photographs corresponds to the equally perfect objects, as seen here in the components of a silver tea set by Marianne Brandt (1924).

plexiglass, media which did not really belong in a metal workshop. Materials were purchased from industry. Moholy encouraged his students to produce unusual metal combinations and employ previously base metals such as alpaca, an economical silver substitute.
The metal workshop's new orientation was reflected in its preoccupation, starting from 1923, with the lamp. The lamp was decidedly not a traditional subject for gold and silversmithery. 'With the approval of Muche and Moholy, work on lighting for the house (Am Horn). ... Moholy suggests standard lamps as uniform as possible (glass, metal)', note the workshop reports. This period saw the creation of the famous Bauhaus table lamp. Following preliminary work by K.J. Jucker, Wilhelm Wagenfeld produced the final version of this lamp. In 1924 it was already being offered in the two versions still available today: either with metal shaft and foot or glass shaft and foot (ills., p. 80 and 81). Bauhaus Ltd. also supplied both models.
It is clearly not possible to settle the – still continuing – dispute over the copyright to the lamp in favour of one or the other designer. In such a small workshop, with a workforce of rarely more than ten, many products were the subject of joint development and continuous discussion, testing and improvement. This applied to the table lamp, too, as proven by the numer-

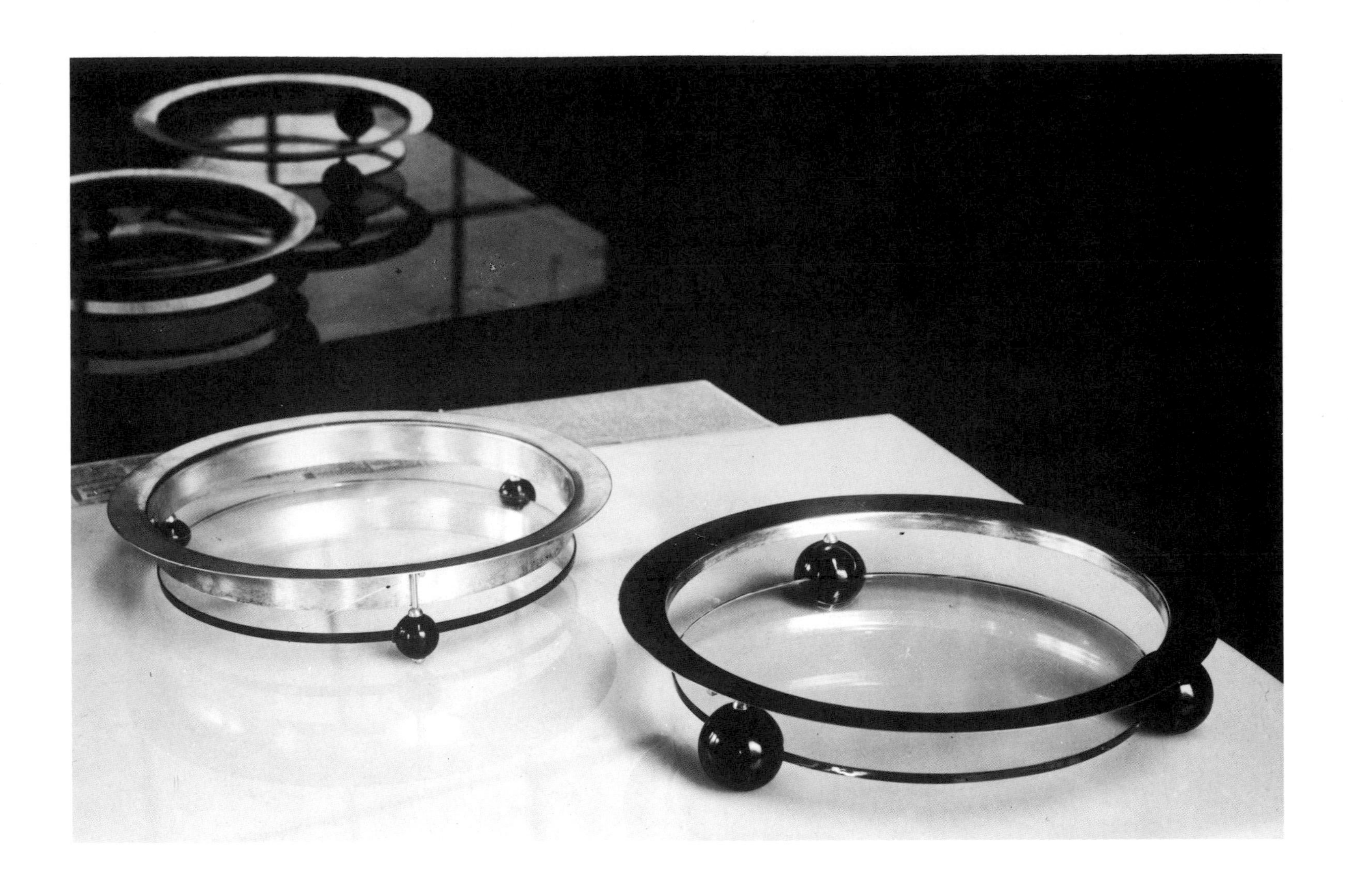

Josef Albers: Fruit bowls, 1924. Glass, metal, black-lacquered wood.

ous photographs which were taken of intermediate versions produced along the way.

Wilhelm Wagenfeld described the 1924 lamp thus: 'The table lamp – a model for machine mass-production – achieved in its form both maximum simplicity and, in terms of time and materials, greatest economy. A round base, cylindrical shaft and spherical shade are its most important components.'[59]

Although the metal objects dating from Itten's time were also composed of circular and spherical elements, their beaten surfaces speak of craftsmanship and the manual manufacturing process. The metal-beating process always remained visible, just as in the many pots by Gyula Pap.

The Bauhaus lamp, tea-essence pot and Albers' fruit bowl (ill., p. 78) deliberately deny any such handicraft character, although all were made entirely by hand. These objects assume the external appearance of machine-manufactured metal parts. The creator of the now famous tea-essence pot (ill., p. 76) was Marianne Brandt who, as a woman, initially experienced particular difficulty in being accepted by the metal workshop. As in so many of the designs conceived at the Weimar Bauhaus, she takes basic geometric elements (here circle, sphere and cylinder) as her creative starting-points. Her combination of different metals was also novel for its time. To start from elementary forms in the search for design solutions today strikes us as somewhat arbitrary. At that time, however, the processes of machine manufacturing were still insufficiently understood and it was believed that such elementary forms were particularly easily mass-produced.

The Bauhaus did not, however, take advantage of the experience in the

Marianne Brandt: Brass ashtray, part nickel-plated, 1924.

design of industrial and functional utensils gathered a few years earlier by artists in the Werkbund and the Werkstätten movement.

Elementary forms and primary colours remained a kind of common ABC which painters, sculptors, architects and designers agreed was binding and which was taught to students in theoretical form classes. It was erroneously assumed that the simplest bases could be used to create universally acceptable prototypes: the chair, the pot, the house. No thought was given to the market factors which make almost every new design soon look out of date. Not until 1928, when Hannes Meyer took over the directorship of the Bauhaus, was it realised that such form teaching could provide only a limited degree of help in solving design problems.

As automatically as students turned to elementary forms and primary colours when starting out on a design, so too they addressed the question of function. Their aim was not style or applied art, but form appropriate to function.

Functional form can be seen particularly clearly in the many different tea and coffee services produced in the metal workshop. A teapot might look completely different to a coffee pot, while cream jug and sugar pot seemed not to match at all. 'Since each of them satisfies our requirements without disturbing the other, their combination creates our style. Their overall unity lies in their relatively best fulfilment of their specific functions', explained Marcel Breuer. Nevertheless, since Bauhaus production up to 1927/28 remained firmly attached to primary forms and colours, the emergence of something like a Bauhaus style was more or less inevitable.

Productive operations appear to have started in the metal workshop during the course of 1924, with orders being executed in part on a job-share basis.

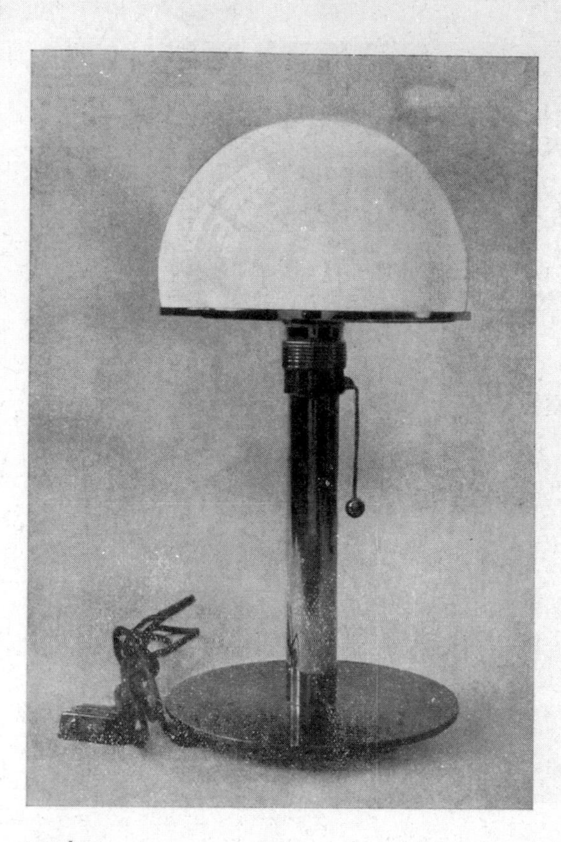

Metallwerkstatt

gesch.
Höhe ca. 35 cm

AUSFÜHRUNG

Messing vernickelt, Glasschirm, Zugfassung

TISCHLAMPE AUS METALL

VORTEILE

1 beste Lichtzerstreuung (genau erprobt) mit Jenaer Schottglas
2 sehr stabil
3 einfachste, gefällige Form
4 praktisch für Schreibtisch, Nachttisch usw.
5 Glocke festgeschraubt, bleibt in jeder Lage unbeweglich

bauhausdruck 'bayer'
din a4 11. 25. 1000

Opposite page: *Karl J. Jucker and Wilhelm Wagenfeld:* Glass table lamp, 1923/4. This lamp clearly illustrates the Bauhaus programme of the time: the emphatic use of industrial materials (metal and glass), the revelation of function in every part (the electric cable is clearly visible inside the glass shaft) and an aesthetic form arising from the harmony of simple forms. Wagenfeld was dispatched to the 1924 Leipzig trade fair with a small collection of lamps; he later recalled how 'dealers and manufacturers laughed over our products. Although they looked like cheap machine products, they were in fact expensive handicrafts. Their criticisms were justified.' This contradiction summarizes both the success and the failure of the years around 1923. Although understood as industrial forms, Bauhaus goods continued to be produced by hand in the workshops. Nevertheless, this lamp represents a milestone on the road to modern industrial form. It became one of the most celebrated examples of early industrial design, and received the Federal Prize for 'Good Form' as recently as 1982.

The table lamps of metal and of glass (right) number among the most famous Bauhaus products. An advertisement (left) was designed in 1925 by Herbert Bayer and included in the 'Catalogue of Designs', which introduced the range of Bauhaus products available. In view of the sophistication of advertising today, the advantages listed under 'Vorteile' strike us as somewhat naïve; they were deliberately intended to sell the lamp on its technical merits.

Rationalization measures were being introduced by June 1924 with the identification of objects as e.g 'MT 8'. At least 43 objects were now ready for reproduction, including tea caddies, dishes, pots, ashtrays (ill., p. 79), coffee and tea services (ill., p. 76) and lamps. Work was deliberately oriented towards trade fairs and exhibitions, such as the important 1924 exhibition, 'Die Form', in which the Werkbund showed the latest trends in design.
In 1924 the Bauhaus, showing products from its workshops, took part successfully for the first time at the Leipzig trade fair – for commercial art and artists, the most important trade fair of the twenties .

Josef Albers described his conference table of 1923 as a combination of artistic-formal and functional arguments: 'Woods of equal strength and width were used for the table legs. The alternating angling of the legs ensures stability and expresses a circularity which is further underlined by the lateral supports. These are attached at the bottom of the legs across the narrow ends of the table, where they are not in the way, and along the top of the long sides of the table, where they can be used as shelves. All overlaps, projecting and receding dimensions match wood diameter, all vertical distances correspond to the width of the boards. All the horizontal wood is dark oak, all the vertical wood light oak.'

The furniture workshop

In 1921 Walter Gropius took over the running of the furniture workshop as Master of Form. He himself had already designed furniture for apartments he had furnished or renovated before the War.

The furniture workshop seems to have been one of the first workshops to accept the need for standardization. The most important evidence for this is the wood-slat chair (ill., p. 55) which Marcel Breuer, one of the workshop's first journeymen, produced in 1922 and which he intended as a prototype for industrial mass-production. The chair is patently indebted to the overwhelming influence of the furniture which Gerrit Rietveld had been producing since 1917. The entirely new, eye-catching appearance of Bauhaus furniture was always presented as the result of functional analysis: sitting had been thoroughly investigated and this was the result. 'The starting-point for the chair was the problem of creating a comfortable seat and combining it with simple design. This led to the formulation of the following requirements:

a) Elastic seat and back rest, but no heavy, expensive or dust-collecting cushioning.

b) Angling of the seat so that the full length of the upper leg is supported without the pressure arising from a horizontal seat.

c) Angled position of the upper half of the body.

d) Spine left free, since any pressure on the spine is both uncomfortable and unhealthy.

These requirements were met by introducing an elastic back support. Of the whole skeleton, only the small of the back and the shoulder-blades are – elastically – supported, while the sensitive spine is left completely free. Everything else arose as an economic solution to the requirements. The design was decisively influenced by the static principle of offsetting the wider dimensions of the wood against the directions of material stretch and pressure exerted by the seated body.'[60]

Innovations in all the most important items of furniture produced after 1924 were justified by such functional analysis. Wilhelm Wagenfeld used a similar argument to explain the non-homogeneous design of a tea service.

Painted chair and table by Marcel Breuer, 1923.

In his chair of 1924 Marcel Breuer combines wood with light plywood. He uses colour to differentiate their functions. White and grey were employed for a number of items of furniture produced in this same year.

Nursery chest by Alma Buscher, 1924, in a page from the 'Catalogue of Designs'. Alma Buscher made intensive studies of children's furniture and toys (ill., p.93).

This total rejection of art as an explanation for form reflected Bauhaus ideology of the time, whereby art was to be absorbed into handicraft and engineering. The word 'art' was to deleted from the dictionary.
One critic of the Bauhaus took the following view: 'The Bauhaus chair is also an artistic creation, and the point is absolutely not because it can't look any different for technical reasons but because that's how the artist wants it to look.'[61] Many items of furniture were painted in clear colours which were intended to emphasize their constructive character. As in all the workshops, work after November 1923 concentrated upon commercial production. The workshop reports are free of the complaints of lack of personnel or equipment which we have heard from other quarters.

Marcel Breuer used Constructivist forms when designing the furniture for this lady's dressing room of 1923, part of the experimental 'Haus Am Horn'. The structure of the furniture is emphasized through the contrast of light rosewood and dark walnut. Breuer completed the dressing-table on the right for his journeyman's examination.

Ernst Gebhardt: Children's daybeds, 1923.

The stained-glass and mural-painting workshop

In the Bauhaus Manifesto, Gropius had announced a further workshop for 'decorators, stained-glass painters, mosaicists and enamellers'. A workshop was indeed set up for glass, and another for mural-painting, but in the course of 1924 the stained-glass workshop was made a subdivision of the mural-painting workshop and thereby lost its independence for good. The reason was undoubtedly the workshop's poor level of productivity.

Paul Klee was Master of Form for a while, but did little. The most important and most beautiful of the products known from this workshop stemmed from the hand of Josef Albers, who took over as Master of Craft in the summer semester of 1923 while also teaching the materials course. Albers' first glass pictures, composed of glass remnants (ill., p. 87), clearly betray the influence of Itten and Klee. For Gropius' two Berlin commissions, the Sommerfeld and Otte houses, Albers created two impressive stained-glass windows, since destroyed (ill., p. 47). Independent of the metal workshop, Josef Albers – who must have been fascinated by glass – designed a fruit dish which combined glass, metal and wood (ill., p. 78) and, a short time later, the first modern glass cups with metal handles, subsequently manufactured on an industrial scale. Albers later developed his own technique for making reproducible glass pictures.

The first Master of Form in the mural-painting workshop was Oskar Schlemmer, with Kandinsky taking over in 1922. One reason for the changeover was the fact that Schlemmer was to assume the running of the theatre workshop in 1923.

Master of Craft for a short while was Oskar Schlemmer's brother, Carl (called Casca – 'Carl Schlemmer from Cannstatt' – for short). Highly respected for his extensive technical and handicraft skills, he remained an important assistant to his brother throughout his life.

In 1922, however, he became involved in an internal dispute with Gropius and was sacked on the spot. His successor was master craftsman Heinrich Beberniss. The activities of this workshop can today be divided into three main areas:

Specialität (Beruf):
Geschlecht:
Nationalität:

Die Werkstatt für Wandmalerei im Staatlichen Bauhaus Weimar bittet zu experimentellen Zwecken der Werkstatt um Beantwortung der folgenden Fragen.

1. Die 3 aufgezeichneten Formen mit 3 Farben auszufüllen – gelb, rot u. blau und zwar so, daß eine Form von einer Farbe vollständig ausgefüllt wird:

2. Wenn möglich eine Begründung dieser Verteilung zu geben

Begründung:

Wassily Kandinsky: Questionnaire issued by the mural-painting workshop, answered by Alfred Arndt, 1923. This questionnaire was evaluated in order to 'scientifically' corroborate Kandinsky's assignment of primary colours to elementary forms.

1. Execution of commissions for other Bauhaus workshops. The toys which were produced in the wood-carving workshop, and which ranked among the Bauhaus' most successful commercial products, were painted by the mural-painting apprentices. This frequently involved considerable quantities: in April 1923, for example, 1000 tops, 30 small boats, 15 large boats and 40 building-block games were painted. Furniture from the joinery was also painted here (ill., p. 83).
2. Simple painting jobs or colour schemes for buildings. After a few experiments with strongly-coloured 'Expressionist' schemes, such as advocated by Bruno Taut, colour schemes were developed which employed delicate, pastel shades. These decorations were oriented to architecture and saw themselves as playing a subservient role. One impressive example was the colourful wall and ceiling scheme proposed for Gropius' Director's Office and published as a colour print. Many other examples of Bauhaus interior decoration have also survived on paper.
3. Free mural design. The Bauhaus exhibition of 1923, for which the stairs, corridors and reception areas of the entire complex were to be decorated in the spirit of Bauhaus thinking, gave students a major opportunity to realize some of their artistic intentions.

The mural-painters were as little interested in figurative painting as the theatre department in conventional drama or the textile department in narrative tapestries. Herbert Bayer decorated the three landings of a back staircase with variations on the yellow triangle, red square and blue circle (ill., p. 90). Two other pupils designed a colour-coded routing system, and

Opposite page: *Josef Albers:* Grid picture, 1922. Glass composition.

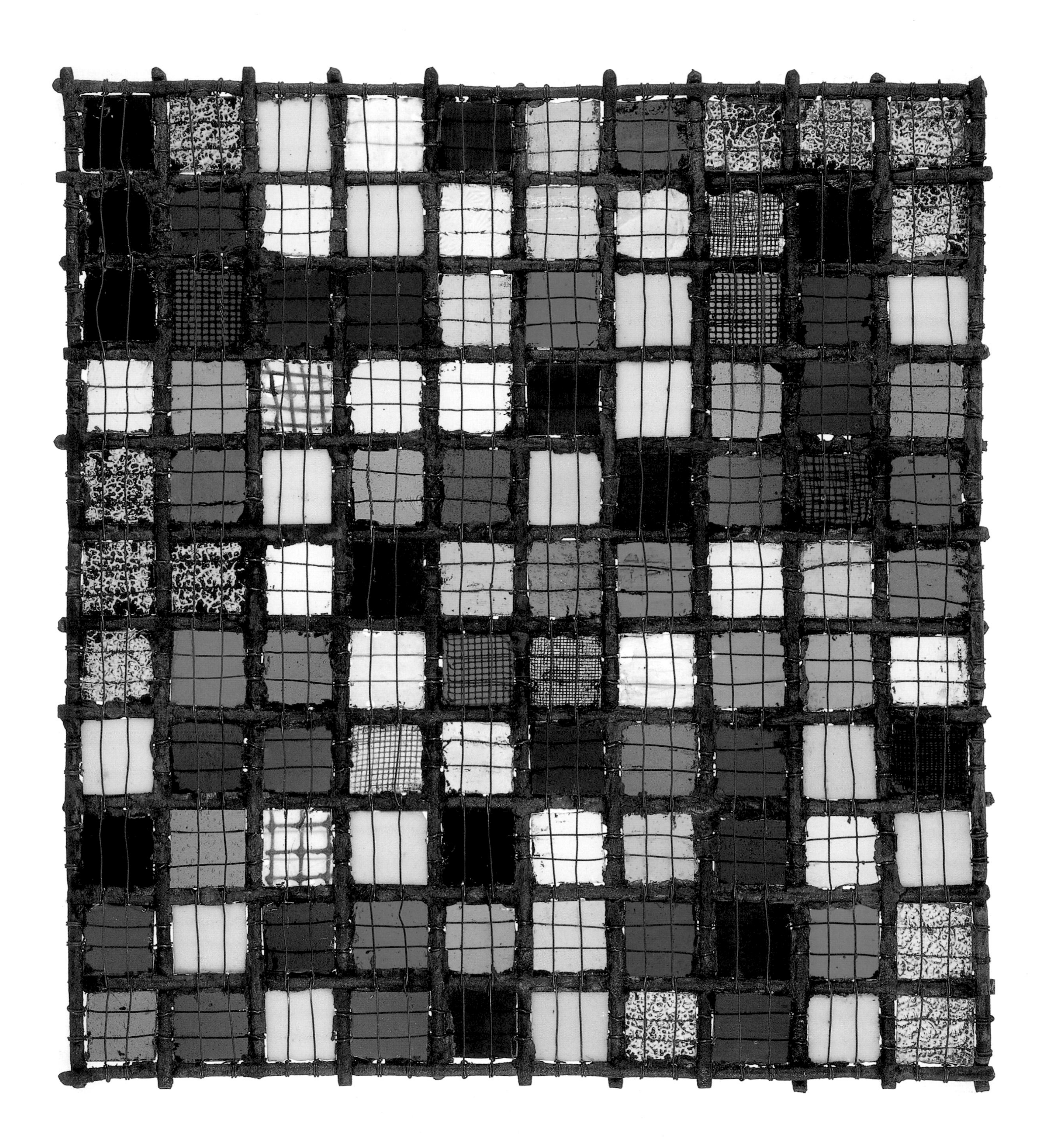

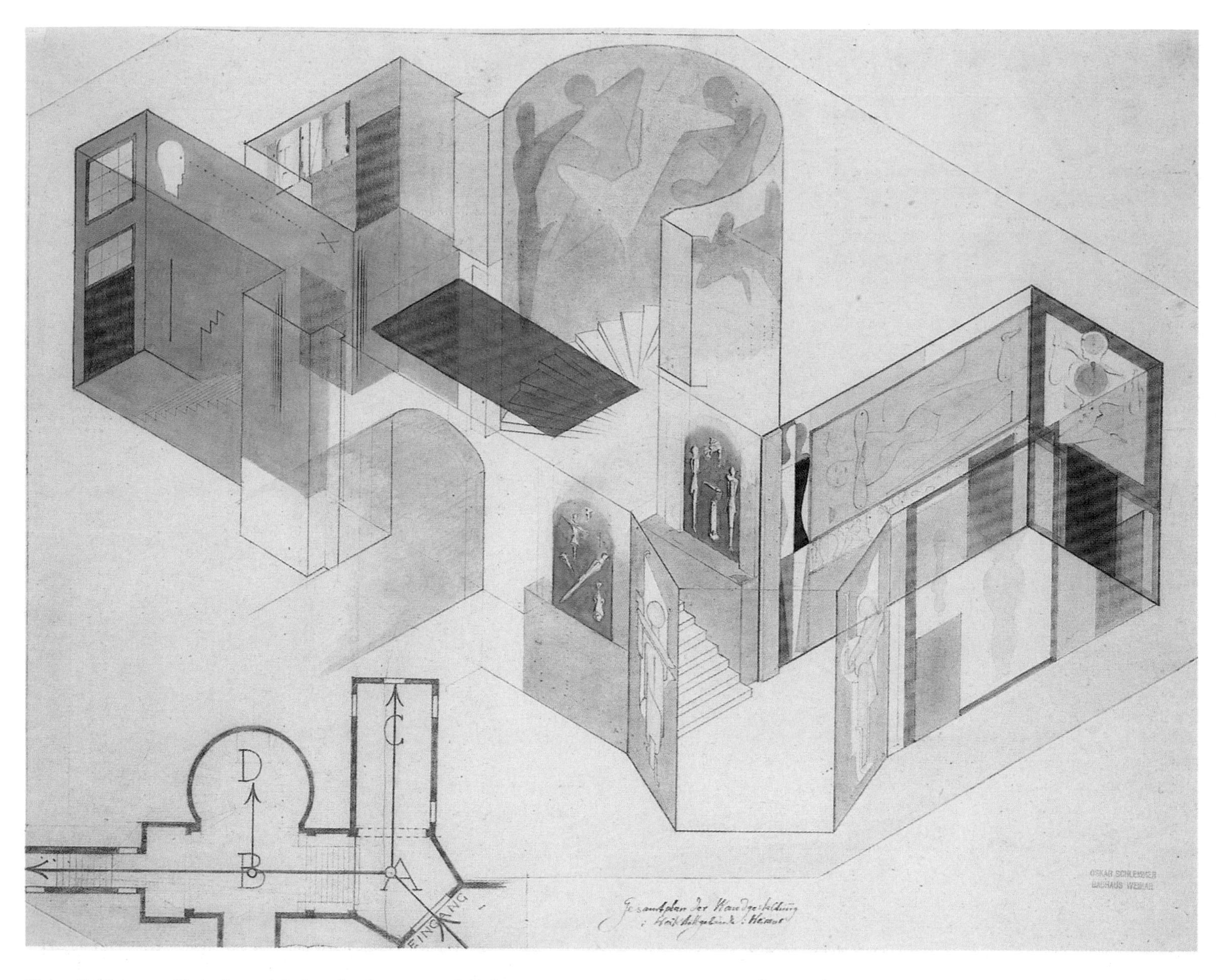

Oskar Schlemmer: Plan of mural designs for the workshop wing of the Weimar State Bauhaus, 1923.

Opposite page: Bauhaus Masters Oskar Schlemmer and Josef Hartwig and their apprentices at work on the entrance to the Bauhaus workshop building, 1923. They can be seen at work on the relief-like elements of Oskar Schlemmer's murals (above).

a third group even incorporated a radiator into their mural. Only Schlemmer retained 'Man' as a subject in his mural-painting.
He, too, contributed a mural as part of the redecoration of the school's Jugendstil premises in the spirit of the Bauhaus. He chose the workshop wing, where he combined painting and sculpture in 'coloured mortar reliefs' (ills., p. 88 and 89). These were executed by Master of Craft Josef Hartwig and a number of students. In these reliefs, Schlemmer played with the contrasts of standing/lying, male/female and man/architecture.
In April 1924 Kandinsky proposed a timetable for the mural-painting workshop which included a comprehensive range of theoretical and practical tasks.
Kandinsky was particularly interested in the relationship between colour and form, a relationship which he wanted to explore systematically. As a first step he distributed a questionnaire in which he asked everyone to mark which elementary form matched which primary colour (ill., p. 86). The majority chose the associations triangle-yellow, circle-blue and square-red. Despite repeated opposition, these arbitrary assignments have remained 'valid' until today. They had been current at the Bauhaus even before the questionnaire was circulated.
The mural-painting workshop was no more able to satisfactorily restructure itself into a teaching workshop and production workshop than were the workshops for stone-sculpture and wood-carving.

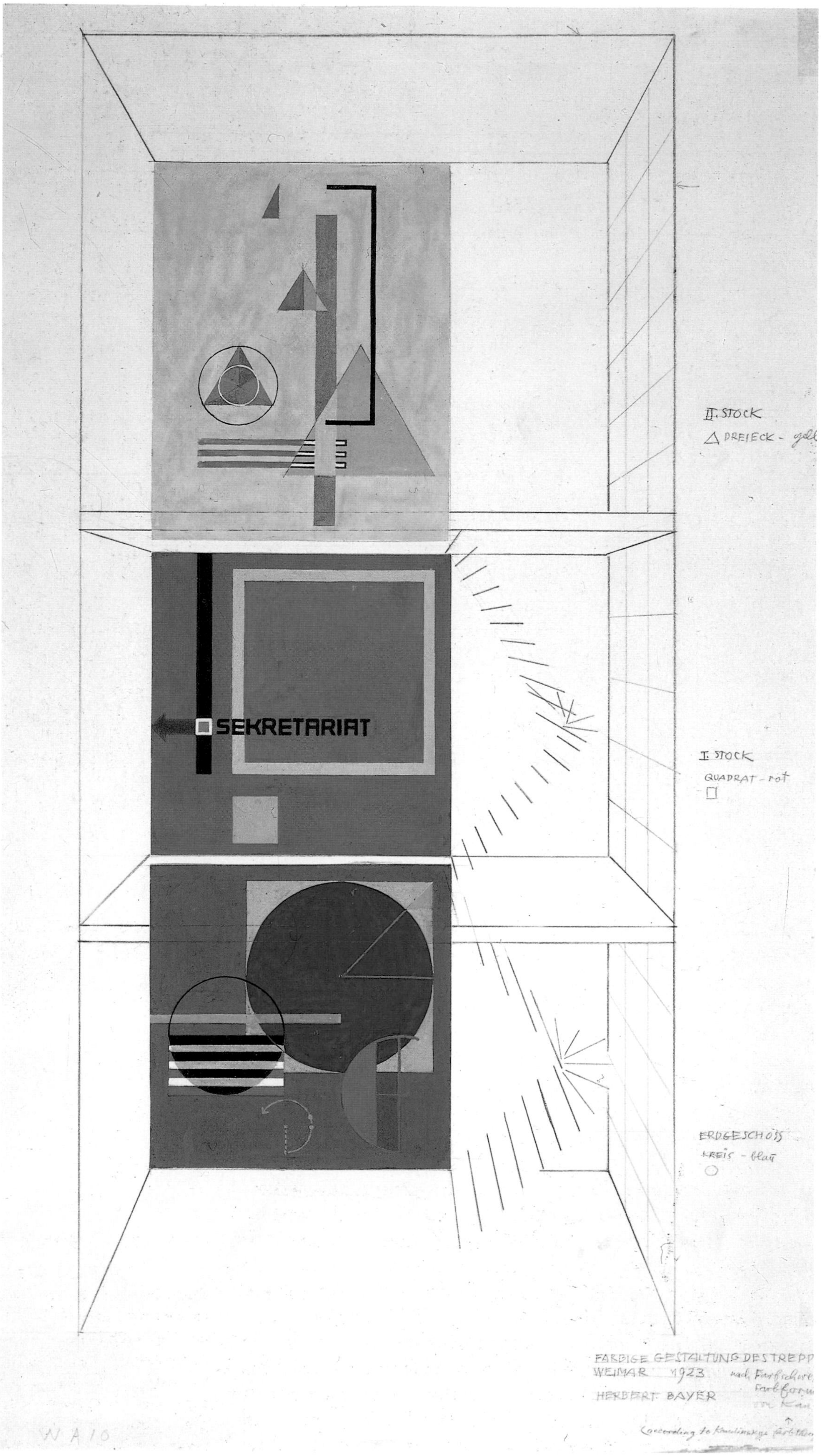

SEKRETARIAT

II. STOCK
△ DREIECK - gelb

I. STOCK
QUADRAT - rot
□

ERDGESCHOSS
KREIS - blau
○

FARBIGE GESTALTUNG DES TREPP
WEIMAR 1923 nach Farbschema
HERBERT BAYER Farbform
im Kan

(according to Kandinsky's farbtheo

WA10

These two workshops were established in accordance with traditional academy convention. Both were headed by master craftsman Josef Hartwig, who was artistically active in his own right.
Oskar Schlemmer was Master of Form of both workshops from 1922 to 1925. He wrote a report on the hopelessness of the situation in the workshops in as early as November 1922. He could see almost no means of practising the Bauhaus concept. Producing free art was out of the question, 'because our conscience prevents us'. 'The problem lies in the lack of large commissions. Perhaps the exhibition will bring some – but only perhaps!'[62]
In the event, the next few years brought neither important commissions from outside nor a meaningful role for the workshop members themselves. Judged overall, work in these two workshops consisted chiefly of assisting the rest of the Bauhaus. They produced architectural models in plaster for buildings designed by Gropius, e.g. for the skyscraper project in Chicago and the theatre in Jena. The commission for the wood-carvings for the Sommerfeld house also came via Gropius' private office. Students also produced lights, masks, cabinets and gravestones, and designed their own Monument to the March Dead for Arnstadt. The few photographs from this workshop (ill., p. 91) reveal that a whole series of purely artistic sculptures were in fact produced in plaster and stone. Itten and Schlemmer had objects made in plaster, and the theatre workshop provided a plentiful flow

The wood-carving and stone-sculpture workshops

Above: Stone-sculpture workshop, around 1923.

Opposite page: *Herbert Bayer:* Mural designs for the back stairwell of the Weimar Bauhaus building, 1923. Herbert Bayer executed these decorations in conjunction with the Bauhaus exhibition of 1923. Their design reflects Kandinsky's theories of colour and form: a blue circle at ground level, red square on the first floor and, on the second floor, the lightest colour, yellow.

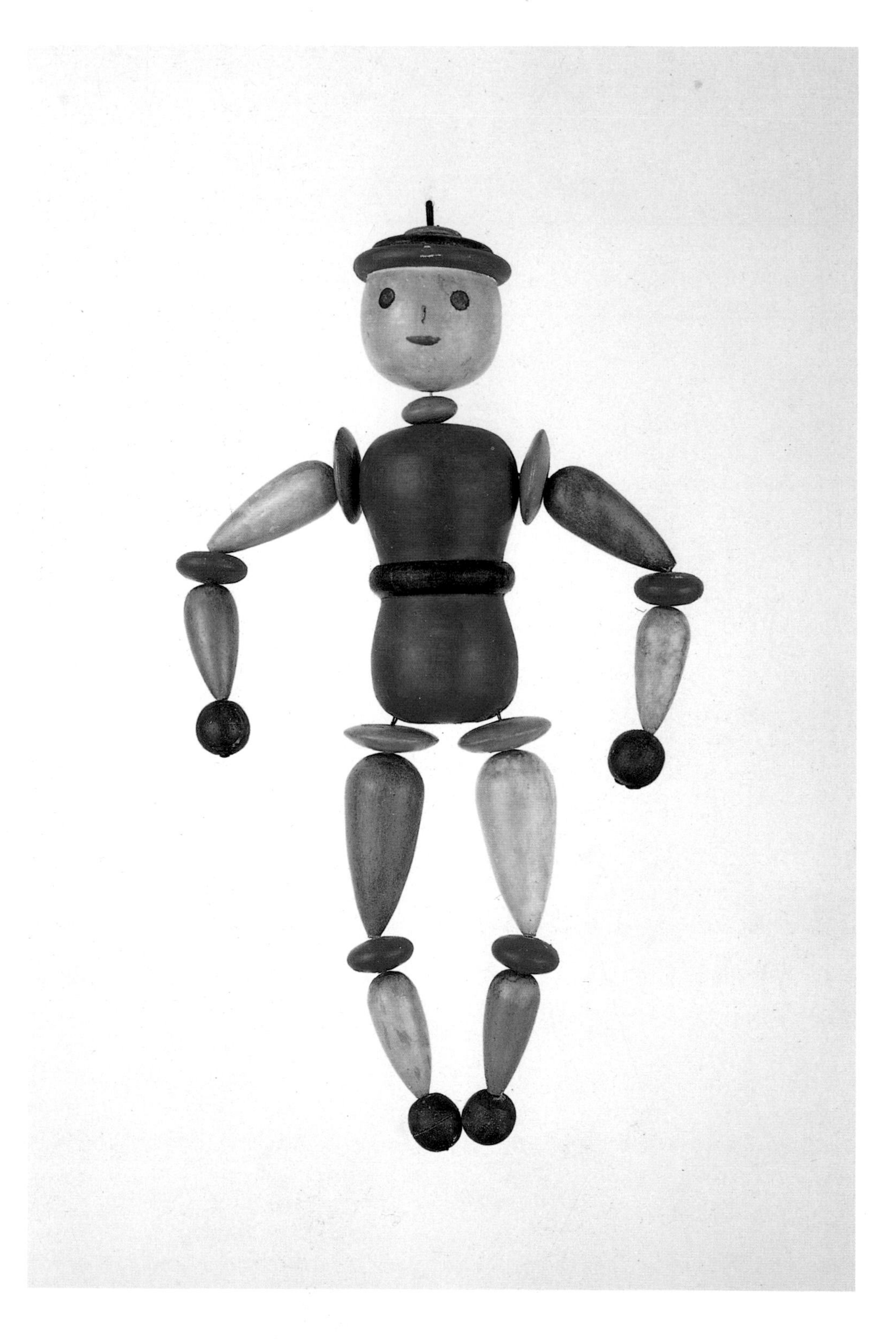

Josef Hartwig (turning) and *Oskar Schlemmer* (painting): Jointed doll, around 1923.

of work: stage masks for Lothar Schreyer, Toni Hergt's beautiful marionettes and Eberhard Schrammen's 'Roundlings'.

The Bauhaus toys developed by Eberhard Schrammen and above all Alma Buscher proved highly successful. A committed follower of the latest pedagogical trends, Alma Buscher designed modern toys for children, some of which were sold through the Pestalozzi Fröbel Verlag (ills., p. 92 and 93).

Buscher rejected fairy-tales as 'an unnecessary burden for a small brain'. She wanted to create toys which were 'unconfusingly clear and specific' and 'as harmonious as possible' in their proportions. The primary colours should also include white 'to heighten the cheerfulness of colour and thus the pleasure of the child'.[63]

A chess set (ill., p. 94) newly-developed by Master of Craft Josef Hartwig

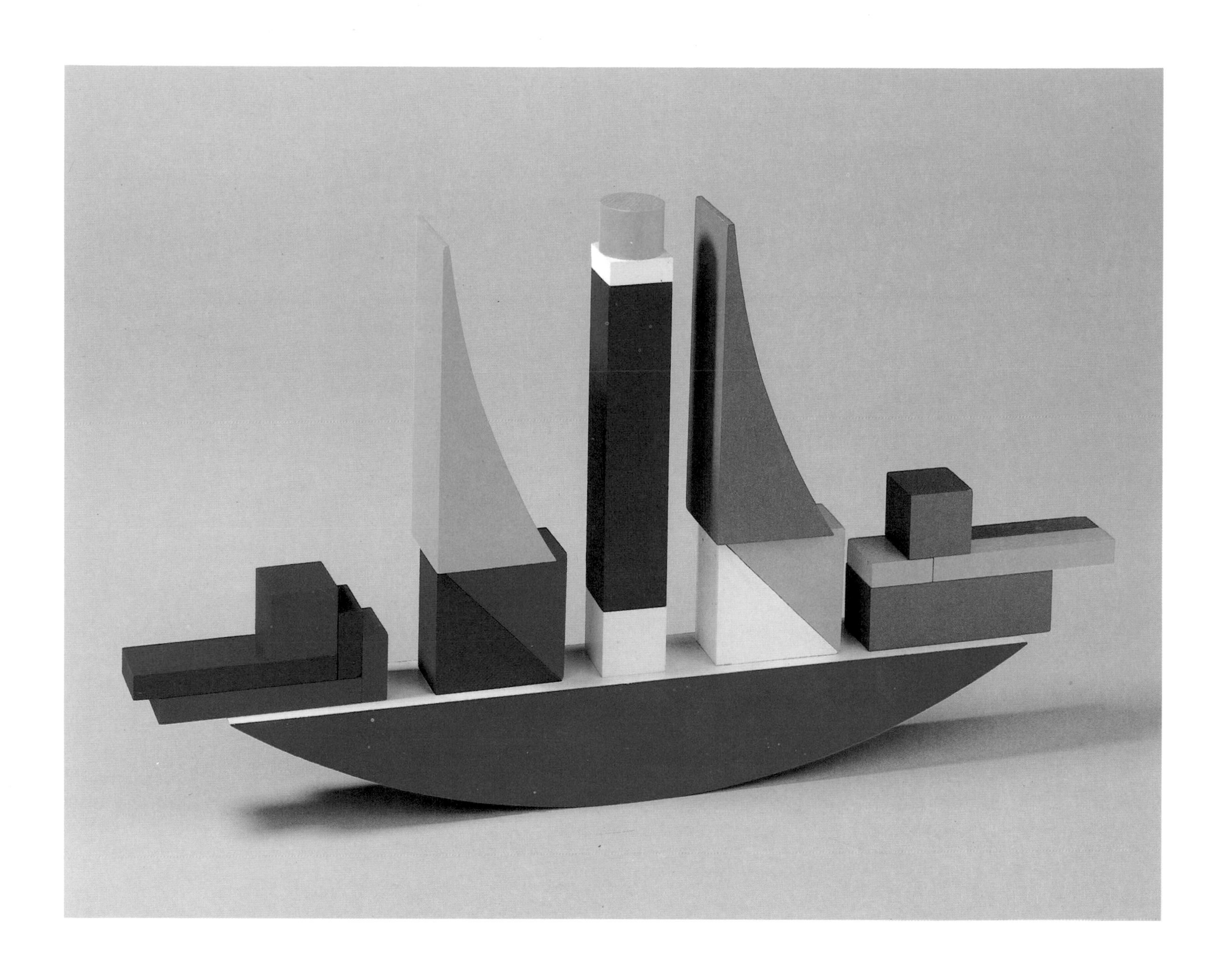

Above: Building-block game by Alma Buscher, 1924.

Below: Set of colourfully-painted wooden blocks from 1924 and, in the foreground, colour tops by Ludwig Hirschfeld-Mack.

Below: Josef Hartwig's chess set from 1924. Joost Schmidt designed the accompanying advertisement (above). The pieces are composed of simple, stereometric bodies, mostly cubes, whose size and combinations illustrate their moves in the game.

was another successful Bauhaus product. Each piece was designed to reflect the directions in which it could move. The chess set was also an example of workshop collaboration; in the joinery workshop, Heinz Nösselt made the chess table (ill., p. 95), while student Joost Schmidt designed posters, printed materials (ill., p. 94) and a publicity leaflet.
With the shift of emphasis towards productive operations, it became increasingly obvious that the earning potential of the stained-glass and mural-painting workshops was virtually non-existent. In Dessau, therefore, they were subsequently refounded as a sculpture workshop.

The bookbinding workshop

Printing and bookbinding were subjects traditionally taught at arts and crafts schools. Both had been offered at van de Velde's former school. The bookbinding workshops were privately owned by master craftsman Otto Dorfner, one of Germany's finest bookbinders. His workshop took

Heinz Nösselt: Chess table, 1924. The chess pieces could be stored below the table. There was also room for an ashtray.

Anny Wottitz: Wood and pergament book cover for 'Chorus Mysticus', 1923.

both Bauhaus students and external apprentices unconnected with the Bauhaus.
Paul Klee became Master of Form of the bookbinding workshops in 1921, but it was not long before fundamental differences of opinion between Dorfner and Klee began to emerge. Both men were artistically independent personalities following entirely different paths. When the problem was discussed at the Council of Masters, Dorfner made it clear that he did not intend to extend his contract with the Bauhaus. Training of the apprentices was completed, however. Dorfner's contract having expired, the Bauhaus

Opposite page: *Lyonel Feininger:* Cover of the portfolio of 'Italian and Russian Artists' in the 'Neue Europäische Graphik' series, 1924.

BAUHAUS DRUCKE
NEUE EUROPAEISCHE GRAPHIK

4te MAPPE =

ITALIENISCHE u. RUSSISCHE KUENSTLER

HERGESTELLT UND HERAUSGEGEBEN
VOM STAATLICHEN BAUHAUS IN WEIMAR
IM JAHRE
1921

ZU BEZIEHEN DURCH
MÜLLER & CO VERLAG
POTSDAM

Wassily Kandinsky: Joyful Arising, colour lithograph from the Bauhaus 'Masters' portfolio, 1923.

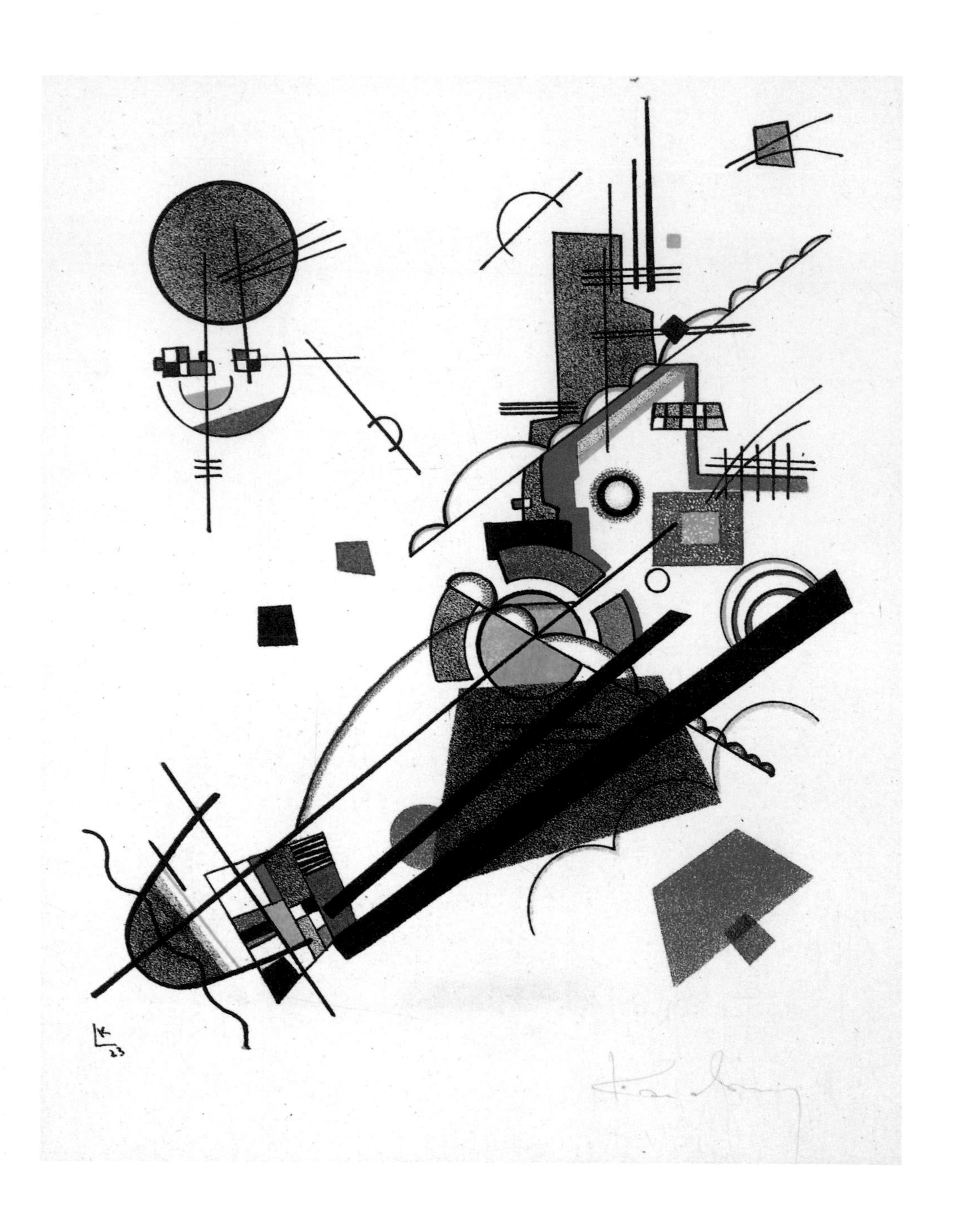

made no attempt to continue this workshop. The concentration on profitability and standardization left little room for a purely handicraft workshop offering no starting-points for modernization.

The graphic printing workshop

The graphic printing workshop was run by Master of Form Lyonel Feininger and Master of Craft Carl Zaubitzer throughout the Weimar period. 'Feininger was an enthusiastic graphic artist, passionately devoted to the woodcut above all (ill., p. 100), which he used both for his large-format prints and to illustrate his own letters. He would even use the lid of a cigar box as a woodcut if he had nothing better to hand.'[64]
The workshop had survived the War well and work could be started immediately. At first apprentices were trained in the techniques of wood-cutting and copperplate engraving; at the end of 1921, however, with Gropius' insistence upon the necessity of commissions for the survival of the school, it was decided to change direction.
The 1922 timetable now read: 'The State Bauhaus art printing workshop no longer accepts apprentices on the basis of articles, as in the other workshops, but trains Bauhaus members in all areas of art printing upon

Oskar Schlemmer: Page from the portfolio 'Play with heads', 1923.

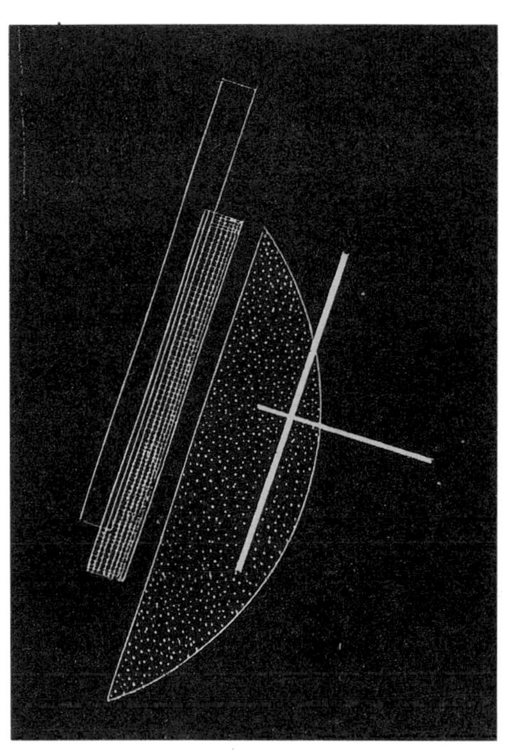

László Moholy-Nagy: Untitled, 1923. Lino cut.

request... The graphic printing workshop is essentially a production workshop and executes commissions for art block printing of all kinds, including whole editions.'[65]
It was during this period that the idea of the five-part 'Neue europäische Graphik' (New European Prints) portfolio series was born (ill., p. 97). The series was issued regularly until 1924, although the forced closure of the Bauhaus meant the last portfolio (II, French artists) remained unfinished. 'Masters of the Weimar State Bauhaus' (I) was followed by two portfolios of works by German artists (III and V) and one devoted to Italian and Russian artists (IV).
Among the countless portfolios produced in the course of the twenties, the Bauhaus series is one of the most outstanding. The portfolios did not prove the financial success that had been hoped for, however, since their publication coincided with Germany's growing inflation. The market was furthermore suffering from nothing short of a glut of graphic prints and the competition was simply too great.
The workshop was healthily occupied with commissions most of the time. Outside artists also had works printed here. Masters commissioned the printing of both single sheets and entire portfolios. The graphic workshop

Oskar Schlemmer: 'Triadic Ballet' costumes in the 'Wieder Metropol' review at the Berlin Metropol theatre, 1926.

movements, but instead specific figurative inventions; the disguise – one could almost call it a chrysalis – was so dominant that body and movement had to "incorporate" it like a sculptural shell.'[68]

A number of students wishing to stage their own work assembled under the name 'Group B'. Their formal solutions in particular retained many traces of Schlemmer's theatrical world, but the content was distinctly their own. While Schlemmer's artistic goals were always metaphysical – namely to bring basic elements of form into harmony with Man and space – his students placed greater emphasis upon mechanization and automation.

These students produced a 'Mechanical Cabaret', premièred at the Bauhaus, and a 'Mechanical Ballet' which was also staged (ill., p. 103). The aim was a direct illustration of the *Zeitgeist:* 'The mechanical ballet sought to give the technical spirit of our age new forms of expression through dance... the machine principle (was) presented and translated into form dance. 'A 'uniform, constant rhythm was selected with no changes of tempo in order to underline the monotony of the mechanical'[69].

The musician and music critic Hans Heinz Stuckenschmidt described the background to the first performance. László Moholy-Nagy had invited him to come to the Bauhaus, where he met, among others, Kurt Schmidt.

'After the first communal meal, I accompanied Kurt Schmidt to his studio. It was full of man-high constructions of cardboard, wire, canvas and wood, all in elementary forms: circles, triangles, squares, rectangles, trapezia, and naturally all in the primary colours yellow, red and blue. Schmidt put on a red square, fastening it with leather straps in such a way that he disappeared behind it. Two of his colleagues did the same with a circle and

Kurt Schmidt, Friedrich Wilhelm Bogler and Georg Teltscher: 'The Mechanical Ballet', 1923.

a triangle. These strange geometric figures, their wearers completely invisible behind them, then danced an eerie round. There was an old piano against the wall. It refused to stay in tune and sounded appalling. I improvised a few chords and aggressive rhythms. The cardboard figures immediately began to react. An abstract dance of square, circle and triangle was performed ad lib. After about a quarter of an hour, Kurt Schmidt got out of his square, rather out of breath but thoroughly satisfied. I had instinctively guessed and performed something he had wanted but only vaguely imagined: a primitive accompaniment roughly corresponding to the primary geometric forms... From now on we rehearsed every day, from morning till night... After two or three weeks the programme of the "Mechanical Ballet", or rather the "Mechanical Cabaret", of which it was a part, had been created.'[70]
'The Man at the Control Panel' (ill., p. 104) also confronted the relationship between man and machine. The creation – the machine – conquers its creator. The 'new man' has become a 'marionette', 'ruled by a higher, non-human and untameable power'[71].
Schlemmer also encouraged the creation of puppet shows, some of whose figures have survived to the present. Such puppets represented the 'typifying exaggeration of the human form'.[72]
Independent of Schlemmer, Moholy and Kandinsky had also concerned themselves with aspects of theatre. Moholy banned the human figure entirely from the stage in his 'Mechanical Eccentric', a piece which was only to appear in score form.
Kandinsky had already published his 'Yellow Sound' in Munich in 1912; a

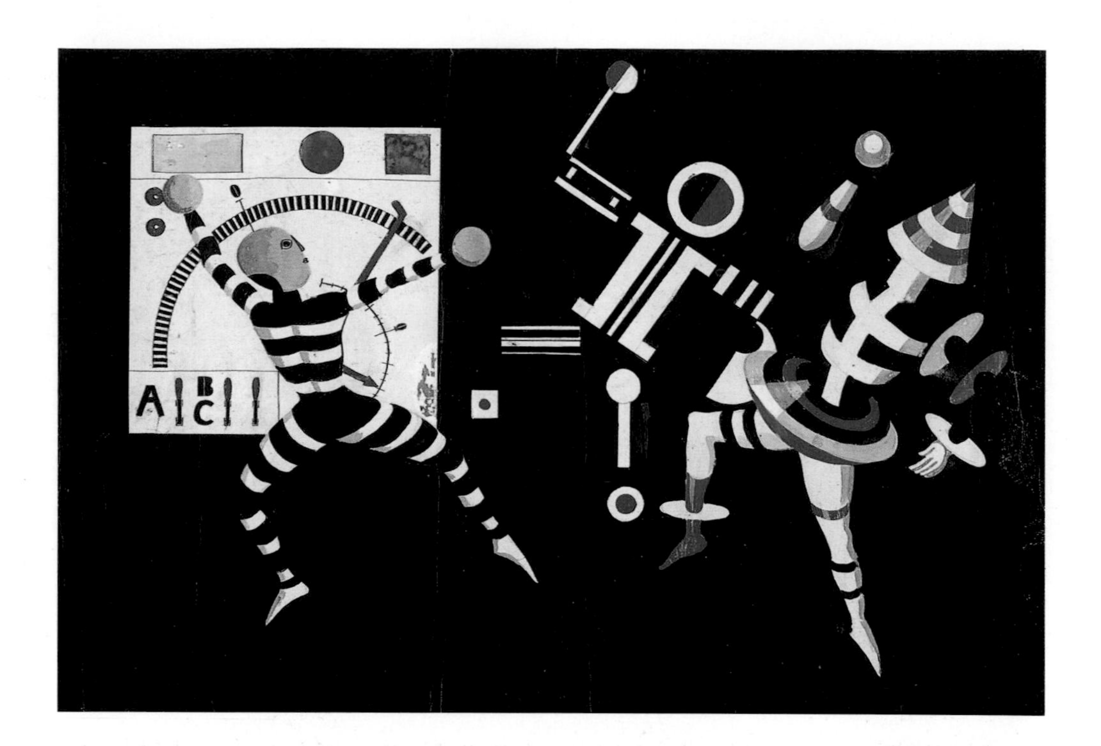

Kurt Schmidt: The Man at the Control Panel, 1924. Scene design, 1924.

Xanti Schawinsky: Circus, around 1924. Scene design.

'stage composition' (there was no generic term such as drama, etc., to describe it), it formed the first contribution to abstract theatre.
In 1923, he published the essay 'On Abstract Theatre Synthesis'. It is a title which contains the key to Kandinsky's understanding of art during his Bauhaus years – 'synthesis'. Behind this concept lay the vision of a *Gesamtkunstwerk,* a total work of art to be created through the combination of all the arts – architecture, painting, sculpture, music, dance and poetry. Kandinsky saw the Bauhaus as an ideal opportunity to achieve this aim. He was actually able to create such a synthesis just once, in 1928, as producer of Mussorgsky's 'Pictures at an Exhibition'.

Bauhaus Exhibition of 1923

In June 1922 a government loan to the Bauhaus was tied to the stipulation that the school held an exhibition of its achievements so far – a sort of proof of its creditworthiness. Over the following months, the energies of the entire school were focussed upon this exhibition, with Gropius declaring an effective state of emergency: an exhibition committee was formed, working hours in the workshops were extended, and no new students were admitted for the 1923 summer semester. At the same time, the Council of Masters decided to include a fully-furnished house within the exhibition. This house was to involve all the workshops in presenting the Bauhaus programme to the public for the first time. Its design was supplied by the painter Georg Muche as the result of a general competition. State-of-the-art building methods and materials were to be employed; the same applied to the fittings inside. The financing of this experimental house in the midst of the inflationary period – the school's government subsidies were insufficient – presented Gropius with a particular problem.

The necessary loans were obtained from the businessman Adolf Sommerfeld in return for the right of first refusal to the house and land. The foundation stone was laid at the beginning of April 1923, and building and decoration completed within just a few months. A Bauhaus creation from top to bottom, the 'Haus am Horn' (as it was named after its location) was the first practical example of new living in Germany.

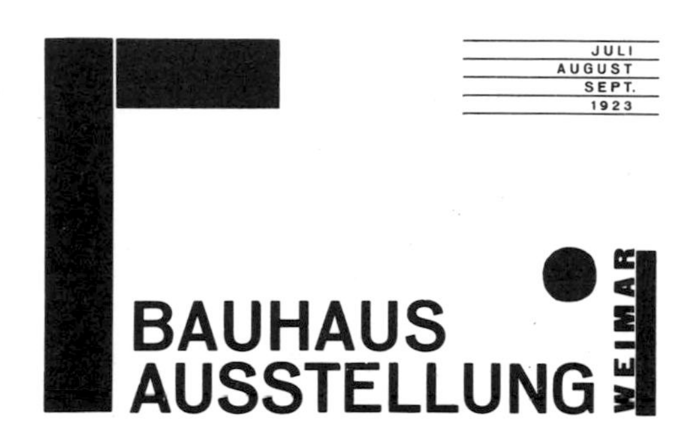

Newspaper advertisement for the 1923 Bauhaus exhibition in Weimar, designed by Herbert Bayer.

The Bauhaus here introduced for the first time much of what we now take for granted. The very ground plan was innovative (ill., p.108). There were almost no corridors, with the rooms instead being laid out around the largest room, the living room. The bathroom was easily reached from the bedroom. Kitchen and dining room were next door. The kitchen was intended solely for cooking purposes, while the dining room was just big enough to contain a table and six to eight chairs. The housewife was even able to keep an eye on the children's room from the kitchen. Alma Buscher furnished the children's room with walls which children could write on and large wooden blocks for building and acting games.

The kitchen was the first modern one of its kind. It featured a continuous worktop in front of the window, chairs which could be fitted under the table to save space and surfaces which were smooth and easy to clean. The latest electrical equipment – a hot-water boiler in the kitchen, a laundry in the cellar – demonstrated the labour-saving advantages of technology. But still opinions differed about the experimental house.

The exterior was compared to a 'white box of sweets', a 'bran factory', a 'whitewashed die' and a 'North Pole station', and generally attracted little positive criticism. Its practical and functional interior fittings (ill., p.108), and in particular the kitchen (ill., p.109), bathroom, children's room and dining room, were better received. But there were still comparisons with 'operating theatres' and technical equipment: 'Tall standard lamps of iron and glass tubes, severe, undimmed by silk shade, recall physics instruments; seats look like looms, furniture recalls printing presses, teapots water gauges.'[73] Despite such objections, however, celebrated critics ultimately judged the house as 'important and significant'.

Gropius was careful to distance himself from the experimental house by declaring that he had been elected to build it by a student majority. And indeed, the ground-plan in particular reveals a number of serious flaws. It was noted, for example, that: 'There is no access to any of the eating or sleeping cells except through the others', and 'the ground-plan might be taken from an architectural comic'. Similarly harsh criticism came from Adolf Behne, previously one of the Bauhaus concept's most ardent apologists, while the reactions of architects J.J.P. Oud and Bruno Taut were predominantly favourable.

Georg Muche (idea) and *Adolf Meyer* (planning and execution): Experimental 'Haus Am Horn', created for the 1923 Bauhaus exhibition. Standing in front of the house are László Moholy-Nagy and Alma Buscher.

Gropius opened the exhibition, which ran from August 15 to the end of September, with a lecture on 'Art and technology, a new unity'. Kandinsky spoke on 'Synthetic art' and the architect and guest speaker J.J.P. Oud talked about modern Dutch architecture. The musical avant-garde was also represented: Paul Hindemith's 'Songs of Mary' received its première, and there was music by Busoni, Ernst Křenek and Igor Stravinsky. Students staged the 'Mechanical Cabaret' and 'Motion pictures', while the undisputed highlight remained the performance of the 'Triadic Ballet'.

An exhibition of pictures by Masters and pupils was held in the Landesmuseum, and coursework and workshop products were on show in the school buildings. Gropius' newly-decorated Director's Office could also be viewed. Schlemmer and students from the workshops for stone-sculpture and mural-painting had decorated virtually all of the school's corridors, staircases and entrance areas with murals and sculptural reliefs.

Gropius also organized an 'International Architecture Exhibition' (ill., p.112) with models and drawings, in which he sought to illustrate the 'line of a functional, dynamic architecture'. The exhibition was intended to show that Bauhaus aims were being independently pursued elsewhere, too. It also featured the first standardized-type housing designs.

While the critic Paul Westheim felt that 'Three days in Weimar and you've seen enough squares for a lifetime', the student Andor Weininger identified two sides to the exhibition: 'As well as the "old" works with their emotional emphasis, there were also new developments to be seen: horizontal-vertical, two-dimensionality, squares and a red cube (as private residence); in short, "Stijl" influence.'

Opposite page: Joost Schmidt's poster for the 1923 Bauhaus exhibition in Weimar, with its round and square motifs, recalls reliefs by Oskar Schlemmer.

STAATLICHES BAUHAUS
AUSSTELLUNG
JULI SEPT
1923
WEIMAR

Radically simple forms and bare – pictureless – walls characterize the rooms of the 'Haus Am Horn'. Here, the living room with furniture by Marcel Breuer and a carpet by Martha Erps-Breuer, 1923.

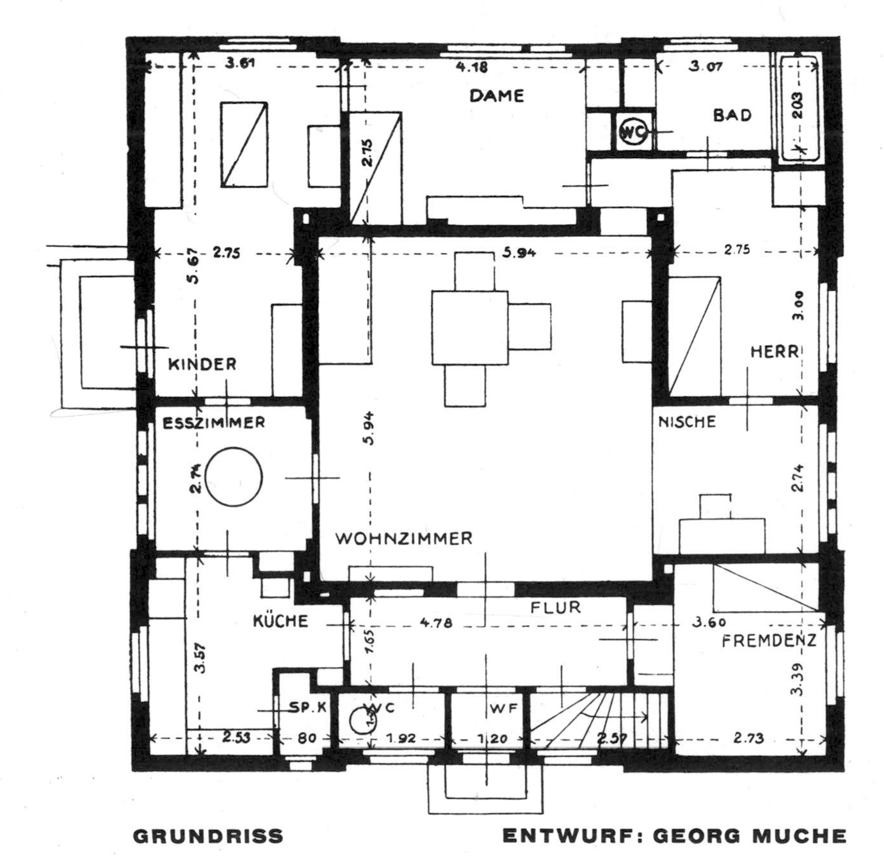

Georg Muche (idea) and *Adolf Meyer* (planning and execution): Ground-plan of the 'Haus Am Horn', 1923. The individual, very small rooms are grouped around a central, clerestory-lit living room containing only one eye-level window in a niche. The square house, its sides 12.7 m long, features separate ladies' and men's sleeping quarters, a kitchen, dining room, children's room and guest room.

Compared to the living room, the 'Haus Am Horn' kitchen still looks practical today. It was designed by Benita Otte and Ernst Gebhardt. Storage containers by Theodor Bogler can be seen on top of the cupboards, as well as dishes made of Jena glass, 1923.

The exhibition was not a financial success, falling as it did during the inflation which reached its peak in summer 1923. But this only heightened its success as an exercise in public relations. Newspaper articles written by journalists from all over the German Reich and abroad filled two fat albums. It was the first time the press had also been able to carry photographs of Bauhaus products, specially released by Gropius to accompany the exhibition.

The Bauhaus also took the 1923 exhibition as an opportunity to give itself a new image. 'New typography' was the cue. Taking De Stijl publications and Russian Constructivism as their starting-points, the printed materials issuing from the Bauhaus now reflected the school's claim to modernity. Black, white and red were the most important colours (ills., p.105 and 107). Significant content was heavily underlined or highlighted. The formerly symmetrical printed page was now composed as an asymmetric equilibrium with blocks, bars and lines as its essential components. The most important source of inspiration behind this new typography was Moholy-Nagy, who knew the Constructivist avant-garde and introduced many of their ideas at the Bauhaus.

View of the entrance side of the theatre renovated by Gropius and Meyer in Jena in 1922.

Architecture at the Weimar Bauhaus

The first project which Gropius was awarded in his capacity as director of the Thuringian Bauhaus was the renovation of the municipal theatre in Jena in 1921 (ill., p.110). It was also the first building in which Gropius and Meyer abandoned the Expressionist log-cabin style of the Berlin Sommerfeld house and oriented themselves instead towards the architecture of De Stijl and Le Corbusier.
The building has since changed, and the theatre that Gropius knew survives only in a small number of photographs. Gropius wrote: 'I have invested far more time and effort in this challenging building than I shall actually be paid for because it is the first I have built in Thuringia since becoming director of the Bauhaus. I have involved all the painters and sculptors I have available to me in the project.'[74]
The decoration of the interior (ill., p.111) was executed by the Bauhaus. 'Through two blue porches, you passed into a light yellow foyer with violet cloakrooms attached. Terracotta-coloured staircases led up to the level of the auditorium, which was painted salmon pink and grey, with a deep blue which was picked up in the curtains.'[75]
Gropius had a ceiling painting by Schlemmer removed at his own expense, even though it was almost completed, after van Doesburg had expressed strong criticism of it. The Bauhaus workshops executed decorating and building work in the theatre interior.
This first modern building by Gropius and Meyer after the War marked a change in direction which characterized both Gropius' own architectural œuvre and the Bauhaus itself.
Although the Bauhaus workshops were involved in decorating the theatre, the actual building commission went to Gropius' private architecture practice. In the years 1922–1925 Gropius continued unsuccessful in his attempts to introduce the architecture course which had originally been proclaimed the Bauhaus aim. Conflicts arose within the Bauhaus, as Fréd Forbát reported in a letter to Gropius: '... among the Masters, or at least among some of them, I sense such a dislike of the architecture studio, which they view as a foreign body within the Bauhaus, that I am thoroughly intimidated.' The much-discussed 'experimental building site' which was to be

Foyer of the theatre renovated by Gropius and Meyer in Jena in 1922.

headed by the architect and – since 1922 – Bauhaus syndic Emil Lange, never materialized. 'The experimental site we want to construct jointly is to provide the opportunity for common work on building, in the sense that all the other Masters of Form as well as him (Lange) can experiment with new formal and technical solutions. However, the Masters of Form generally lack the technical ability to be able to transform their formal ideas into reality.'[76]

Adolf Meyer continued to teach as an Associate Master, however, and Ernst Schumann gave another one-semester course on technical drawing and architectural design in 1924/25.

In order to be able – despite the opposition of the authorities – to begin with the planning of a 'rural estate' which would offer the 'members of the Bauhaus, and in particular the students, better living conditions', Gropius organized the foundation of a Bauhaus Estate Cooperative which was joined by both Masters and students, including Klee, Schreyer, Muche, Börner, Oskar and Casca Schlemmer, Meyer, Albers and the Bauhaus friend and publisher Bruno Adler and his wife Tery. This limited company employed the Hungarian architect Fréd Forbát and commissioned him to plan the estate.

'As the principle on which the future estate housing was to be based, Gropius stipulated the standardization of individual components from which different types of buildings could be composed. In our case this meant standardizing the mould for slag-concrete casting. As well as this technical argument, however, the architectural advantage of employing a uniform module for the entire estate played no insignificant role... My layout, jointly developed with Gropius [ill., p. 112], was spaciously planned. In addition to 20 detached houses located on the hillside, space was reserved for approx. 50 one-family terraced houses on the plateau to the north and student housing for 40 students was planned around a space in the middle of the estate. Of all of these, only the detached houses on the hillside came into immediate question and my first commission was to plan these.

In my layout, the smallest housing unit – three rooms and kitchen – featured

The 'International Architecture Exhibition' organized by Gropius within the framework of the 1923 Bauhaus exhibition represented the first display of modern architecture in the twenties. On the wall can be seen the plan of the Bauhaus estate; in front are models of the modular housing units of 1923. On the right are photographs of buildings by Erich Mendelsohn and Erwin Gutkind.

a large, central, square living area flanked on three sides by lower bedrooms and side rooms. The larger units had 1-2 more rooms, whereby the central living room was then surrounded on all four sides. Alternatively, or at the same time, a second floor could be added to part or all of the original bungalow unit and a two-storey family house created. We applied for planning permission for four of these two-storey units in mid-July, but ran into difficulties with the municipal building authorities, who opposed the flat roof design. I continued my work, however, and began studying the constructional components of the various spatial combinations in perspective drawings in order to improve the plans from an architectural point of view, technical problems having been basically overcome. I also made plaster models of the eight room cells and combined these into a wide range of different housing configurations...'[77]
It was 'built of six components' and could be 'combined in various ways... Gropius called this system a "large-scale building set", with which different "living machines" could be composed depending on requirements and the number of residents.'[78] At the large Bauhaus exhibition of 1923, Forbát's standardized housing units, with their 'spatial cells', were exhibited as 'honeycomb architecture' (ill., p. 112). However, extensive opposition from both municipal and state authorities ensured they were never built. 'The city would approve no grants, the state would therefore guarantee no loan, and the planned sale of land to the Cooperative thus never took place.'[79] In 1924, as a protest against the lack of an architecture department at the Bauhaus, an 'architecture study group' was formed whose members included the painter Georg Muche, Marcel Breuer from the joinery workshop and Farkas Molnár. Muche, who in 1924 was the first Bauhaus Master to visit the USA, designed a multi-storey apartment building. Breuer, too, worked on a similar project. In the Germany of the

twenties, neither design stood even the slightest chance of practical implementation.

The strangulation of the Weimar Bauhaus

The result of the Thuringian elections of 10 February 1924 was to seal the political fate of the Bauhaus. The right-wing conservative parties, who had long been demanding the closure of the Bauhaus because of the Communist and Bolshevist tendencies they saw at work there, were to achieve their ambition through a series of steps. On 20 March 1924, Public Education Minister and Minister-President Richard Leutheusser told Gropius that his dismissal was virtually a foregone conclusion. On 18 March 1924, Gropius was indeed informed that his contract was to be terminated on 31 March 1925 with the possibility of renewal on a six-monthly basis. Soon afterwards the previous level of Bauhaus funding was cut by half, from 100,000 to 50,000 Marks.
These two moves made it impossible for the Bauhaus to plan for the long term while at the same time cleverly avoiding the political outcry risked by immediate closure. 'The Bauhaus was thus slowly but surely strangled to death', wrote the former public education minister Max Greil, who had always supported the Bauhaus. In this hopeless situation the Bauhaus Masters took a dramatic political step; in a press release of 26 December, they announced that they considered their contracts with the State of Thuringia dissolved as from March 1925. They thus effectively handed in their notice, a move to which they were not legally entitled but which was designed to mobilize the political and cultural publics. 'The Bauhaus Masters accuse the Thuringian Government of having approved and encouraged the subversion of the objective, entirely non-political cultural work of the Bauhaus through party-political intrigues.'[80] The Bauhaus had in fact been supported throughout by the SPD, USPD, and even the Communists. Conservatives from both the extreme right and centre had opposed the reform-oriented Bauhaus right from the start, as indeed they had opposed many other comparable institutions in the educational reform movement.
The Bauhaus itself experienced the start of a phase of internal unrest and increased activity. Would the Bauhaus really shut down at the end of March 1925? Students concentrated upon finishing their education, while a number of Masters began looking for teaching posts at other institutions.
Gropius tried to deflect the political threat of closure, which had been looming since spring 1924, with a proposal for the government. He suggested founding a limited company which would carry the costs of now quite extensive Bauhaus productive operations. This would relieve the financial burden on the government, leaving it only tuition costs and teacher salaries to pay.
The company was to have a capital of 150,000 Marks, of which Gropius had raised 121,000 Marks by early December 1924. The largest shareholders were the General German Trades Union Congress and Adolf Sommerfeld. Gropius was confident of the financial success of such a limited company. He believed '... that Bauhaus products have now conquered the market. With the business suitably organized on a private-enterprise basis and the provision of sufficient working capital, there is nothing to prevent healthy sales ... A marketing organization is available ...'[81]
The state – suggested the Bauhaus – could invest its possessory right to the equipment in the workshops as its shareholding.
Although Gropius was able to put forward his ideas in a number of discussion sessions, he was clearly the victim of stalling tactics. Since it was the government's declared political intention to close the Bauhaus, it had no interest in securing the school's material future.

On his 41st birthday in 1924 Gropius was given a portfolio of works by Bauhaus Masters. The contributors took as their inspiration the above photograph from the Vossische Zeitung of 1924. Seldom is the variety of artistic positions held at the Bauhaus so clearly illustrated as in this portfolio, whose range encompasses the artistic extremes of Feininger's playfulness and Moholy-Nagy's cool Constructivism (right). More than just a birthday present, the portfolio was also a demonstration of the Masters' solidarity with Gropius in what was then a politically very difficult situation. At the same time the portfolio celebrates the first five years of the Bauhaus' existence.

Not until Dessau was Gropius able to found his Bauhaus Ltd. He also started a 'Society of Friends of the Bauhaus', a politico-cultural lobby with a committee of famous names. Even Albert Einstein was a member – probably at Moholy's request. But neither this initiative nor the publication of the 'Pressestimmen für das staatliche Bauhaus' (Voices of the press for the State Bauhaus) had the desired effect.

Despite internal crises, despite a permanent shortage of funds and political animosity, the Weimar Bauhaus had successfully improved its livelihood during the first six years of its existence.

The 'two-Master system' and the integration of theory and practice had been a success. During these years the Bauhaus produced a series of creative solutions which changed the face of design in the twenties and thirties.

In the workshops, type, norm and function were the catchwords behind creative experimentation. Elementary forms and primary colours remained important bases of design activity, ultimately leading to the emergence – contrary to Gropius' intentions – of a certain 'Bauhaus style'.

Bauhaus finances during these years remained unsatisfactory, however. Commercial efforts to free the Bauhaus from its dependence on state funding failed on a number of scores. Lack of working capital and workshop equipment, lack of commercial experience and the effects of inflation were all equally to blame. In many of its designs the Bauhaus was years ahead of its time, and it was similarly long before its successes were felt.

The modern design which developed in Germany in the wake of the 1918 Revolution was viewed by the conservative parties as 'Bolshevist' and 'left-wing'. These parties were opposed to the Bauhaus right from the start and fought the school at every political opportunity. Although Gropius denied that modern design had a political character, he was unable to protect the Bauhaus – by now a symbol of the modern age – against attack.

Georg Muche: Sheet from the portfolio for Walter Gropius, 1924.

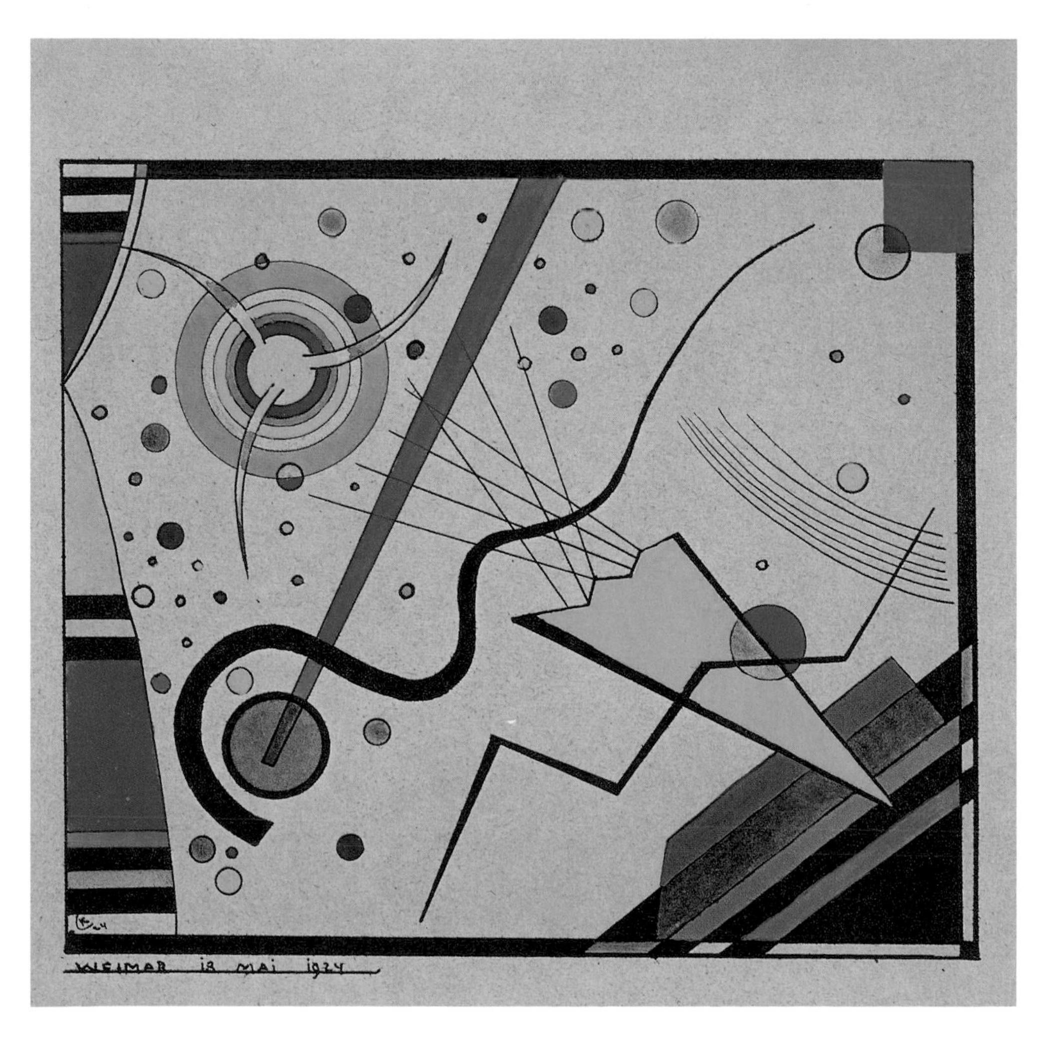

Wassily Kandinsky: Sheet from the portfolio for Walter Gropius, 1924.

Above: *Oskar Schlemmer:* Sheet from the portfolio for Walter Gropius, 1924.

Below: *Lyonel Feininger:* Sheet from the portfolio for Walter Gropius, 1924.

Opposite page: *Paul Klee:* Sheet from the portfolio for Walter Gropius, 1924.

Lösung „ee." der Geburtstags Aufgabe

Facing, previous page: Façade of the workshop wing of the Dessau Bauhaus. Photograph by Lucia Moholy, 1926.

The Weimar Masters had terminated their contracts before considering their future options. The move could easily have spelled the end of the Bauhaus. But the fame of this new type of school proved such that, in the course of the next few months, a number of cities expressed interest in giving the Bauhaus a home. From 'Dessau, Frankfurt/Main, Mannheim, Munich, Darmstadt, Krefeld, Hamburg, Hagen/Westphalia . . . came encouragement and offers to continue the work of the Bauhaus'[82]. Ultimately, however, the only offer of substance was to come from Dessau, a city governed by the Social Democrats and whose mayor, Fritz Hesse, expressed his personal support for the Bauhaus. The body of Masters (ill., p.135) agreed to the move, and what had been a state school now became a municipal institution. Dessau was then, as now, a centre for mechanical engineering. The engineering and aircraft company, Junkers, was one of its major industries. The region was also home to a number of large chemical factories, such as IG Farben, whose employees lived in Dessau. In 1925 the city had a population of some 50,000; by 1928 this figure had grown to 80,000. An acute housing crisis was coupled with a lack of developmental urban planning. One of the reasons behind the City of Dessau's rapid decision to adopt the Bauhaus was its shortage of accommodation; Gropius was at that time arguing for the technicalization and rationalization of residential architecture, and his ideas fell on eager ears. It was not long before he was commissioned to build a model estate in the Törten district of Dessau.

Gropius was only to head the Bauhaus in Dessau for another three years, from March 1925 to March 1928. During this period the school reached another pinnacle in its career. The new school building designed by Gropius, and the Masters' houses he built for the Bauhaus teaching staff, became the epitome of modern architecture in Germany. The Bauhaus became a site of pilgrimage, attracting hundreds of visitors every month from home and – increasingly – abroad. Bauhaus students gave regular guided tours. The Törten estate offered Gropius his first opportunity to demonstrate industrialized building techniques, and the labour exchange he built for the City of Dessau (1927-29) was his most logical and attractive example of functional architecture.

The Bauhaus building in Dessau

'The City of Dessau has approved the building of a joint complex to house the new Bauhaus and the already existing handicrafts and trades school, which is now to be run by the Bauhaus; it has also approved the construction of detached houses and a studio apartment block for students.'[83] This commission from the City of Dessau enabled Gropius and the Bauhaus to test in practice their aim to develop everything from the simplest domestic

Preliminary design for the Bauhaus building in a drawing from Gropius' architecture practice, 1925.

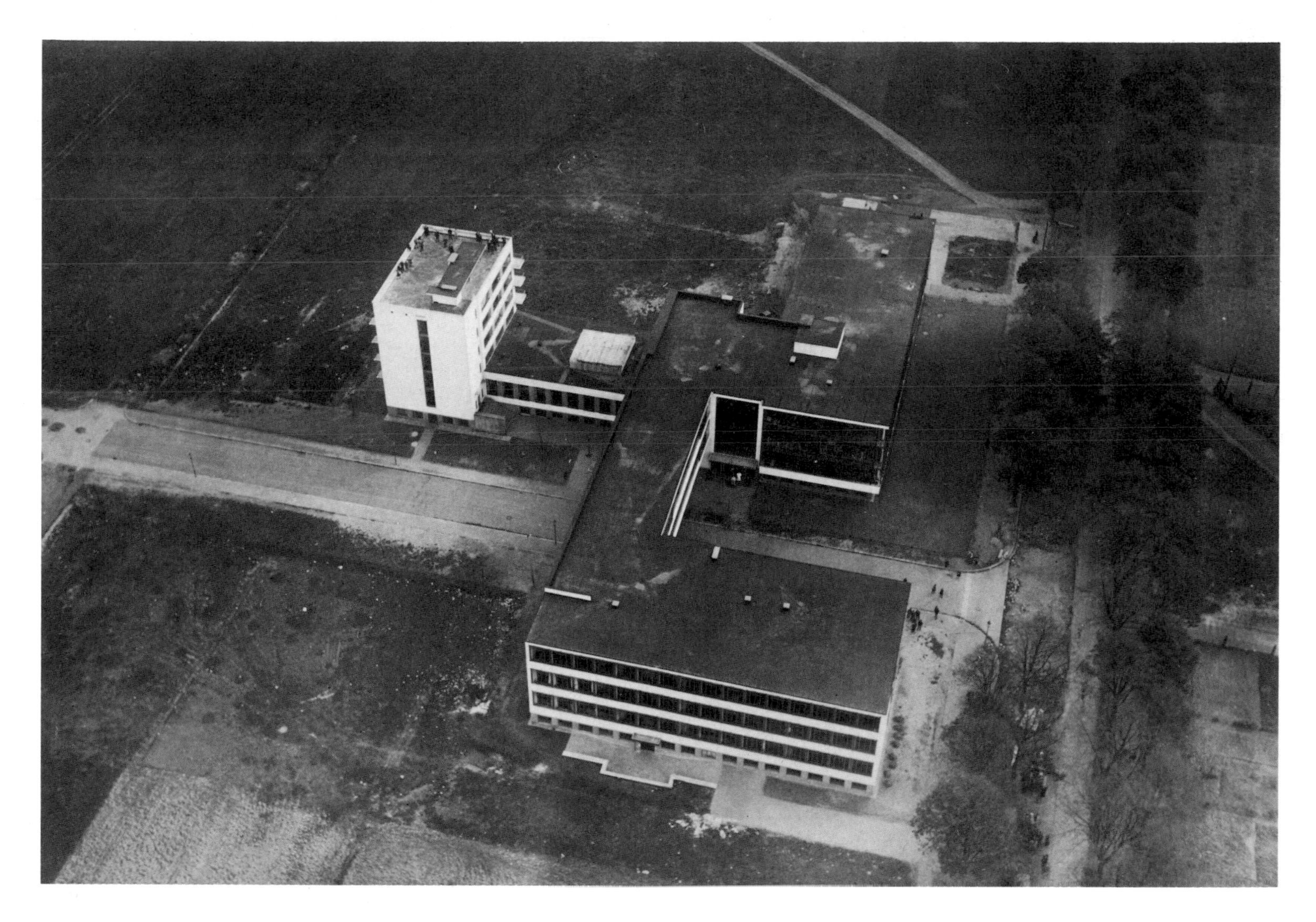

The Dessau Bauhaus building designed by Walter Gropius, 1925/26. Describing the free layout of the different compositional elements, Gropius compared the Bauhaus with historical architecture. 'The typical building of the Renaissance or Baroque has a symmetrical façade and an approach leading up to its central axis. ... a building produced in the spirit of our own times rejects the imposing model of the symmetrical façade. You have to walk right round the whole building in order to appreciate its corporeality and the function of its members.'

utensil to the finished building. After the move to Dessau, where it officially opened on 1 April 1925, the entire Bauhaus was now set to work exclusively on this project, as earlier on the Haus Am Horn.

Even now there was still no architecture department – Gropius was not to introduce one until 1 April 1927 – and thus the entire planning and execution of the project was carried out from Gropius' private architecture offices.

A preliminary sketch completed in 1925 (ill., p.120) already contained what were subsequently built as the three main sections of the new Bauhaus complex: the spacious, four-storey workshop wing with its glazed façade, the arts and crafts school wing, and the raised joint administrative section linking the two. The three-wing building, in which the individual functional areas are clearly separated, was completed only a short while later (ill., p.121). In addition to the arts and crafts, workshop and administrative sections of the original version, it was also given a five-storey student accommodation block, called the studio building. An auditorium, theatre and canteen were also located on the first floor; these could be opened up to create an interconnecting 'party area'. Working, living, eating, sport, parties and theatre were thus united under one roof in a 'miniature world' which expressed Gropius' belief that 'to build is to shape the patterns of life'[84].

Gropius particularly liked to show off his Bauhaus building in aerial photographs (ill., p.121) since these best revealed both the clear distinction between the individual sections and the logic of the overall layout. 'You have to walk right round the whole building in order to appreciate its corporeality and the function of its members', said Gropius. The 'rigorous

The Bauhaus building seen from the south-west: workshop wing. In 1927 Rudolf Arnheim wrote of the Bauhaus: 'It is a triumph of purity, clarity and generosity. Looking in through the large windows, you can see people hard at work or relaxing in private. Every object displays its construction, no screw is concealed, no decorative chasing hides the raw material being worked. It is very tempting to see this architectural honesty as moral, too.'

clarity with which Gropius isolated the different functions and sought to illustrate their nature through materials and design makes the Bauhaus building one of the most significant and influential buildings of the 20th century'[85].

But despite such emphasis upon the purely functional inspiration behind the Bauhaus building, the glazing of the entire street-facing façade of its workshop wing repesented what was considered then – as now – a sensational climax of artistic design. Visitors experienced the Bauhaus as an enormous, floating, sparklingly transparent cube. In the words of a contemporary visitor: 'I arrive in *Dessau* at dawn. Fog hangs over the city. Our headlights occasionally penetrate the damp air. But the eye is drawn to a dazzling beam of light. A *giant light cube:* the new Bauhaus building. Later, with sunshine and blue sky, the building remains a focal point of lightness and brightness. Glass, glass and more glass, radiating dazzling white light from every wall. I have never seen such a light reflector. And the *weight of the walls is neutralized* by two factors, namely the high glass walls openly revealing the light steel structure of the building and the radiating whiteness... The huge complex creates a special, almost unforgettable impression *by night,* as on the day of its opening, when every room was illuminated, creating a cube of light which was delineated in all its transparency by the iron grid of its exterior structure.'[86]

The official opening of the Bauhaus on 4 and 5 December 1926 was accompanied by great festivities. A programme of exhibitions, musical events and performances by the Bauhaus theatre workshop were

organized to entertain guests from far and wide. The chief object of admiration was the Bauhaus building itself and the recently-completed Masters' houses nearby. All the fittings had been produced in the Bauhaus workshops. The mural-painting class had been responsible for decorating the Bauhaus building, as one report describes: 'The individual classrooms, and above all the *library,* are gently shaded in light tones. Beams are logically highlighted in specific colour shades. The school's dining room works particularly well: the tripartition of the ceiling is picked out in the colours red and black while, where there are no windows, the walls are entirely white.'[87] All the furnishings for the studios, auditorium, canteen and workshops were produced in the joinery workshop under the direction of Marcel Breuer. A particular highlight was the tubular steel furniture here on show to the general public for the first time. Inspired by the handlebars of his bicycle and with the help of the local Junkers factory, Breuer combined bent tubular steel with seating, back-support and armrests of taut cloth. Contemporaries viewed this tubular steel furniture as the *non plus ultra* of seat technology. All the lamp designs came from the metal workshop, many from ideas by Max Krajewski and Marianne Brandt. The printing workshop was responsible for sign-making. The Bauhaus ideal – the collaboration of all the arts on the building – was here realized in all its clarity and modernity, and the universally-discussed concepts of new architecture, new living and new life were translated into real life with conviction and without compromise.

The Bauhaus building seen from the south-east. On the left, the start of the workshop wing (glass façade); next, the administration and architecture section (continuous line of windows) and, on the right, the student accommodation block. The connecting section below (individual large windows) housed the canteen and auditorium.

Photographs of the interior of the Dessau Bauhaus. Top left, the staircase of the building-trades school; below, the view from the stairwell window. Top right, the canteen; below right, the auditorium with seating by Marcel Breuer and ceiling lighting by Max Krajewski.

Masters' houses

Municipal funding had also allowed Gropius to build a group of Masters' houses (ills., pp.126-129) in a small pinewood within walking distance of the new Bauhaus building. These consisted of three pairs of semi-detached houses with studios, each for two professors, and one detached house for himself. At the beginning, Klee and Kandinsky shared one house, Muche and Schlemmer another, and Feininger and Moholy-Nagy the third. The ground-plans of these mirror-image semi-detached houses met at a 90° angle to each other and thus served to illustrate Gropius' concept of the 'large-scale building set', even though it was not possible to use prefabricated elements in their construction.
The houses, which the Masters rented from the municipal authorities, were furnished with remarkable generosity, astounding even the artists. Schlemmer wrote: 'I was shocked when I saw the houses! I could imagine the homeless standing here one day watching the haughty artists sunning themselves on the roofs of their villas.'[88]
Klee later complained about the size of his heating bills, and he and Kandinsky sought to obtain a rent rebate from the municipal authorities. Some of the artists supplied their own interior colour schemes. Klee had his studio painted yellow and black; Kandinsky chose a rather eccentric decoration scheme, and even Muche experimented with colourful mural designs. Muche's bedroom was painted to a scheme by Breuer. Of her home, Nina Kandinsky recalled: 'The living room was painted light pink, with a niche in gold leaf. The bedroom was painted almond green, Kandinsky's study light yellow and the studio and guest room light grey. The walls of my own small room were a luminous light pink... each room an

Left and right: *Walter Gropius:* Gropius' house, 1925/26. On the left, a view from the south-west showing a side entrance and the upper and lower balconies. On the right, view of the north front from the street, with the main entrance. Photographs by Lucia Moholy.

architectural whole.'[89] A contemporary visitor described the artists' estate thus: 'Everywhere the same purposeful horizontals, the same flat roofs and incisive straight lines of the frameless doors and windows, repeatedly surpassed by the glass wall of a studio. A living-machine objectivity whose coldly uniform essence nevertheless incorporates, as an artistic component, the attractive play of light and shadow set in motion by the not yet grubbed trees.'[90]

Gropius' house was destroyed in the Second World War. The remaining houses were preserved, but have been drastically altered and are now in poor condition. Some of the Masters, including Gropius, Muche and Moholy, used the new buildings and the move as an opportunity to furnish their private apartments in the spirit of the Bauhaus. Gropius' house (ills., p. 126 and 127) was particularly impressively equipped, with a guest apartment, janitor's rooms in the basement, a maid's room and a garage. It became a sort of demonstration model which was shown to visitors and was even made the subject of a film.

The critic Max Osborn compared the Masters' houses with the experimental house of 1923: 'I still think back to the experimental house at the Weimar exhibition of 1923, and how positively unfriendly, orthodox-puritanical, empty and cold it looked. The houses now express contentment and comfort in both their spatial organization and interior decoration.'[91] But whether the Bauhaus had indeed changed, or whether critics and public alike were simply growing more accustomed to the modern style of living, is another question.

Walter Gropius: Bauhaus Masters' houses, 1925/26, view from the road.

Photograph of the topping-out ceremony for the Masters' houses in October 1925.

The families of the Bauhaus Masters in one of the Masters' houses.

Georg and El Muche on the balcony of their Masters' house.

Inside the Masters' houses. Above, the living room in Gropius' house; below, Wassily and Nina Kandinsky in the dining room of their home. Marcel Breuer designed the interiors and furnishings of the Masters' houses. Gropius' house was a demonstration of modern living, both in its thoughtful details and its technical fittings. Gropius saw his lavish house as a model of the lifestyle of the future: 'Much of what we today consider luxury will tomorrow be the norm!'

Above: Josef and Anni Albers' living room, around 1929.

Below: Paul Klee in the studio of his Masters' house, photographed by Lucia Moholy in 1926.

Törten estate

As part of the celebrations accompanying the opening of the new Bauhaus, visitors were allowed to view both the inside and outside of the first houses to be completed on the Törten estate. In the first construction phase of 1926, 60 detached houses were erected. The estate itself had been designed by Gropius. It was purely residential (lacking schools) and consisted of simple, one-storey detached houses with garden. The Konsum building, a three-storey block with shops, was added later. In the course of the – altogether three – construction phases of the Törten estate, Gropius was able to test, for the first time, a concept central to the solution of the current critical housing shortage. For years now, Gropius had been studying ways of cutting building costs by rationalizing work at the building site, by using prefabricated materials and through standardization.

Precise work and time schedules drawn up for the building of the Törten estate were largely kept to. The pace of manual and machine work was carefully coordinated. Since the construction site contained natural deposits of gravel and sand, building blocks could be manufactured on site. Despite such precise and accurate planning, the small scale of the commission meant that Gropius' rationalization measures produced no noticeable economies. However, the houses themselves were cheap enough for even workers to afford. In a second construction phase in 1927 another 100 houses were built; a further 156 were added in a third phase in 1928. In these second and third phases Gropius was able to rectify a number of earlier design weaknesses, such as excessively high window parapets and poorly-functioning heating. These early problems nevertheless provided his political opponents with ammunition for years to come, with damaging consequences even for his successor, Hannes Meyer, who was subsequently only awarded one small-scale municipal commission.

The Bauhaus workshops equipped a model apartment in Törten with furnishings which could be ordered from the Bauhaus. The simple living room also doubled as an eating area. Walls were partially covered with fabric and floors were fitted with mats instead of carpets. The traditional bulky

A model apartment in the estate. The apartment is furnished with standardized furniture made of differently-coloured stained and polished woods.

Above: View of the Törten estate, Dessau.

Below: Two houses in the Törten estate dating from the building phase of 1927.

sideboard was replaced by an asymmetric cabinet with partly open shelving.

School reforms of 1925 and 1927

Work at the Dessau Bauhaus was essentially a direct continuation of work in Weimar. The Bauhaus wanted to further the development of modern housing in all its aspects – from simple domestic utensils to the finished apartment block. This was to be achieved 'through systematic experiment at both theoretical and practical levels – in formal, technical and economic fields'[92]. In Weimar Gropius had regularly assessed the efficiency of the Bauhaus and introduced several amendments to the curriculum. The aims of the Bauhaus were continuously measured against the changing world outside. Now, directly after the move to Dessau (1925), and again in 1927 following the occupation of its new premises, Gropius was to introduce further far-reaching changes.

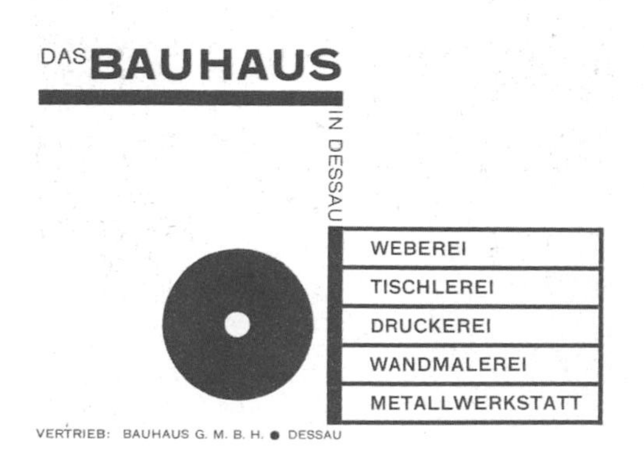

Joost Schmidt: Postcard advertising the distribution of Bauhaus products via 'Bauhaus GmbH'.

The number of workshops at the Bauhaus was now reduced to six: joinery, metal, mural-painting, textiles, book and art printing, and sculpture. 'Theatre' was not mentioned in the 1925 timetable (ill., p.136) but was subsequently reintroduced. As from 1925 four of the departments were headed by former students, called 'Young Masters'. Hinnerk Scheper ran the mural-painting workshop, Marcel Breuer the joinery workshop, Joost Schmidt a sculpture workshop and Herbert Bayer the workshop for printing and advertising. All had successfully completed the tandem system of training in Weimar and were now to be responsible for educating a new generation in the Bauhaus philosophy. In 1927, when Muche left the Bauhaus, Gunta Stölzl was finally able to become Young Master in sole charge of the weaving workshop.

Gropius did not relinquish his aim of making the Bauhaus a going productive concern. The division of workshop activities into teaching and production which had been introduced in Weimar was now written into every timetable.

In November 1925 Gropius was able to found his long-planned limited company, with money chiefly provided by Adolf Sommerfeld. 'Bauhaus GmbH' had a capital of only 20,000 Marks, however. One of its first actions was to print a 'Catalogue of Designs' containing short descriptions and a photograph of all the main Bauhaus products available (ills., p. 80 and 84). The catalogue was designed by Herbert Bayer and printed at the Bauhaus.

The foundation of the limited company, and the appointment of a syndic to represent it, created an organizational basis for the profitable exploitation of Bauhaus products. But it was precisely here that problems arose: turnover fell far short of expectations, and thus the Bauhaus profits for which the municipal authorities had already budgeted were in fact much lower than calculated. Profits from work by the limited company and product licences only finally materialized several years behind schedule.

At about the same time as the opening of the new school building, Gropius decided the Bauhaus should be given the subtitle 'Hochschule für Gestaltung' – Institute of Design. National Art Curator Edwin Redslob, a confirmed Bauhaus supporter, agreed to such a revaluation. From its previous status of municipal school the Bauhaus was now elevated to the same rank as conventional fine art academies, technical colleges and arts and crafts schools. It dropped its earlier use of the terms apprentice, journeyman and master, although some students continued to conclude articles of apprenticeship with chambers of handicrafts. They were now simply called 'students', while the Masters became 'professors'.

Gropius achieved a further success in the following months. He appointed

Masters on the roof of the Bauhaus building. From left to right: Josef Albers, Hinnerk Scheper, Georg Muche, László Moholy-Nagy, Herbert Bayer, Joost Schmidt, Walter Gropius, Marcel Breuer, Wassily Kandinsky, Paul Klee, Lyonel Feininger, Gunta Stölzl and Oskar Schlemmer.

the Swiss architect Hannes Meyer to take over, as from April 1927, the architecture department which was at last to be opened. These two factors precipitated a fundamental revision of the teaching curriculum.
In a printed brochure of 1927 the Bauhaus timetable has been completely reorganized. Architecture is named in first place, subdivided into building ('bau') and interior decoration ('inneneinrichtung'). The metal, textiles, joinery and mural-painting workshops were all grouped under this latter heading. Advertising appears as the second single main category. It was in fact a new name for the old printing workshop, and now included the sculpture workshop and, later, the photography workshop. Theatre, in third place, had never been assigned such an important role in a Bauhaus timetable as now.
A further innovation was the 'Seminar for free sculptural and pictorial design' in fourth place, a synonym for the 'free painting classes' demanded by Klee and Kandinsky. In 1925 the two painters had expressed the wish to teach, in addition to the standard course on form, some kind of painting class – in other words, an entirely traditional field which the Bauhaus had previously rejected out of hand. The new 'Seminar' in the 1927 semester plan now gave them their opportunity. It was later taught as a 'free painting class', given privately once a week by Klee or Kandinsky. Both Masters had meanwhile been released from their workshop commitments as Masters of Form. For the first time, a final diploma was introduced for the architecture course. Similar diplomas were later awarded for other subjects, too. The main teaching emphasis was thus shifted to architecture, although a surprising amount of space was nevertheless reserved for 'free subjects'. In practice the revised timetable made little initial impact since the architecture department contained only a small number of students.
Gropius' successors also started – with different weightings – from similar teaching plans, whereby architecture was both the centre and the summit of

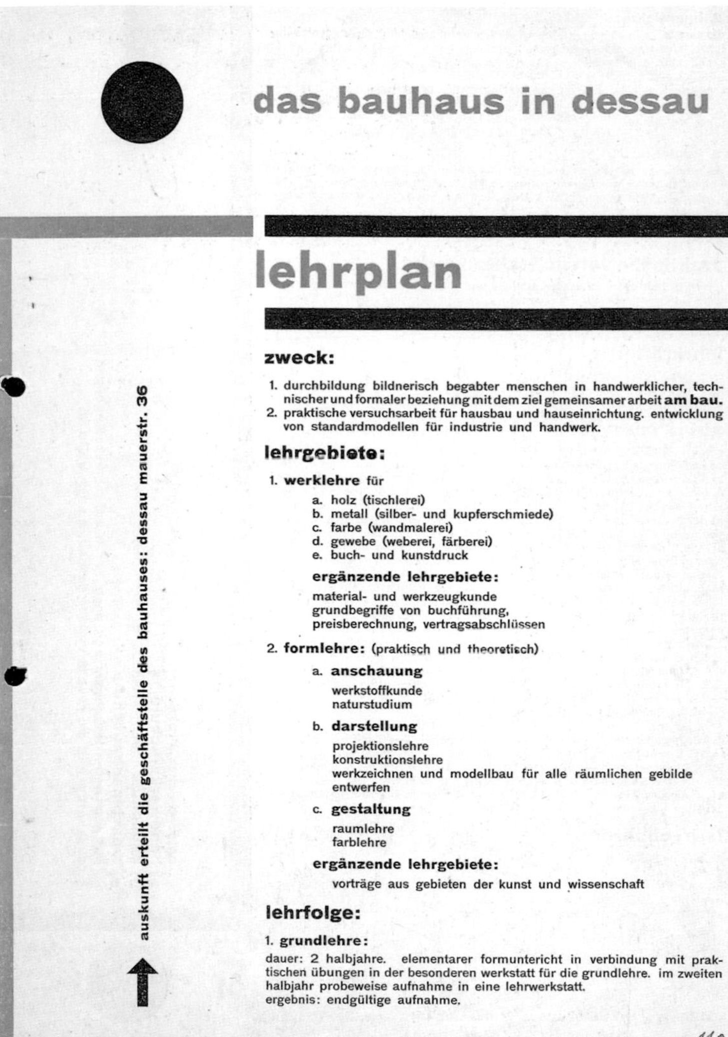

das bauhaus in dessau

lehrplan

zweck:

1. durchbildung bildnerisch begabter menschen in handwerklicher, technischer und formaler beziehung mit dem ziel gemeinsamer arbeit **am bau.**
2. praktische versuchsarbeit für hausbau und hauseinrichtung. entwicklung von standardmodellen für industrie und handwerk.

lehrgebiete:

1. **werklehre** für
   - a. holz (tischlerei)
   - b. metall (silber- und kupferschmiede)
   - c. farbe (wandmalerei)
   - d. gewebe (weberei, färberei)
   - e. buch- und kunstdruck

   ergänzende lehrgebiete:
   material- und werkzeugkunde
   grundbegriffe von buchführung,
   preisberechnung, vertragsabschlüssen

2. **formlehre:** (praktisch und theoretisch)
   - a. **anschauung**
     werkstoffkunde
     naturstudium
   - b. **darstellung**
     projektionslehre
     konstruktionslehre
     werkzeichnen und modellbau für alle räumlichen gebilde entwerfen
   - c. **gestaltung**
     raumlehre
     farblehre

   ergänzende lehrgebiete:
   vorträge aus gebieten der kunst und wissenschaft

lehrfolge:

1. **grundlehre:**
dauer: 2 halbjahre. elementarer formunterricht in verbindung mit praktischen übungen in der besonderen werkstatt für die grundlehre. im zweiten halbjahr probeweise aufnahme in eine lehrwerkstatt.
ergebnis: endgültige aufnahme.

auskunft erteilt die geschäftsstelle des bauhauses: dessau mauerstr. 36

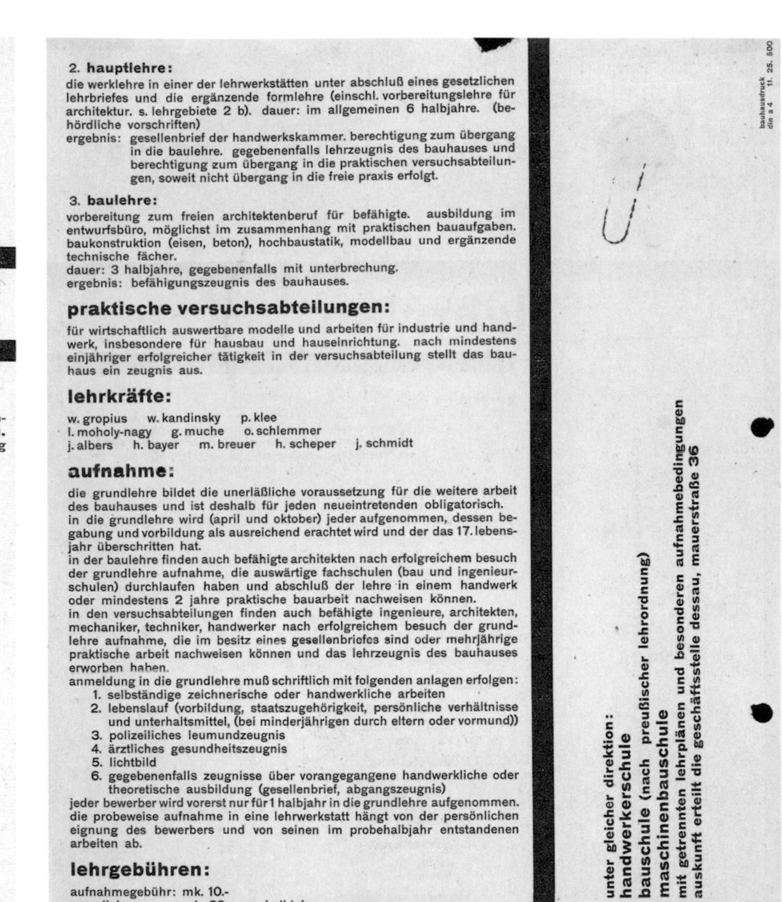

2. **hauptlehre:**
die werklehre in einer der lehrwerkstätten unter abschluß eines gesetzlichen lehrbriefes und die ergänzende formlehre (einschl. vorbereitungslehre für architektur. s. lehrgebiete 2 b). dauer: im allgemeinen 6 halbjahre. (behördliche vorschriften)
ergebnis: gesellenbrief der handwerkskammer. berechtigung zum übergang in die baulehre. gegebenenfalls lehrzeugnis des bauhauses und berechtigung zum übergang in die praktischen versuchsabteilungen, soweit nicht übergang in die freie praxis erfolgt.

3. **baulehre:**
vorbereitung zum freien architektenberuf für befähigte. ausbildung im entwurfsbüro, möglichst im zusammenhang mit praktischen bauaufgaben. baukonstruktion (eisen, beton), hochbaustatik, modellbau und ergänzende technische fächer.
dauer: 3 halbjahre, gegebenenfalls mit unterbrechung.
ergebnis: befähigungszeugnis des bauhauses.

praktische versuchsabteilungen:

für wirtschaftlich auswertbare modelle und arbeiten für industrie und handwerk, insbesondere für hausbau und hauseinrichtung. nach mindestens einjähriger erfolgreicher tätigkeit in der versuchsabteilung stellt das bauhaus ein zeugnis aus.

lehrkräfte:

w. gropius   w. kandinsky   p. klee
l. moholy-nagy   g. muche   o. schlemmer
j. albers   h. bayer   m. breuer   h. scheper   j. schmidt

aufnahme:

die grundlehre bildet die unerläßliche voraussetzung für die weitere arbeit des bauhauses und ist deshalb für jeden neueintretenden obligatorisch.
in die grundlehre wird (april und oktober) jeder aufgenommen, dessen begabung und vorbildung als ausreichend erachtet wird und der das 17. lebensjahr überschritten hat.
in der baulehre finden auch befähigte architekten nach erfolgreichem besuch der grundlehre aufnahme, die auswärtige fachschulen (bau und ingenieurschulen) durchlaufen haben und abschluß der lehre in einem handwerk oder mindestens 2 jahre praktische bauarbeit nachweisen können.
in den versuchsabteilungen finden auch befähigte ingenieure, architekten, mechaniker, techniker, handwerker nach erfolgreichem besuch der grundlehre aufnahme, die im besitz eines gesellenbriefes sind oder mehrjährige praktische arbeit nachweisen können und das lehrzeugnis des bauhauses erworben haben.
anmeldung in die grundlehre muß schriftlich mit folgenden anlagen erfolgen:
1. selbständige zeichnerische oder handwerkliche arbeiten
2. lebenslauf (vorbildung, staatszugehörigkeit, persönliche verhältnisse und unterhaltsmittel, (bei minderjährigen durch eltern oder vormund))
3. polizeiliches leumundzeugnis
4. ärztliches gesundheitszeugnis
5. lichtbild
6. gegebenenfalls zeugnisse über vorangegangene handwerkliche oder theoretische ausbildung (gesellenbrief, abgangszeugnis)

jeder bewerber wird vorerst nur für 1 halbjahr in die grundlehre aufgenommen. die probeweise aufnahme in eine lehrwerkstatt hängt von der persönlichen eignung des bewerbers und von seinen im probehalbjahr entstandenen arbeiten ab.

lehrgebühren:

aufnahmegebühr: mk. 10.-
grundlehre: mk. 30.- pro halbjahr
hauptlehre: frei. verdienstmöglichkeit aus verwerteter arbeit
baulehre: mk. 50.- pro halbjahr
versuchsabteilungen: gewinn aus der verwertung der selbstgefertigten modelle oder arbeiten.

unter gleicher direktion:
a) handwerkerschule
b) bauschule (nach preußischer lehrordnung)
c) maschinenbauschule
mit getrennten lehrplänen und besonderen aufnahmebedingungen
auskunft erteilt die geschäftsstelle dessau, mauerstraße 36

die leitung des bauhauses in dessau   walter gropius

Above: The timetable of November 1925 mentions only five workshops instead of the previous ten. Also new was the practical experiments department in which models were to be developed for trade and industry.

semesterplan

	1. semester	2. semester	3. semester	4. semester	5. semester u. folg.
1 architektur a. bau b. inneneinrichtung	vermittlung der grundbegriffe der gestaltung allgemeine einführung: a) abstrakte formelemente analytisches zeichnen ca. 2 std. b) werklehre, materialübungen ca. 12 std. allgemeine fächer: a) darstellende geometrie ca. 4 std. b) schrift ca. 2 std. c) physik oder chemie ca. 2 std. d) gymnastik oder tanz (fakultativ) ca. 2-4 std.	einführung in die specialausbildung praktische arbeit in einer bauhauswerkstatt ca. 18 std. vorträge und übungen: a) primäre gestaltung der fläche ca. 2 std. b) volumen raumkonstruktion ca. 2 std. allgemeine fächer: a) darstellende geometrie ca. 2 std. b) fachzeichnen ca. 2 std. c) schrift ca. 2 std. d) physik oder chemie ca. 2 std. für fortgeschrittene: baukonstruktion ca. 4 std. statik ca. 2 std. übungen ca. 2 std.	spezialausbildung a. bau: prakt. arbeit in einer werkst. 18 std. baukonstr. 4 „ statik 4 „ entwurf 4 „ veranschlag. 2 „ baustofflehre 2 „ b. inneneinrichtg.: praktische arbeit in einer werkstatt, mit entwerfen, detaillieren, kalkulieren 36 std. fachzeichnen 2 „	spezialausbildung unter bevorzug. der theorie entwurfsatelier mit anschließender baupraxis einzelvorträge über baukonstruktion eisenbetonbau statik wärmelehre installation veranschlagen ausschreibung normenlehre sonderkurse über stadtbau verkehr wirtschaftliche betriebsführung praktische arbeit wie im 3. semester 18 std. gestaltungslehre fachzeichnen fachwissen reifere (siehe ableitungsplan 1a vorbedingung 1–3) können bereits nach dem 1. semester auf antrag an den lehrgängen des 4. semesters teilnehmen.	erhöhte spezialausbildung wie im 4. semester mit wachsender selbständigkeit der aufgaben wie im 4. semester wie 4. semester selbständige laboratoriumsarbeit in der werkstatt 36 std.
2 reklame			einführung in das werbewesen untersuchung der werbemittel praktische übungen	wie im 3. semester und einzelvorlesungen über fachgebiete	selbständige mitarbeit an praktischen werbeaufgaben
3 bühne			werkstattarbeit gymnastisch-tänzerische, musikalische, sprachliche übungen	werkstattarbeit choreographie dramaturgie bühnenwissenschaft	werkstattarbeit, selbständige mitarbeit an bühnenaufgaben und aufführungen
4 seminar für freie plastische und malerische gestaltung			korrektur eigener arbeiten nach vereinbarung selbstwahl der meister praktische arbeit in einer werkstatt 18 std.	wie im 3. semester ohne werkstatt	wie im 4. semester

The cover of the Bauhaus brochure, designed by Herbert Bayer, 1927. The semester plan published in this brochure (opposite page, below) made the first mention of the architecture department opened in April 1927. The workshops were amalgamated under the heading of interior design ('inneneinrichtung') and ranked after building ('bau') beneath the overall heading of architecture.

the curriculum. This emphasis upon architecture – and upon developing models for industry – probably discouraged many women students from attending the Bauhaus. Indeed, the following years saw a steady decline in their numbers.

Bauhaus books – Bauhaus journal

Gropius and Moholy-Nagy had planned a series of 'bauhausbücher' (ill., p.138) while still in Weimar. This series of books was intended to treat 'artistic, scientific and technical aspects of various specialist fields' in a total of 50 volumes; the Bauhaus portfolio series had covered the most important modern painters and graphic artists in a similar way. All but two of the first eight volumes, published simultaneously in Dessau in 1925, were written by Masters themselves. They offered a comprehensive picture of architecture, theatre, photography and the activities of the Bauhaus workshops. Moholy designed the typography of almost all the books.

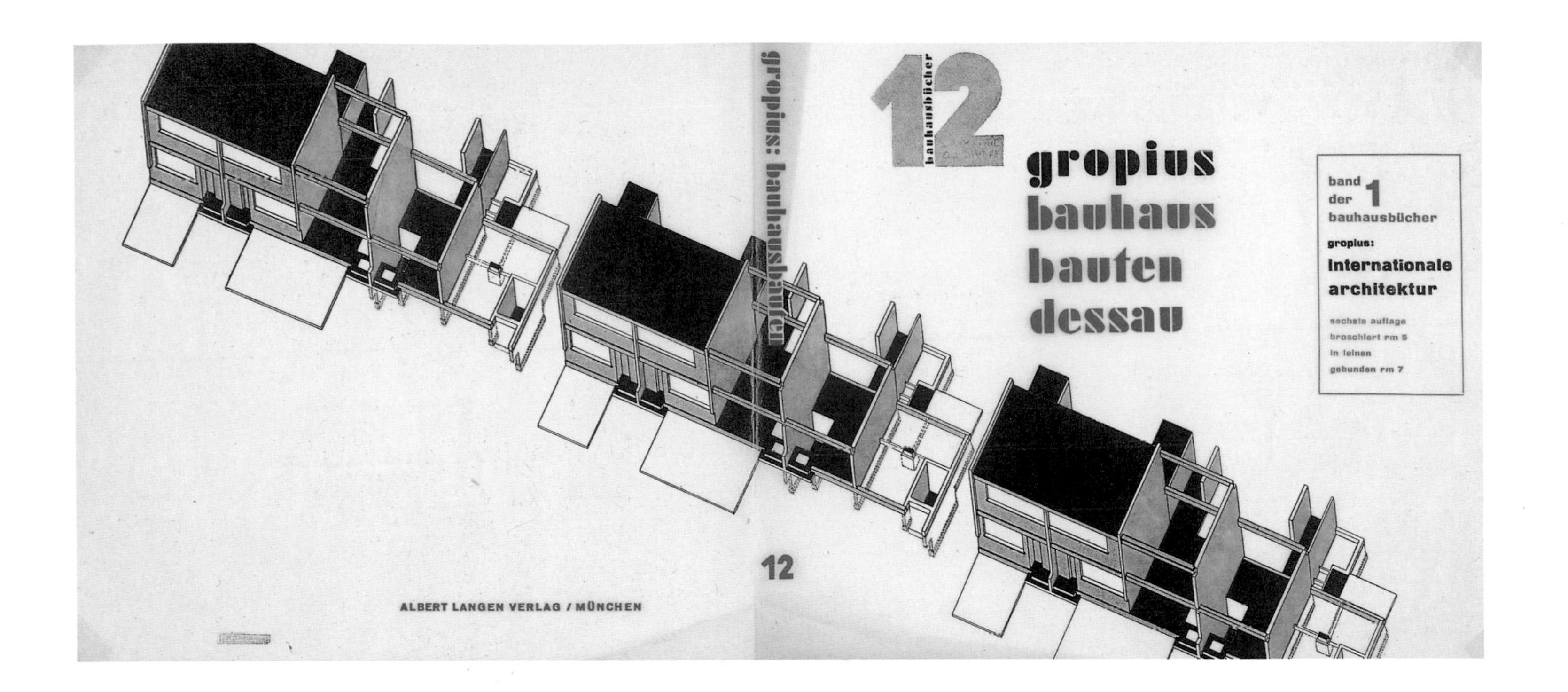

Bauhaus book jackets for 'Bauhausbauten Dessau' by Gropius (1930) and 'von material zu architektur' by Moholy-Nagy (1929), both designed by Moholy-Nagy. Jacket for Gropius' 'Internationale Architektur' (1925) designed by Farkas Molnár.

Moholy, however, who was chiefly concerned with getting new authors, wanted to make the future volumes a cross-section of the new age. Interrelated modern currents were all to be documented in word and image. Moholy gave the individual guest authors a large degree of freedom, allowing them to design their own covers and even page make-up if they so wished. A total of fourteen volumes were published in the period up to 1930.

Coinciding with the opening of the school's new building the Bauhaus launched its first official journal, the 'bauhaus' quarterly (ill., p. 139). It contained information about the Bauhaus, its latest products and commissions, and welcomed contributions from guest authors. At the beginning almost every issue was devoted to a particular theme: the first number (edited by Gropius, designed by Moholy-Nagy) briefly introduced all the workshops, while issue 1927/3 was compiled by Schlemmer and dedicated to theatre. The content of the next issue was dictated by Hannes Meyer, newly appointed as head of architecture, while Herbert Bayer devoted the following number, 1928/1, entirely to advertising. The next six issues

Cover for the 'bauhaus' journal published from the end of 1926 to 1931. In this virtuoso design for the first issue of 1928, Herbert Bayer takes the tools of his graphic art to illustrate a variety of representational levels and means.

appeared under the new director of the Bauhaus, Hannes Meyer. Only three slim issues could be financed under Mies van der Rohe.
At the end of 1925 the Bauhaus decided to abolish capital letters and only to use printed materials satisfying existing DIN norms. The bottom of every piece of Bauhaus writing paper carried the line: 'we only use small characters because it saves time. moreover, why have 2 alphabets when one will do? why write capitals if we cannot speak capitals?'
These advertising and design initiatives can today be viewed as exercises in 'image' and 'public relations'. But we should also remember the political context in which the Bauhaus was then operating. In Dessau, as earlier in Weimar, there soon appeared a local initiative which opposed and slandered the Bauhaus. In the medium-sized city of Dessau, the Bauhaus slowly but surely lost its political backing. Publicizing its successful achievements was thus part of its fight for survival. Another aspect of this fight was the revival of the 'Society of Friends' originally founded in Weimar. It was now expanded; its number of members increased and the Bauhaus became the

regular receiver of sizeable donations. From 1926 onwards, the Society financed the publication of the 'bauhaus' journal, purchased Bauhaus products and organized numerous events.

Preliminary courses by Josef Albers and László Moholy-Nagy in Dessau

The preliminary courses and the classes given by Kandinsky and Klee remained a major part of the basic curriculum in Dessau and also had to be completed by some of the more advanced students. Over the course of the Dessau period the individual teachers developed and, in some cases, fundamentally revised the content of their teaching. From the students' point of view, courses were more intensive and more demanding. As earlier in this book for Weimar, so the teaching now given by Klee, Kandinsky, Albers and Moholy in Dessau will be outlined once more below.
At the core of the preliminary training given to Bauhaus students lay Josef Albers' *Vorkurs* (ill., p. 65). In Weimar, following the resignation of Johannes Itten, the Council of Masters had voted to extend the *Vorkurs* to one year. The time spent on technical aspects of handicrafts training was thereby to be increased so that students would be better prepared for work in the workshops.
Albers, a former elementary-school teacher, came to the Bauhaus hoping to become a painter. Having completed Itten's *Vorkurs* he joined the stained-glass workshop, whose poor record in commissions was soon to cost it its independence. As from autumn 1923 Albers taught the first semester of the *Vorkurs,* consisting of 18 lessons a week, while Moholy taught the second semester (8 lessons a week). Albers' timetable included visits to craftsmen and factories. Without machines, and using the simplest, most conventional tools, pupils designed containers, toys and small utensils, at first using just one material and later in combinations. In this way students familiarized themselves with the inherent properties of each material and the basic rules of design.
In Dessau Albers and Moholy continued to share the teaching of the *Vorkurs,* which remained a year in length. In the second semester, students were permitted to join workshops for a trial period. Albers now taught on four mornings a week for a total of 12 lessons. His course was obligatory for all first-semester students. Moholy-Nagy taught the second-semester students just four lessons a week. When Moholy-Nagy left the Bauhaus in 1928, Albers took over the teaching of the entire *Vorkurs,* which he then ran until the school's closure in 1933.
Although Albers naturally adopted some elements – such as the study of materials – from Itten's *Vorkurs,* he systemized them in a completely new way, as can be seen in his approach to material studies. From 1927 onwards students were no longer permitted to work with materials at random, but instead had to progress through glass, paper (ill., p.142) and metal (ill., p.140) in strict order. They worked solely with glass in the first month and paper in the second, while in the third month they were allowed to use two materials which their studies had shown to be related. Not until the fourth month were students free to choose their own materials.
Albers observed: 'Materials must be worked in such a way that there is no wastage: the chief principle is economy. The final form arises from the tensions of cut and folded material.'

In this hanging sculpture by Hin Bredendieck from Moholy-Nagy's class (1928), glass tubes and metal wire are incorporated into an elastic system. Moholy described the work, hung on slender metal wire, as the preliminary form of a floating sculpture: material and volume relationships existed only within the individual parts, not with the external world as e.g. through a base.

While the main aim of Albers' teaching was the creative and economic handling of materials, Moholy-Nagy concentrated his exercises – still called 'Design studies' in 1924 – on organization in space. As under Itten and Albers, texture studies were created to encourage a feeling for materials, but the majority of the three-dimensional, sculptural objects which have survived in photographs are better described as simple spatial exer-

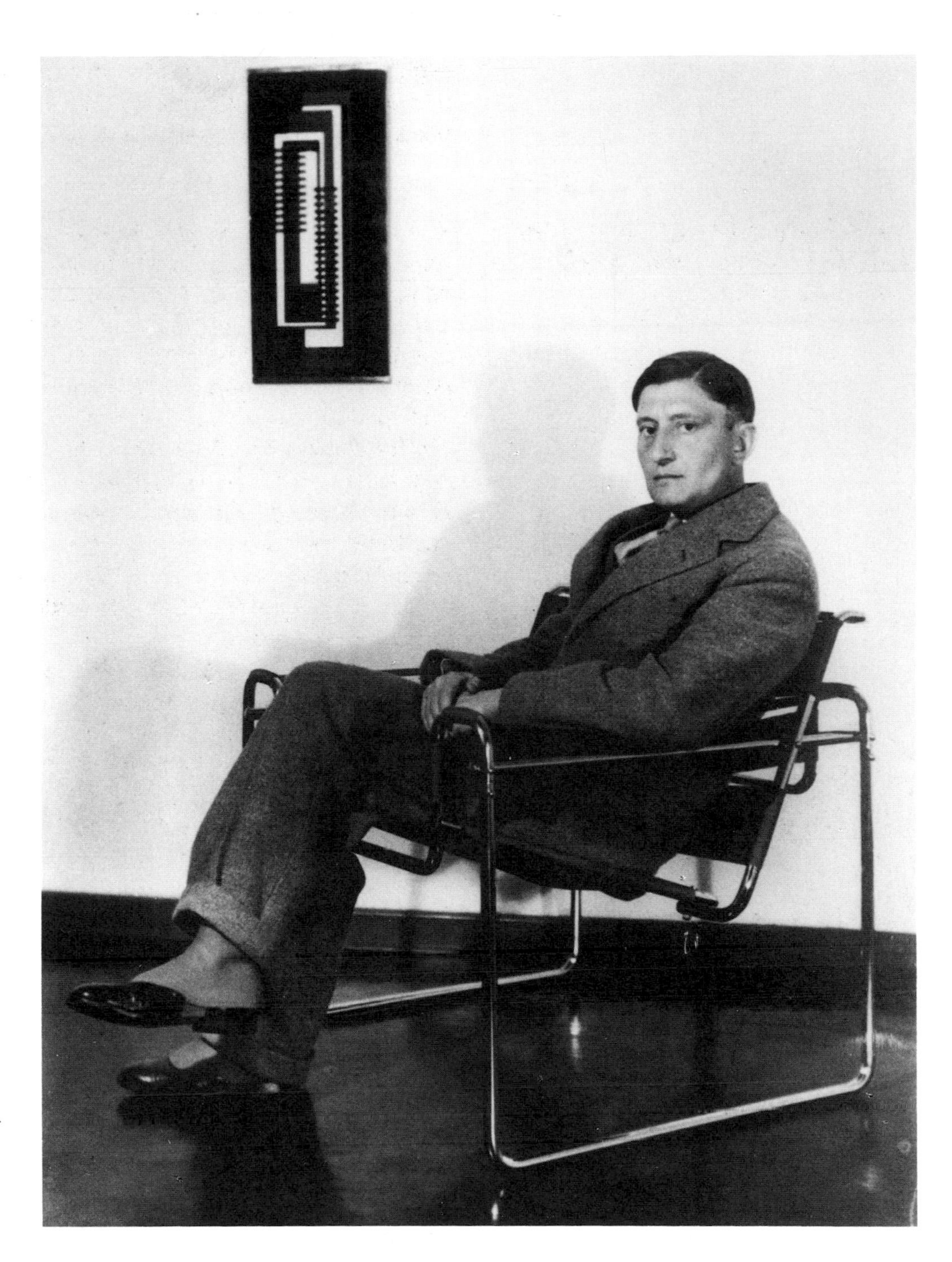

Josef Albers in his Dessau studio in 1928, photographed by Umbo in the latest version of the tubular steel chair by Marcel Breuer. The glass picture on the wall is by Albers himself, from the year 1927.

cises. Glass, plexiglass, wood, metal and wire were employed to produce a variety of harmonious, usually asymmetrical objects, 'equilibrium exercises', studies on 'floating sculptures' and 'volume and space studies'.
Albers' teaching had a particular and profound influence on many students and their subsequent work. The painter Hannes Beckmann described his first lesson with Albers thus: 'I can still clearly remember my first day at the school. Josef Albers entered the room with a bundle of newspapers under one arm, which he gave out to the students. He then turned to us with roughly the following words: "Ladies and gentlemen, we are poor, not rich. We cannot afford to waste either time or materials. We must make the best out of the worst. Every work of art starts from a specific material, and we must therefore first study how that material is constituted. To this end, we shall first simply experiment – without trying to produce anything. For the present we shall focus on skill, not beauty. The complexity of the form is dependent upon the material with which we are working. Bear in mind that you often achieve more by doing less. Our studies should inspire construc-

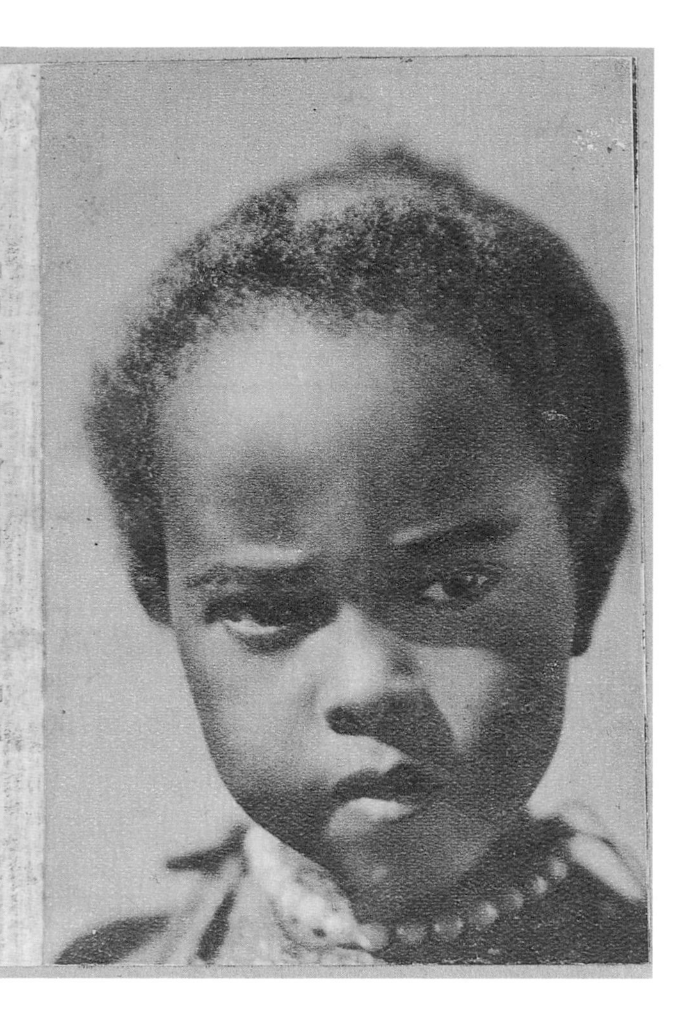

Hans Kessler: Study from Albers' preliminary course. Transformation of a newspaper, 1931.

Opposite page: Gustav Hassenpflug produced this paper creation in 1928 as part of Albers' preliminary course. Height 80-90 cm. A sheet of paper has been rendered stable through skillful cutting and folding. There is no wastage; positive and negative forms are equally valid parts of the formal solution, which is also conceived as an 'illusion of penetration'.

tive thinking. Have I made myself clear? I would now like you to take the newspaper you have just been given and make something out of it which is more than it is now. I would also like you to respect the material, to employ it in a meaningful way and thereby consider its characteristic qualities. If you can do so without the aid of knives, scissors or glue, so much the better. Good luck!". Hours later he returned, and had us lay out the results of our efforts on the floor. There were masks, boats, castles, airplanes, animals and numerous cleverly devised little figures. He dismissed it all as childish rubbish and said that a lot of it would have been better made using other materials. He then picked out one, very simple-looking piece of work by a young Hungarian architect. He had done nothing more than fold the material from top to bottom so that it stood up like a pair of wings. Josef Albers now explained how well the material had been understood, how well it had been used and how folding was a particularly appropriate process to apply to paper since it made what was such a soft material rigid, indeed so rigid that it could be stood on its narrowest point – its edge. He also explained how a newspaper lying on a table has only one visually active side, the rest being invisible. But with the paper standing up, both sides had become visually active. The paper had thus lost its boring exterior, its tired appearance. The preliminary course was like group therapy.

By comparing all the solutions found by the other students, we quickly learned the most worthwhile way to solve a task. And we learned to criticize ourselves; that was considered more important than criticizing others. The "brainwashing" which we thus underwent in the preliminary course undoubtedly taught us to think more clearly.'[93]

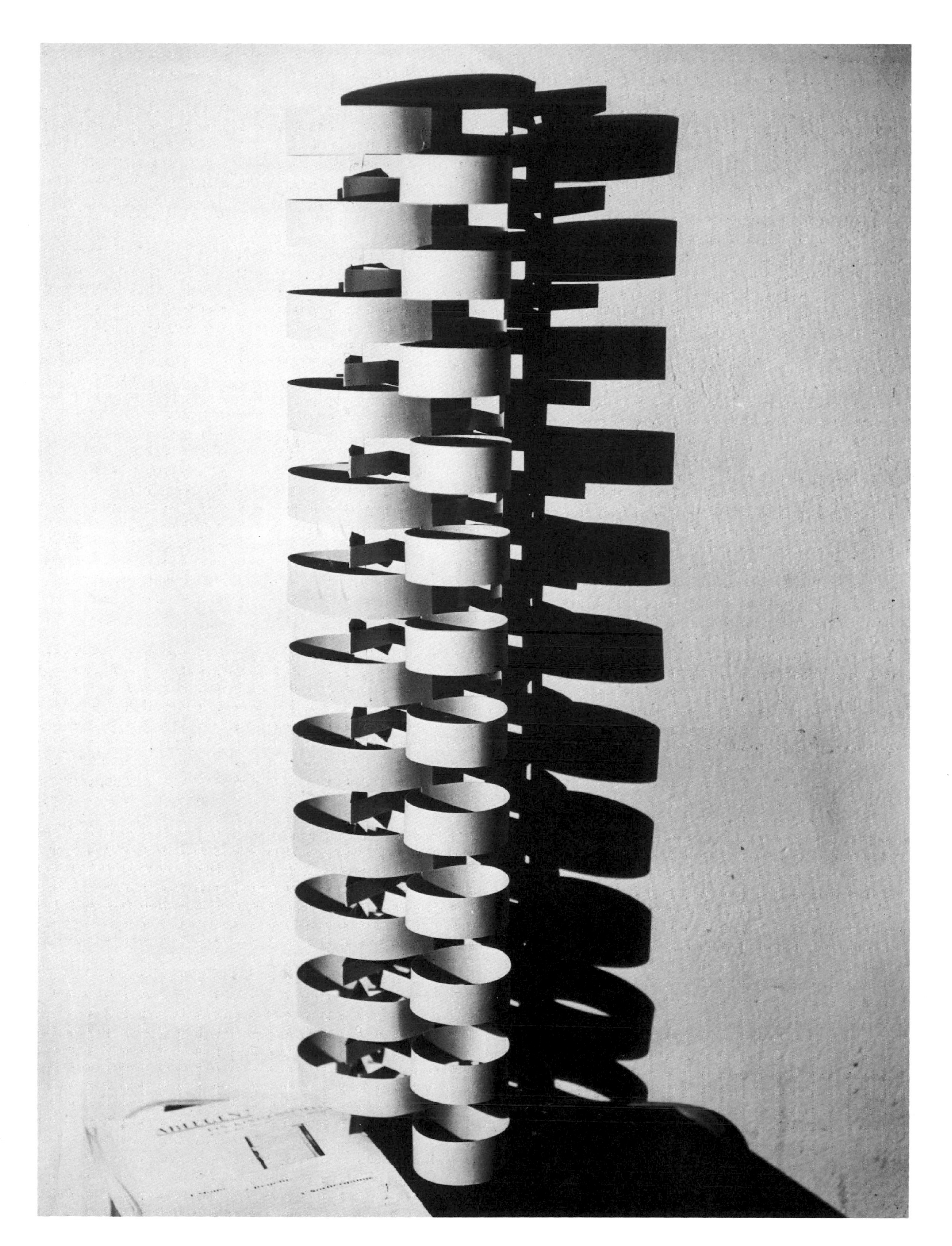

Lena Meyer-Bergner: Exercise from Klee's class: Radiation/modified centre, 1927.

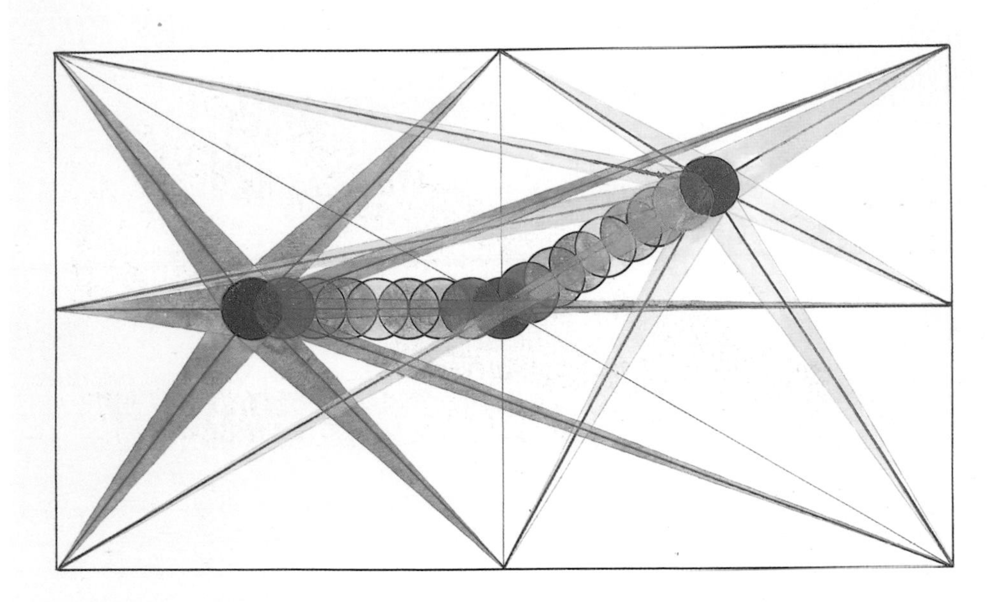

Classes by Paul Klee and Wassily Kandinsky in Dessau

Klee was in charge of teaching the second-semester *Vorkurs* students throughout almost his entire career at the Dessau Bauhaus. His particular field of activity was the 'theory' pictorial form course whose main themes he had developed in Weimar and which also included colour theory, studied in the example of a chromatic sphere. In the winter semester of 1927 this field of activity widened; following Muche's departure, Klee ran the form classes for the weaving workshop. He almost always subdivided his courses into two classes, one for junior students (in their 2nd and 3rd semesters) and one for senior students in the 4th and 5th semesters.

As from May 1926 Klee also taught the free painting classes he had personally requested. Ten students signed up for the first course. These classes, too, he gave throughout his stay at the Bauhaus.

Ernst Kállai: Caricature of Paul Klee as Bauhaus Buddha, 1929.

Unlike Kandinsky, who set the same exercises year after year in his analytical drawing class (1922 onwards) and colour theory class (1925 onwards) with very little change, Klee was continually modifying his classroom teaching, in part with the help of specialist literature which he procured himself. Klee's usual method was to give a few demonstrations himself and then set his pupils to solve tasks through drawing and colour (ills., p. 144 and 145). The underlying aim was to explore, in the broadest possible sense, the laws of planar design and colour theory in terms which were initially simple – 'Weaving. Third semester. Black-and-white colour scales' – and later more complex: 'Fourth to fifth semester. Formal expression with light-dark' and finally 'First ellipsis construction' and 'Inner ellipsis construction'.[94] Pupils had to translate these ideas into their woven designs and choice of colours. Klee also judged the finished fabrics: 'There was some criticism of weaving materials; an eminent number of new ideas were introduced, some particularly good. Women can be extraordinarily hard-working.' Such condescension did not prevent Klee from himself buying numerous Bauhaus textiles, such as a carpet by Ida Kerkovius and a cover by Otti Berger.

Although, in his letters, Klee often remarked disparagingly about his own teaching – 'I do everthing by halves – art, making money, teaching, writing letters...' – he was nevertheless personally committed to the idea and aims of the school. 'The Bauhaus will never calm down; if it does, it's finished.

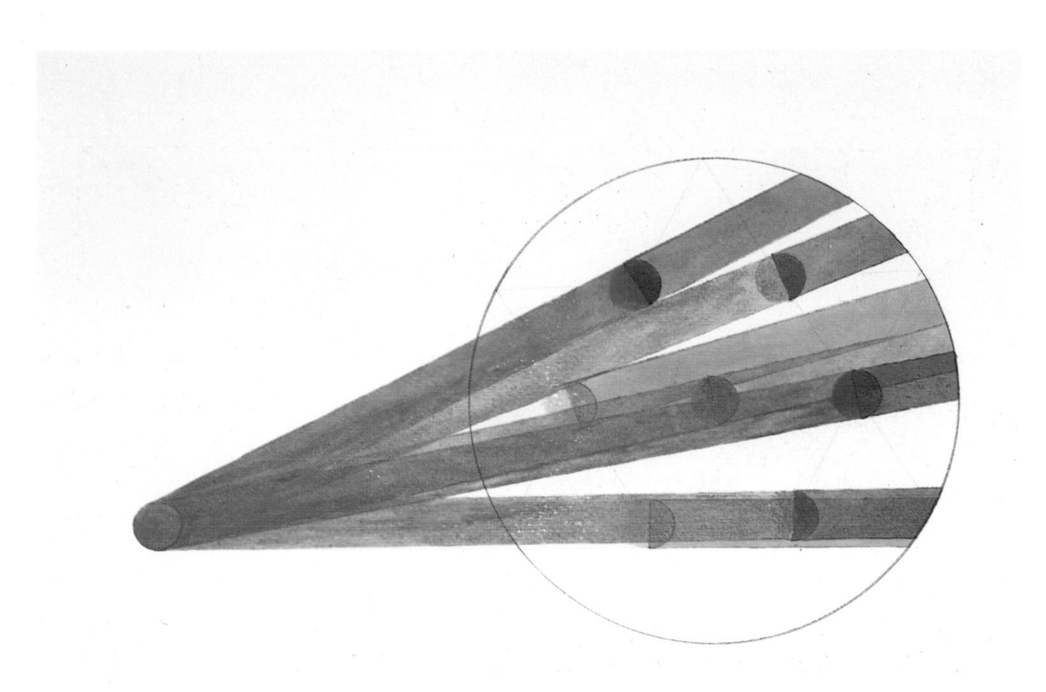

Lena Meyer-Bergner: Exercise from Klee's class: Exposure obscuration, 1927.

Everyone involved with it must make their own contribution, even if they don't want to.'

The author Ernst Kállai, for a short while editor of the Bauhaus journal, caricatured Klee as a sort of Buddha with reverent women students kneeling before him (ill., p. 144). But despite his reclusive nature, Klee always played an active role as critical observer and commentator on the fundamental changes taking place at the school.

As in Weimar Klee's free art and classroom teachings remained in a state of constant interplay. Klee originally hoped to unify his experiences with a closed system. But his investigations widened into an 'infinite natural history', with results deriving as much from science as from art – two areas from which no single system could be created.

Kandinsky's teaching also fell under the heading of form theory, which in Dessau was compulsory for students in the second semester and above. Like Klee, Kandinsky also taught a free painting class as from 1927. It is interesting to note that, in contrast to a suprisingly large number of 'analytical drawings', almost no colour-theory exercises have survived from Kandinsky's Weimar teaching, suggesting that he developed such exercises only gradually. The Bauhaus Archiv in Berlin contains over 200 examples of colour-theory exercises executed by students from Kandinsky's classes in Dessau. Unlike the – almost impossible to categorize – exercises which have survived from Klee's lectures and classes, the tasks set by Kandinsky can be grouped under four main headings: colour systems and sequences (ill., p.147), the correspondence of colour and form (ill., p.146), the interplay of colours, and colour and space.

Kandinsky's starting points were frequently the three primary colours of red, blue and yellow, together with black and white. He followed Goethe's colour theory, according to which the two colours of blue and yellow represent the strongest pair of opposites.

It is not easy to evaluate the significance of Kandinsky's teaching. Kandinsky's course, like Albers' class, came under heavy criticism in particular under the directorship of Hannes Meyer. Kandinsky sought to respond to such criticism and he allowed students to discuss problems encountered in their workshop activities in his lessons.

Lothar Lang: Free green form and yellow triangle. Exercise from Kandinsky's class, around 1926/27.
Lang simultaneously contrasts form and colour: the small triangle is yellow because this form best illustrates the colour's properties – stinging, sharp, pointed. The green plane, considered immobile and calming, has to assert itself through its extension and restless contours.

Monika Bella Broner: Experiment in colouring secondary forms, 1931. Starting from the assignment of primary colours to elementary forms, as specified by Kandinsky himself, colours were sought which corresponded to intermediate forms, whereby a sort of 'colour and form circle' arose.

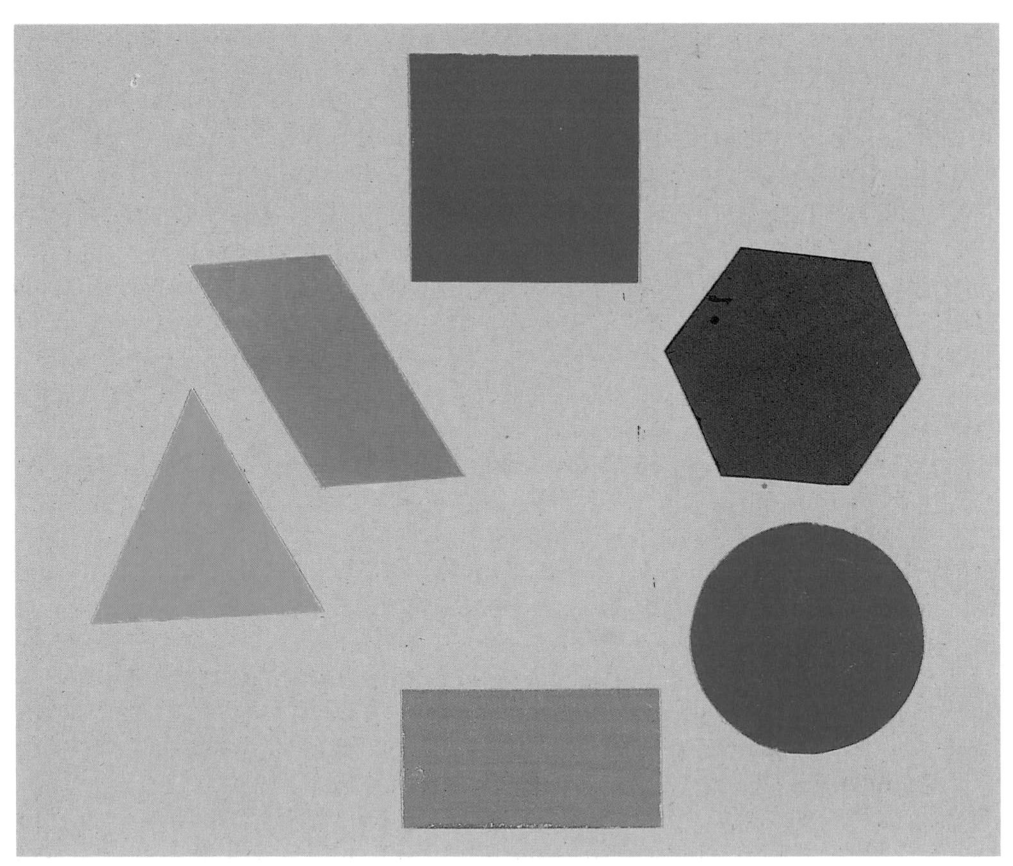

Production and teaching in the workshops

When the Bauhaus moved to Dessau in March/April 1925, it first had to make do with provisional premises in an old department store in the Mauerstrasse. Only a proportion of pupils – albeit many of the most talented – followed the school from its idyllic setting in Weimar to the dirty, industrial city of Dessau. And although Lyonel Feininger, the previous head of the graphic printing workshop, moved to Dessau with the Bauhaus, it was no longer as an active member of the Bauhaus teaching staff.
The commercially ineffective workshops of the Weimar Bauhaus were now abandoned (glass, wood and stone). The graphic printing workshop was also left behind since, although lucrative, it was only capable of reproduction work. In its place a printing workshop was set up in which creative work was also possible.
The wood-carving and stone-sculpture workshops were effectively modernized under the single heading of 'sculpture' workshop. Both financial and pedagogical arguments were thus respected.
The most far-reaching changes were to be felt in two workshops in particular: the printing workshop under Herbert Bayer, with its entirely new orientation, and the weaving workshop. The weaving workshop had been fully re-equipped from the technical point of view; it also became the earliest workshop to offer a proper training course, designed and implemented by Gunta Stölzl. In both workshops young people were being trained for professions which had effectively never existed before.
These Bauhaus years saw not only the production of new industrial designs for furniture, metal, textiles and modern printed materials but, at the same time, the formulation of new training courses and the preparation of new

Lothar Lang: Colour chart. Study from Kandinsky's class, 1926/27. The three primary colours of yellow, red and blue and the secondary colours of orange, green and violet are ranged between a light and a dark pole.

professions which would operate at the interface of design and technology in the widest possible sense.

The printing and advertising workshop

In Dessau the former Weimar art-printing workshop was transformed into a printing workshop, later to call itself the printing and advertising workshop. It now included a small composition department using a sans-serif script in all type sizes, together with a platen press and rotary proof press. Max Gebhard described the activities in the workshop: 'All the students working here set their own designs and printed them under instruction... There was much experimentation with printing-together, overprinting and compositions using large wooden type. All the printed materials, forms, posters and publicity brochures needed for Bauhaus purposes were printed in the school's printing workshop on the basis of designs by Herbert Bayer or the students.'[95]
Design and execution thus took place under one roof; this 'made it possible to structure the preconditions for a new job description: graphic design'[96].
According to Max Gebhard there was no teaching in the classroom sense. Instead, Herbert Bayer tirelessly monitored and directed work on the commissions currently under execution.
Bayer devoted himself energetically to the emerging science of advertising psychology. His teaching covered topics such as 'Systematics of advertising' and 'Effects on consciousness'.
Stylistically speaking, the workshop was now using the 'new', 'elementary'

Herbert Bayer: Poster for a lecture by Hans Poelzig at the Bauhaus, 1926.

Erich Comeriner: Typographical collage, 1927. This collage was probably produced not as a poster for Grel Palucca but as a free study.

Herbert Bayer: Design for a universal type, 1926. Rejecting historical forms and individual 'old-style and fancy types', Bayer sought to create an internationally valid and legible style of lettering with this universal type. 'Like modern machines, architecture and the cinema, so too must type be an expression of our exact times.'

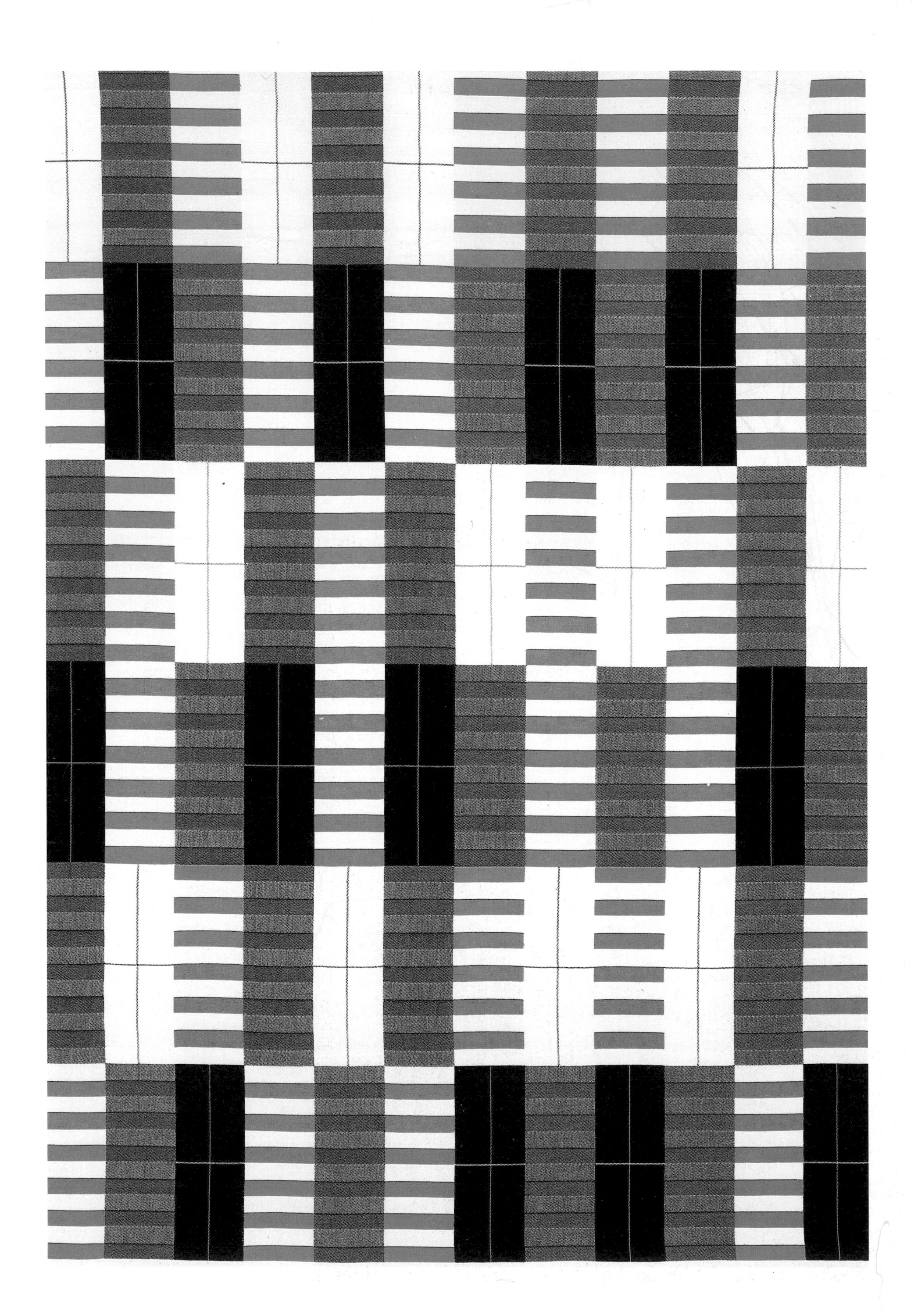

typography which Moholy had first introduced at the Bauhaus. Red and black were the dominant colours; other compositional elements included sans-serif type (joined later by futura) and the use of photos and typographical material such as points, rules, bold rules and screens. Arrangement on the plane now respected not the rules of symmetry but the significance of the text, and might be angled or vertical.

The textile workshop

While the printing and advertising workshop had no registered apprentices, articles of apprenticeship were required in the weaving workshop before students could commence its three-year training course. At the end, students could take their apprentice's final qualifying examination as well as get a Bauhaus diploma. Although Gunta Stölzl was not made Young Master of the weaving workshop until 1927, both the organization and content of the weaving course rested in her hands as from 1925. Master weaver Wanke was responsible for technical matters. Gunta Stölzl introduced a very wide range of loom systems suitable for both learning and production purposes, as well as designing the three-year training course. This course was divided into two stages, the first in a teaching workshop and the second in an experimental and model workshop.
Gunta Stölzl also taught classes in weave and material theory and – since the Bauhaus had its own dye-works – in dyeing.
With the start of work in Dessau, the weaving workshop moved over to industrial design. The design process was in part systemized with e.g. one warp worked by a number of students and one material woven in different colours. Woven fabrics were mounted as marketing samples and numbered consecutively together with details of their price and measurements. Students were thus taken through every stage of the production process – from dyeing, through weaving, right up to ordering materials. At the same time, in Klee's form classes, they learned the rules of patterning and colour design.
A profession was thus created within the textile industry which had rarely been found before – designer. Thanks to their basic training on the hand loom, however, students were equally capable of running small, artistic crafts workshops. Self-employment was at that time an option which many women preferred to a full-time position in trade and industry.

Opposite page: This wall-hanging by Anni Albers from 1926 is a triple weave in which superimposed fabrics are held together by linking threads. Where the material lies double, it vaults sculpturally forward. Anni Albers uses just four colours in blocks and stripes in this formally rigorous but lively carpet.

Group photograph from the weaving workshop. Back row, centre: Gunta Stölzl; next to her, technical master weaver Wanke.

Many items of furniture were produced in two versions, such as Marcel Breuer's folding easy chair of 1927 (above), developed from his first tubular steel chair.

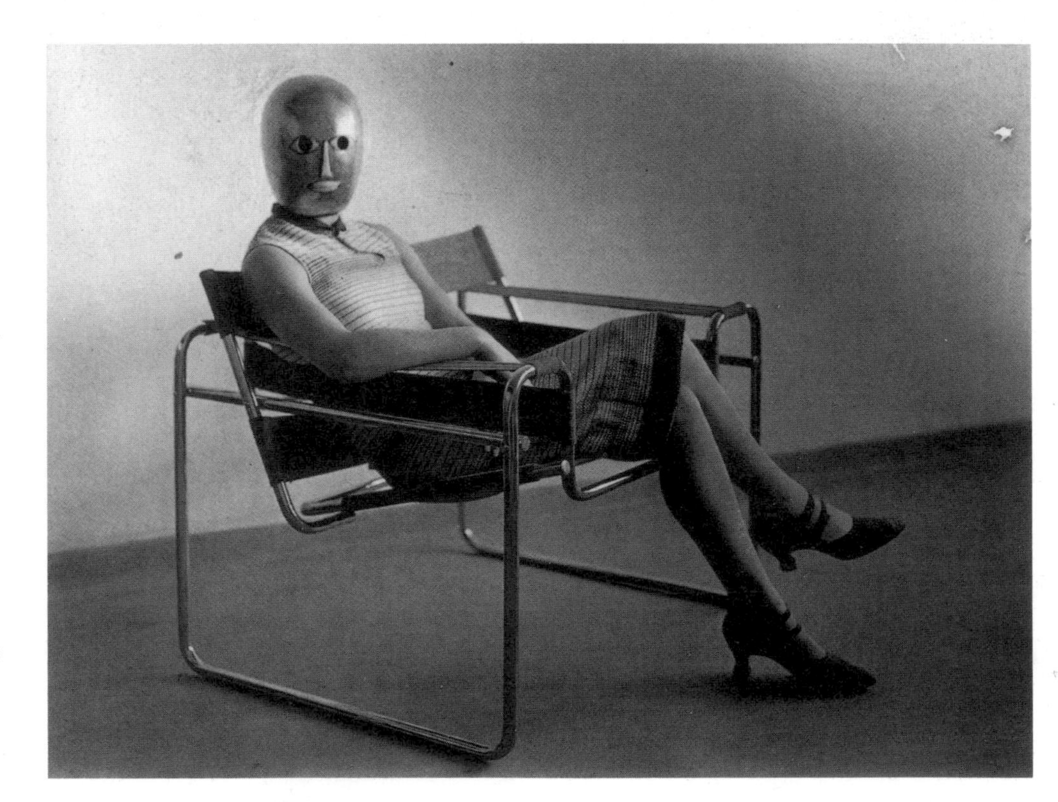

Woman with a mask by Schlemmer seated in one of Marcel Breuer's first tubular steel chairs. This picture was taken by Erich Consemüller, who took several hundred photographs for the Bauhaus' archives.

Two-cord cotton yarn. This very strong cotton fabric was developed for the tubular steel chairs. Textiles woven at the Bauhaus were given a lead seal.

The joinery, metal, mural-painting and sculpture workshops

Under the direction of Marcel Breuer the joinery workshop achieved two outstanding successes in Dessau: firstly its furnishing of the new Bauhaus building and Masters' houses and secondly its further development of tubular steel furniture. The now classic interiors of the Masters' houses inhabited by Gropius, Moholy, Muche and Kandinsky are highlights in the history of 'New Living'. Clear, pictureless walls and expansive windows with large glass panes created generously-sized rooms containing just a few choice items of furniture. Space and furniture seemed to mutually reinforce the effect of the other and at the same time maintain a delicate equilibrium. These interiors were presented as hygienic, easy-to-maintain, practical and functional. The whole, however, was a sophisticated art form which made life itself a work of art. To fulfil their role in everyday life, furnishings had once again to become simple and cheap. The lead was

Left: Ceiling light by Max Krajewski, 1925. Photo: Lucia Moholy.

Right: *Marianne Brandt:* Ball lamp with safety chain, around 1927. Photo: Lucia Moholy.

Opposite page: *Marianne Brandt and Hans Przyrembel:* Hanging lamp with pull, 1926.

here taken by the furniture workshop; in response to the call for greater productivity, the joinery was the first to print a brochure advertising its available range of tubular steel furniture. In addition to his first 'Wassily' chair (as it was subsequently named) (ill., p.152), Breuer went on to systematically design all conceivable sorts of furniture in two versions: theatre seating, easy chairs, tables, chairs, stools. Since the licensing rights to his tubular steel furniture lay with Breuer himself – and not the Bauhaus –, he tried marketing it himself. It was an attempt which soon failed. Had Breuer sold these rights to the Bauhaus instead of Lengye, a dealer who later passed them on to the Thonet company, the history of the Bauhaus might have been quite different; the high licensing revenues would have placed the school on a secure financial footing.
The technical equipment available to the metal workshop had meanwhile been greatly improved, enabling activities to concentrate upon problems of industrial manufacturing. The chief emphasis lay upon the development of new types of lights (ills., p. 154 and 155); in 1927 the first contract was signed with the Berlin company Schwintzer and Gräff, who manufactured various models to Bauhaus designs.
Little is known about the teaching given in the new mural-painting workshop headed by Hinnerk Scheper. Students were taught colour theory and systematically familiarized themselves with colour materials and the differ-

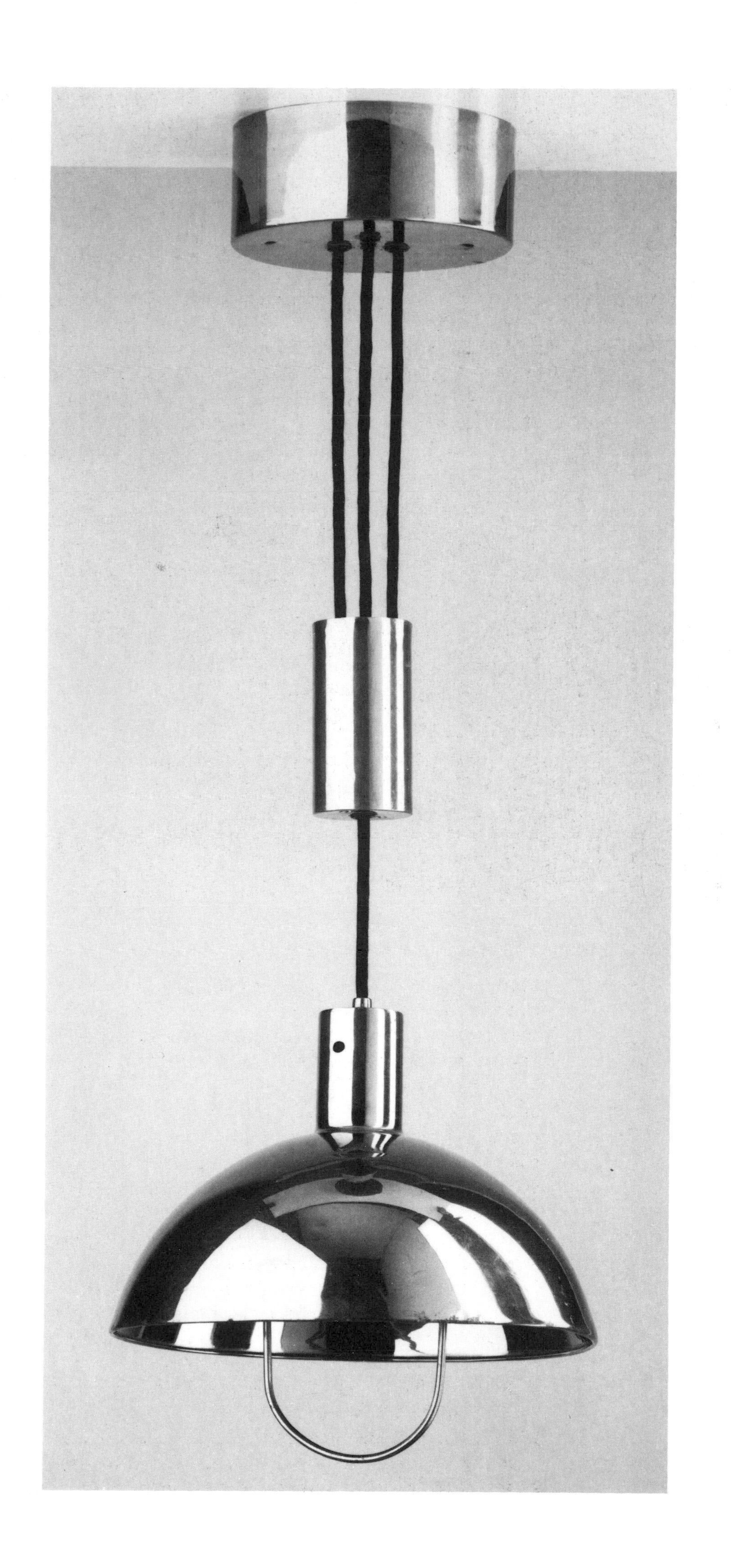

ent behaviours of colours and grounds. A frescoed wall thus produced a different effect to one painted with distemper, for example. The workshop carried out all the decorating work at the Bauhaus as well as numerous external commissions. Many interesting projects were never to see the light of day; a sort of colour-coded routing system which Scheper developed for the Bauhaus building was just one of these.
In 1925 a free sculpture workshop was set up under the direction of Joost Schmidt; a lack of equipment kept its activities to a minimum. The workshop formed the setting for some first experiments in photography, with students Loew and Ehrlich taking pictures of sculptural objects. Joost Schmidt used photography to explore distortion, reflection and rotation in three-dimensional bodies (ills., p.157). It was not until much later, from the winter semester of 1930/31 onwards, that the results were to be applied to perspective drawing and the production of publicity materials.

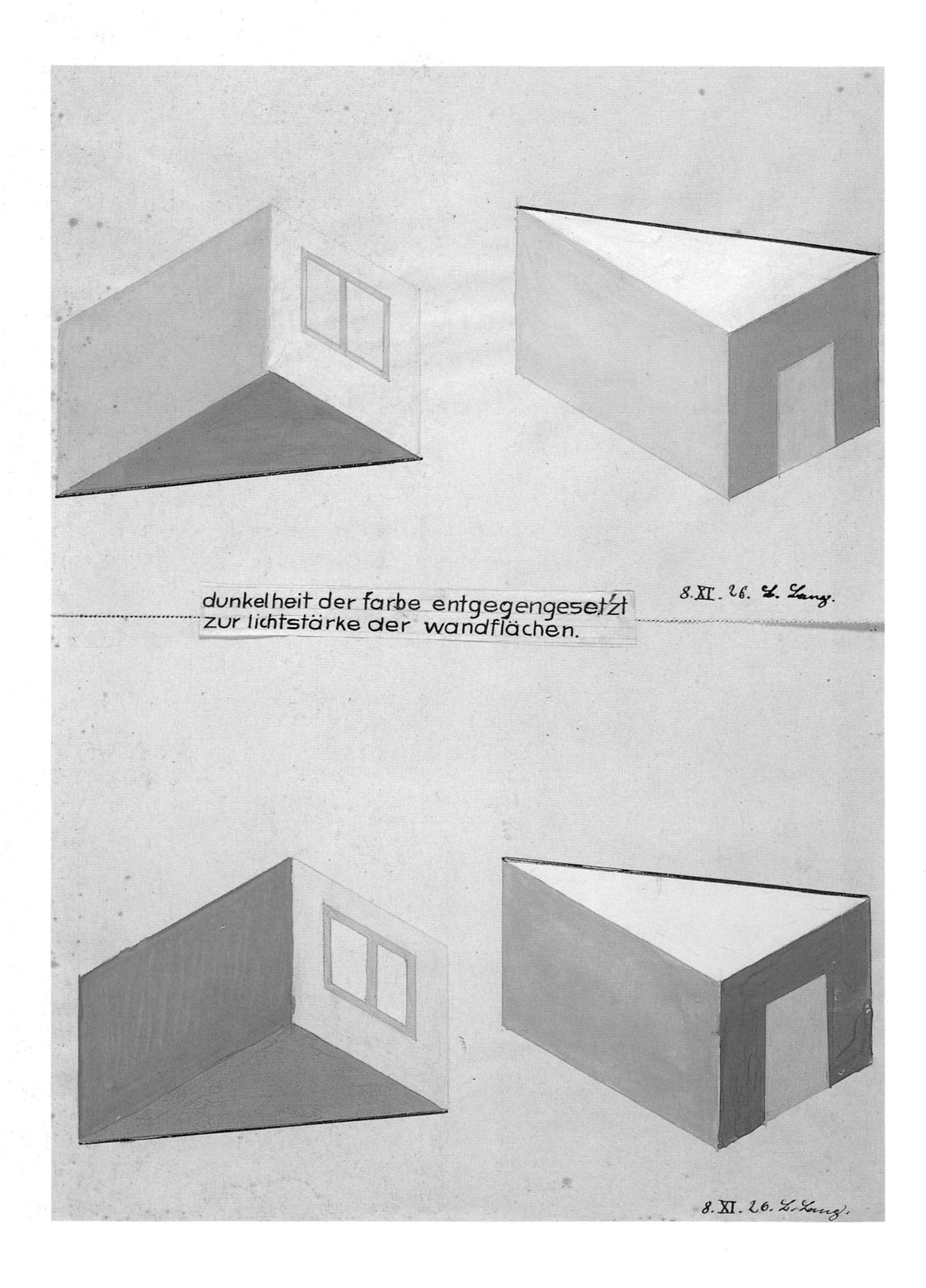

Lothar Lang produced these colour studies in 1926 while a student in the mural-painting workshop.

Studies in composition and lighting effects using elementary bodies from the sculpture workshop, around 1928.

Theatre at the Dessau Bauhaus

The first prospectuses and programmes issued by the Dessau Bauhaus made no mention of theatre. Gropius wanted to close the theatre workshop for financial reasons; it seemed to him to be the most dispensable part of the Bauhaus and had no income to show for itself. In the end, however, a financial settlement was reached, although Schlemmer – unlike Klee and Kandinsky – subsequently complained loudly about his poor salary. In the 1927 timetable theatre reappeared as a major part of Bauhaus teaching.
As early as 1923 Schlemmer had outlined a proposed theatre course which on paper sounded very similar to Schreyer's ideas, but whose results were utterly different. He called for the 'exploration of the basic elements of theatrical creation and design: space, form, colour, sound, movement, light.'[97] Schlemmer thus yielded to the current Bauhaus trend towards 'elementarization' and analysis, and the Bauhaus philosophy stimulated the development of his own work. But it was not until Dessau that Schlemmer actually started to explore these basic elements in his Bauhaus dances. Within the space of a few years, Schlemmer developed his now classic series of – in part 'fundamental-systemizing' – Bauhaus dances (ills., p. 158 and 159): the Form dance, Gesture dance, Space dance, Stick dance, Scenery dance and Hoop dance, together with the Module Play and Box Promenade. These dances were developed with students, but Schlemmer also liked to rehearse with trained dancers and actors. The Bauhaus theatre workshop achieved its greatest success with a tour in 1929 (ill., p.186) through a large number of German cities and Switzerland. In these dances, Man appeared 'not as the vehicle of individual expression, but – standardized through costume and mask – as the prototype of a certain attitude towards the formal stage elements... What occurs in the way of plot is developed out of the visual elements.'[98] 'Thus Schlemmer achieved – not unlike Chaplin – a synthesis of man and marionette, of natural and artificial figure, in which he could employ his entire range of expression: from aethereal grace to monumental weight, from grotesque ornamentation to hieratic perfection.'[99]

In 'Equilibristics', masked members of the theatre workshop performed exercises with simple props. In the background, Schlemmer's large mask. The setting for this scene was the Bauhaus theatre.

Scene from a performance of 'Form Dance', 1927. The dancers are Oskar Schlemmer, Werner Siedhoff and Walter Kaminsky.

Scene from 'Gesture Dance', 1927.

Difficult times 1926/1927

In an article published in the first number of the 'bauhaus' journal of 1926, the painter Georg Muche argued that the creative artist was superfluous when it came to designing forms for industry. The form process started not from the elementary forms and primary colours investigated by the artists, but from the working of the machine. Muche's aim was a redefinition of the role of the fine artist since – as a painter – he, too, was Master of Form of a workshop. His verdict on the artist's role: 'The artistic form element is a foreign body in the industrial product. Technical requirements make art a useless extra.'[100] It was a development to which the Bauhaus had in fact already responded: the painter Masters of Form (with the exception of Moholy-Nagy) had been replaced by Young Masters, and Klee and Kandinsky were no longer in charge of workshops. Muche wrote his article because he wanted to 'save' art. His repudiation of the fine artists at the Bauhaus – Muche was himself soon to resign because he was having problems in his weaving workshop and wanted to return to painting – indicates the shift in emphasis that was be felt during the following years at the Bauhaus. The role of the painter was increasingly modified. Under the directorship of Walter Gropius' successor, Hannes Meyer, the design process was to start first and foremost from social and scientific concerns. Ise Gropius noted: 'The days of the painter at the Bauhaus appear to be truly over. They are estranged from the actual core of present activities and their influence is more restricting than inspiring.'[101] When Moholy-Nagy wrote a sort of farewell speech to the Bauhaus in 1928, he observed that the only reason Klee and Kandinsky were still there was 'to create atmosphere'. About a year later, Schlemmer said of their teaching: 'What else is it but the key to their own kingdoms?'

The Young Masters, paid considerably less than the 'Old' Masters, pressed new demands: salaries on the same scale as Klee and Kandinsky, their own Masters' houses, the title of professor. Schlemmer had to content himself with a pitiful wage. The social standing of the painters appeared out of all proportion to their contribution to the Bauhaus as a whole. This led more or less directly to the questioning of their value for the design process.

Despite impressive appearances at the opening of the Bauhaus in Dessau, many workshops were clearly operating ineffectively. After touring the workshops in January 1926 Gropius wrote a report to all Masters which spoke of a 'deplorable state of affairs'. He wanted to see 'strong leadership' in all the workshops. But a certain lack of direction appeared to have set in, particularly among the more senior and talented pupils. The residual body of Weimar students inhabited the studio block with 'the constant feeling that there was nothing left for them to do', as student representative Hans Volger wrote in a letter to Gropius. They called in particular for the introduction of an architecture course, since they felt that only after architectural training would their education be complete, only then would they be qualified to translate the Bauhaus philosophy into real life. The lack of an architecture department – supposed to be the ultimate stage of the Bauhaus programme – cast doubt upon the whole meaning and aim of the school. In the event, an architecture department was introduced just a short while later. Its teacher, Hannes Meyer, was soon to replace Gropius as director. With his social understanding of architecture he also succeeded in remotivating students in the workshops and increasing productivity.

The problems which were experienced at the Bauhaus around 1926/27 also had their specific financial causes.

When the City of Dessau adopted the Bauhaus in 1925, it made the school a relatively modest financial commitment. In planning the budget for the next few years, Gropius had calculated with revenues from productive operations which subsequently failed to match predictions. It was not until 1929

Opposite page: A student with mask and props from Bauhaus dances, photographed by Lux Feininger.

that productive operations became truly profitable. Many Bauhaus products appeared on the market too soon; they were either too modern or technically still too immature for industrial mass-production. The financial crisis was such that, in August 1926, Gropius proposed that Masters should help the Bauhaus by taking a 10% cut in salary. A circular asking for donations of materials was sent round industry. There were internal discussions about which workshops could be closed. 'Bearing in mind the assurances given to the municipal council, there was no question of an increase in grant'[102], remembered mayor Fritz Hesse of 1926. Although the higher numbers of students meant a greater earnings potential, materials and equipment were still lacking. But here, too, Hesse refused a grant, as he was also to reject the possibility of an increase in budget for 1928.
Ise Gropius observed in her diary that the Bauhaus 'can neither live nor die on its budget'. In 1927, instead of the State subsidy of 30,000 Marks it had hoped for, the Bauhaus was only paid 10,000 Marks.
In December 1927 Gropius weighed up what could be done at the Bauhaus 'to inject some fresher blood into the whole', but did not wish to preach to his successor: 'It is possible that Meyer will develop something quite new; it certainly won't stay the old Bauhaus.'

Walter Gropius' resignation

When Gropius announced his resignation from the post of Bauhaus director in January/February 1928, the school – just one year in its new building – was at the height of its fame and was enjoying growing international celebrity.

Herbert Bayer: Cover for the portfolio 'Nine Years' Bauhaus'. This chronicle of the years since 1919 was compiled for Walter Gropius in 1928 by both Masters and students.

Hugo Erfurth: Walter Gropius, 1928.

Gropius' sudden announcement caused bewilderment among both students and Masters. A Bauhaus without Gropius seemed unthinkable. In explaining his decision, Gropius reasoned that the Bauhaus was now securely established and that he wanted to devote more time to building. Indeed, he was planning to found a 'house-building factory' with Adolf Sommerfeld; the contracts for the third Törten building phase and the Dessau labour exchange were up for decision and were to be awarded to him shortly after his resignation.
In retrospect, it is clear that a succession of internal problems of a fundamental nature had built up over the Dessau years which, although not the cause of Gropius' resignation, nevertheless needed to be resolved if the Bauhaus was to continue to develop successfully. Hannes Meyer, the Swiss architect whom Gropius proposed as his successor, now had to find their solution.

8934

Hannes Meyer:
Necessities, not Luxuries

Hannes Meyer (ill., p.167) remains the 'unknown Bauhaus director' even today. Histories of the Bauhaus often condense his over three-year career at the Bauhaus – from April 1927 to August 1930 – into just one sentence. In actual fact Meyer spent a few months longer at the Bauhaus than his successor to the directorship, Ludwig Mies van der Rohe. Meyer's disappearance from the history books is explained not by his activities as architect or Bauhaus director, but by his political sympathies. He was sacked by the Dessau municipal authorities in 1930 because it was feared that the activities of Communist students at the Bauhaus could cost them valuable votes. Other figures behind Meyer's dismissal included Albers and Kandinsky, as well as Gropius, who sought to diminish and falsify Meyer's contribution to the Bauhaus right up to the last years of his life. It is only more recently that a reassessment of Meyer's role has begun in West and East Germany.

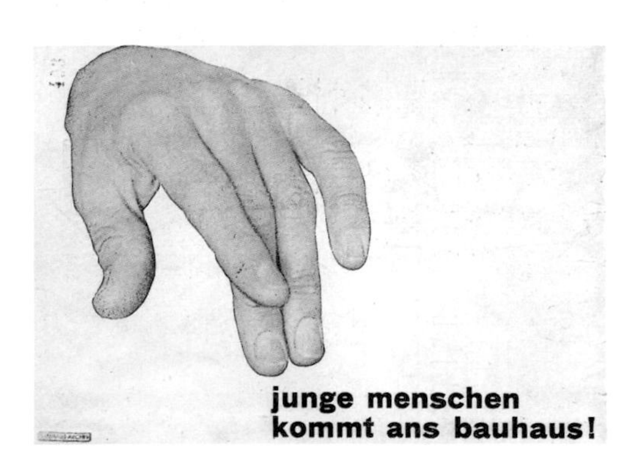

In 1929 Hannes Meyer put together a brochure on the Bauhaus. The hand is taken from a photograph by Lyonel Feininger.

Meyer was Swiss, a member of an old Basle family which had produced a large number of architects. In Metzendorf's office he had worked on the planning of the Margaretenhöhe estate for Krupp in Essen. In 1919 he was commissioned to build the Freidorf co-operative estate near Basle. The co-operative movement was at that time attempting to beat its own path between Capitalism and Socialism and was a theoretical and practical philosophy which Meyer profoundly supported. In the next few years he joined the group centred around the Swiss architectural journal 'ABC Beiträge zum Bauen', whose authors included Mart Stam, El Lissitzky and Hans Schmidt. Inspired by the most important contemporary avant-garde artists of Dutch De Stijl and Russian Constructivism, 'ABC' developed the idea of a radically functional architecture which entirely rejected the concept of 'art'. Its members believed that architecture was the result of systematic planning, that it should arise from the materials employed and the needs of the user. Why, then, did Gropius appoint the Swiss architect to the Bauhaus? Gropius had spent months looking for someone to head what was to be the new department of architecture. His first choice, the Dutch architect Mart Stam, had declined the position. Stam attended the opening of the new Bauhaus building with Meyer and now recommended his colleague for the job. A short while later Hannes Meyer visited the Bauhaus a second time: 'Hannes Meyer here since yesterday to have a good look at the Bauhaus and decide if he is coming or not. Gave a short talk about his buildings, of which he has brought some sketches. His design for the League of Nations building in Geneva seems particularly outstanding. Gr(opius) is highly satisfied and finds more than he expected, especially where practical experience is concerned… At a personal level he seems very nice, albeit a bit wooden like all Swiss. Very clear, open, definite, no great tensions or contradictions in his character.'[103] But Meyer was not afraid to criticize what he saw at the Bauhaus: 'I find myself extremely critical of most of… the work exhibited for the opening celebrations… A lot reminds me immediately of "Dornach – Rudolf Steiner", in other words, sectarian and aesthetic…'[104] Not long afterwards, however, he decided to accept the appointment. He started work at the beginning of April in the summer semester of 1927. He was in charge of the newly-established architecture department. He immediately laid down the guidelines for his subsequent Bauhaus activities: 'The fundamental direction of my teaching will be absolutely towards the functional-collectivist-constructive…'

The initially harmonious, if not entirely uncritical relationship between Gropius and Meyer was not to develop further. 'With very few exceptions, we operate absolutely independently of one another... Gropius lives an entirely separate life to me. We do not get on at all', wrote Meyer to Willi Baumeister in November 1927. One of the problems may well have been

Facing, previous page: *Hannes Meyer, Hans Wittwer and the Dessau Bauhaus building department:* German Trades Union school in Bernau, near Berlin, 1928-1930.

Pages 168 and 169: In 1930, Meyer illustrated the organization of the Bauhaus in a chart which reflects the reorientation of design teaching towards scientific considerations.
The entire plan is laid out between the two poles of art and science. Sport, theatre and the Bauhaus chapel in the first circle on the left offer physical and spiritual refreshment. After completing the – now expanded – *Vorkurs,* students could enter one of the workshop areas represented by the four circles on the right. Weaving ('weberei') and advertising ('reklame') are independent fields, while metal, joinery and mural-painting are amalgamated under the heading of interior design ('ausbau'). This is followed by the fourth and final circle, dedicated to architecture ('bauabteilung'). The total length of study was increased.
This chart, with its 'work circles' or 'cells', lacks the symbolic Utopian goal of the 'Bau' (building) of Gropius' days. Meyer's programme now leads to the practical 'werk' (work) actually created (extreme right).

Hannes Meyer while visiting the site of the German Trades Union school in 1927.

that Meyer and his department lacked a building commission. 'For 3/4 of a year now we have done nothing but theory in our building department and have had to sit and watch while Gropius' private practice is permanently busy.'[105] Gropius nevertheless suggested Meyer as his successor as director at the beginning of 1928. This recommendation may have been inspired by Meyer's professional and teaching qualifications. Students and the Council of Masters were equally ready for new ideas. Meyer, after just nine months at the school, accepted the job, and his new position was confirmed shortly afterwards by both the City of Dessau and the Council of Masters.

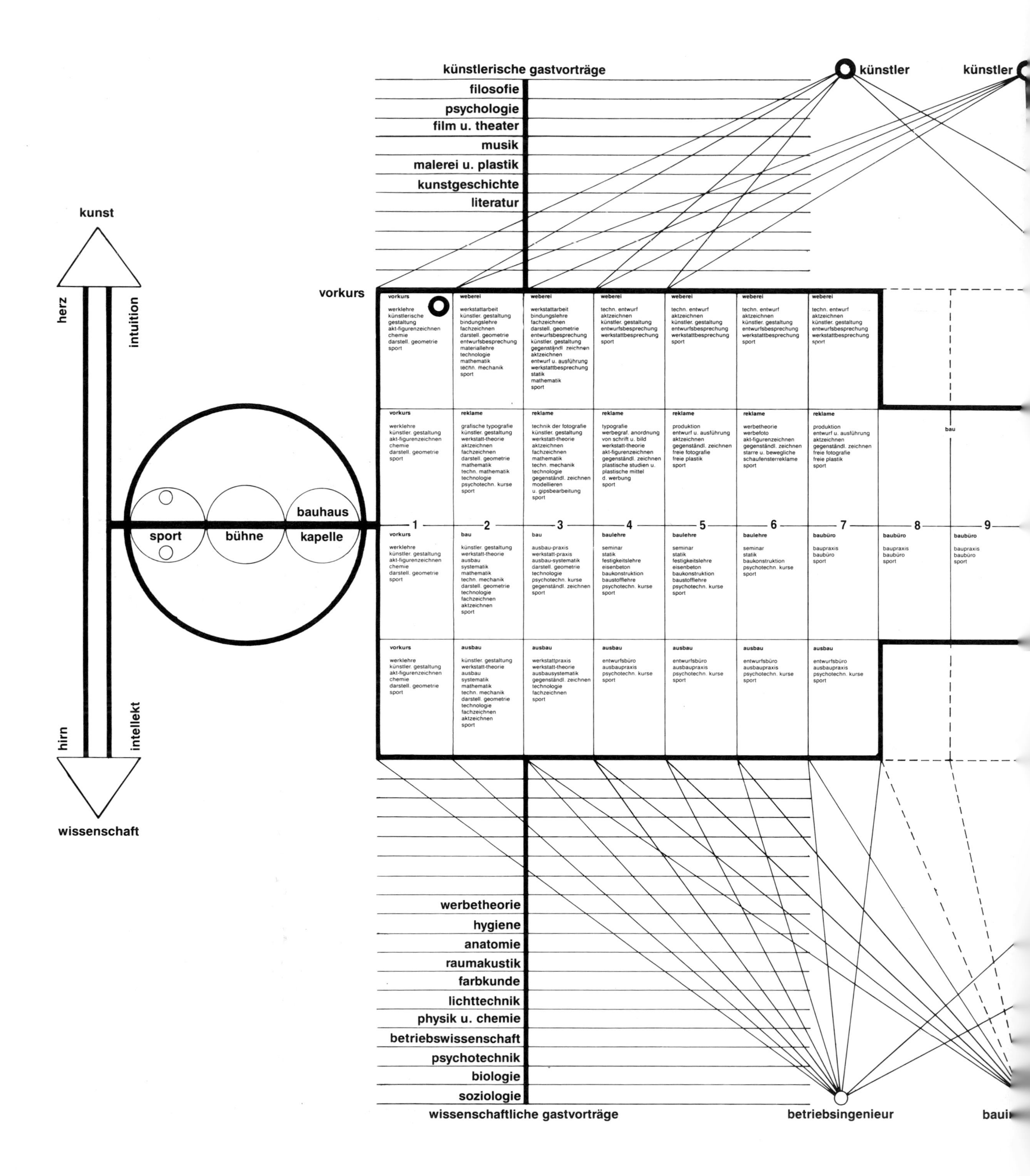
künstlerische gastvorträge
filosofie
psychologie
film u. theater
musik
malerei u. plastik
kunstgeschichte
literatur
künstler
künstler
kunst
herz
intuition
hirn
intellekt
wissenschaft
vorkurs
sport
bühne
bauhaus
kapelle
vorkurs
werklehre
künstlerische gestaltung
akt-figurenzeichnen
chemie
darstell. geometrie
sport
weberei
werkstattarbeit
künstler. gestaltung
bindungslehre
fachzeichnen
darstell. geometrie
entwurfsbesprechung
materiallehre
technologie
mathematik
techn. mechanik
sport
weberei
werkstattarbeit
bindungslehre
fachzeichnen
darstell. geometrie
entwurfsbesprechung
künstler. gestaltung
gegenständl. zeichnen
aktzeichnen
entwurf u. ausführung
werkstattbesprechung
statik
mathematik
sport
weberei
techn. entwurf
aktzeichnen
künstler. gestaltung
entwurfsbesprechung
werkstattbesprechung
sport
weberei
techn. entwurf
aktzeichnen
künstler. gestaltung
entwurfsbesprechung
werkstattbesprechung
sport
weberei
techn. entwurf
aktzeichnen
künstler. gestaltung
entwurfsbesprechung
werkstattbesprechung
sport
weberei
techn. entwurf
aktzeichnen
künstler. gestaltung
entwurfsbesprechung
werkstattbesprechung
sport
vorkurs
werklehre
künstler. gestaltung
akt-figurenzeichnen
chemie
darstell. geometrie
sport
reklame
grafische typografie
künstler. gestaltung
werkstatt-theorie
aktzeichnen
fachzeichnen
darstell. geometrie
mathematik
techn. mathematik
technologie
psychotechn. kurse
sport
reklame
technik der fotografie
künstler. gestaltung
werkstatt-theorie
aktzeichnen
fachzeichnen
mathematik
techn. mechanik
technologie
gegenständl. zeichnen
modellieren
u. gipsbearbeitung
sport
reklame
typografie
werbegraf. anordnung
von schrift u. bild
werkstatt-theorie
akt-figurenzeichnen
gegenständl. zeichnen
plastische studien u.
plastische mittel
d. werbung
sport
reklame
produktion
entwurf u. ausführung
aktzeichnen
gegenständl. zeichnen
freie fotografie
freie plastik
sport
reklame
werbetheorie
werbefoto
akt-figurenzeichnen
gegenständl. zeichnen
starre u. bewegliche
schaufensterreklame
sport
reklame
produktion
entwurf u. ausführung
aktzeichnen
gegenständl. zeichnen
freie fotografie
freie plastik
sport
bau
1
2
3
4
5
6
7
8
9
vorkurs
werklehre
künstler. gestaltung
akt-figurenzeichnen
chemie
darstell. geometrie
sport
bau
künstler. gestaltung
werkstatt-theorie
ausbau
systematik
mathematik
techn. mechanik
darstell. geometrie
technologie
fachzeichnen
aktzeichnen
sport
bau
ausbau-praxis
werkstatt-praxis
ausbau-systematik
darstell. geometrie
technologie
psychotechn. kurse
gegenständl. zeichnen
sport
baulehre
seminar
statik
festigkeitslehre
eisenbeton
baukonstruktion
baustofflehre
psychotechn. kurse
sport
baulehre
seminar
statik
festigkeitslehre
eisenbeton
baukonstruktion
baustofflehre
psychotechn. kurse
sport
baulehre
seminar
statik
baukonstruktion
psychotechn. kurse
sport
baubüro
baupraxis
baubüro
sport
baubüro
baupraxis
baubüro
sport
baubüro
baupraxis
baubüro
sport
vorkurs
werklehre
künstler. gestaltung
akt-figurenzeichnen
chemie
darstell. geometrie
sport
ausbau
künstler. gestaltung
werkstatt-theorie
ausbau
systematik
mathematik
techn. mechanik
darstell. geometrie
technologie
fachzeichnen
aktzeichnen
sport
ausbau
werkstattpraxis
werkstatt-theorie
ausbausystematik
gegenständl. zeichnen
technologie
fachzeichnen
sport
ausbau
entwurfsbüro
ausbaupraxis
psychotechn. kurse
sport
ausbau
entwurfsbüro
ausbaupraxis
psychotechn. kurse
sport
ausbau
entwurfsbüro
ausbaupraxis
psychotechn. kurse
sport
ausbau
entwurfsbüro
ausbaupraxis
psychotechn. kurse
sport
werbetheorie
hygiene
anatomie
raumakustik
farbkunde
lichttechnik
physik u. chemie
betriebswissenschaft
psychotechnik
biologie
soziologie
wissenschaftliche gastvorträge
betriebsingenieur

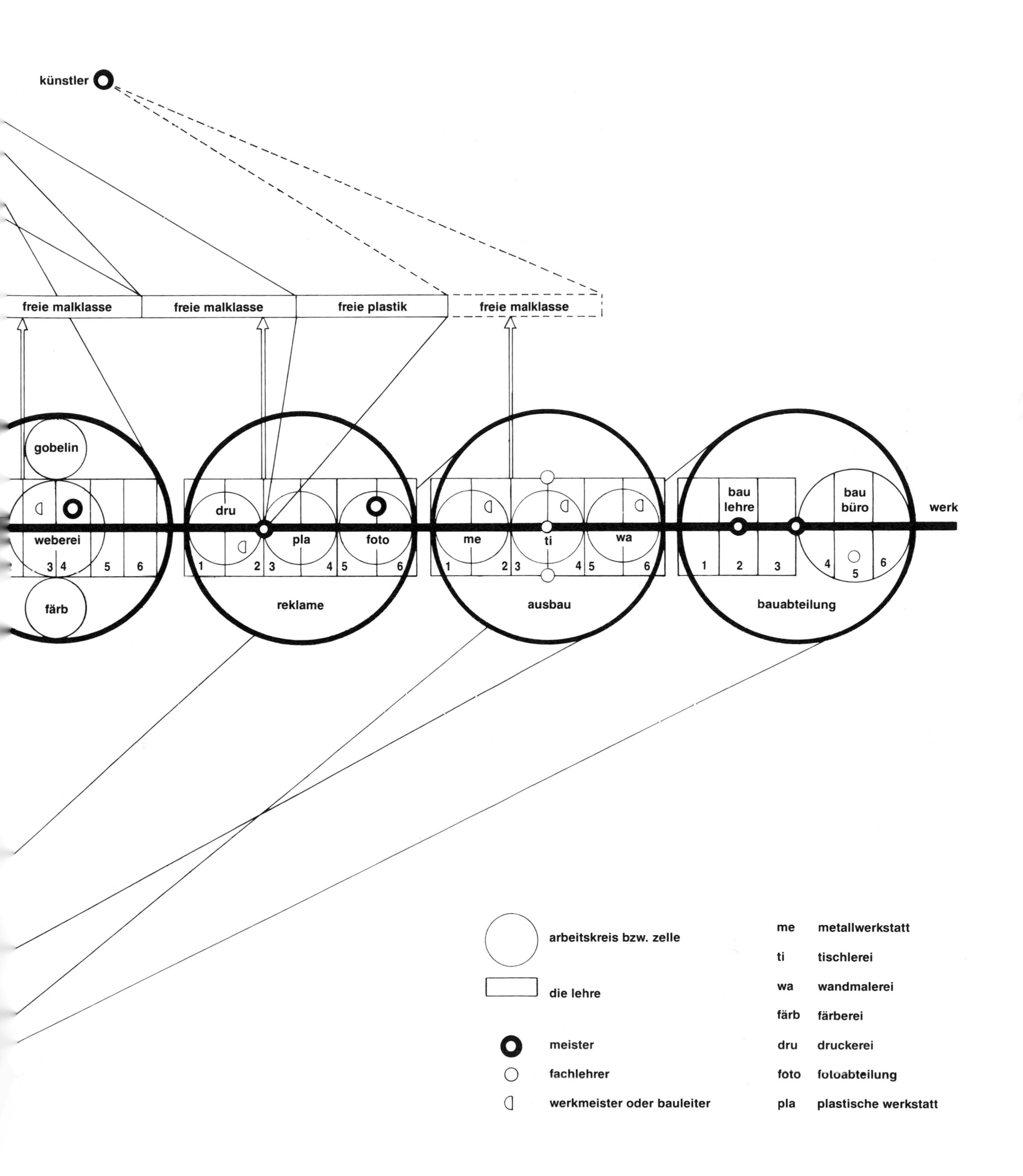

künstler
freie malklasse
freie malklasse
freie plastik
freie malklasse
gobelin
weberei
färb
3 4 5 6
dru
pla
foto
1 2 3 4 5 6
reklame
me
ti
wa
1 2 3 4 5 6
ausbau
bau lehre
bau büro
1 2 3 4 5 6
bauabteilung
werk
arbeitskreis bzw. zelle
die lehre
meister
fachlehrer
werkmeister oder bauleiter
me metallwerkstatt
ti tischlerei
wa wandmalerei
färb färberei
dru druckerei
foto fotoabteilung
pla plastische werkstatt

The student Irene Blühova in the student's common room furnished by Hans Volger and the building office in 1930.

Reorganization of the Bauhaus

Even before he had taken up his new post, Meyer had summed up the situation at the Bauhaus in a letter to Adolf Behne: 'The future of the Bauhaus has become the subject of violent internal dispute. I agree with the students and the majority of Masters that we must take an absolutely categorical stand against the bogus-advertising-theatricalness of the previous Bauhaus. Our budget is so modest that we cannot afford the luxury of all this private publicity and so many considerations.'[106]

Once Bauhaus director, Hannes Mayer initiated an immediate and thorough reform of the school's internal structure. Intensive discussions were opened as early as January 1928 and continued, with student participation, for several weeks. In the summer semester that year Meyer implemented five fundamental organizational changes:

1. Expansion of the preliminary course. Klee and Kandinsky had their teaching hours increased and the course material for the first (Kandinsky), second (Klee), third (Schlemmer) and fourth semesters (Kandinsky) firmly specified.

First-semester students now had to attend Albers' 12-lesson-a-week materials course (*Vorkurs)* as well as Kandinsky's 'Abstract form elements' and 'Analytical drawing' classes. They also had a compulsory lettering class with Joost Schmidt. In the summer semester of 1930, an obligatory course was introduced on 'Representation and Norm' (taught by Hans Volger). In their second semester, students continued their studies with Albers and Joost Schmidt as well as starting a new theoretical course on the 'Elementary design of the plane' with Klee. As had been the case since 1924, new students could join a workshop in their second semester. The third semester introduced life drawing classes by Schlemmer, as well as his course on 'Man'. Schlemmer sought to present Man as a triple unity, teaching his physical nature via proportion and movement, his emotional nature via psychology, and his intellectual existence via philosophy and intellectual history. Technology and politics did not feature in this idealized vision of holistic man. The course was taught for barely a year since Schlemmer left the Bauhaus in summer 1929.
Fourth-semester students had to take another course from Kandinsky. Meyer saw the tuition given by these four teachers as forming the 'artistic pole' of the Bauhaus curriculum.
2. For students in the workshops, tuition was now organized between the two poles of science and art. One day of the week – Monday – was devoted to the arts, while Friday was reserved for the sciences. Tuesday to Thursday were spent in the workshops, with students working an eight-hour day corresponding to industrial conditions. On Saturdays there was sport (ill., p.171). Now extended to seven semesters, the total period of study was the longest yet. Innovations here included the clear distinction between science and art and the increasingly scientific orientation of design activities, which Meyer encouraged through a series of new appointments and guest lecturers.
3. The architecture department was divided into two parts: architectural theory and practical building. The entire architecture course was to last nine semesters. Although initially small, this department was the most important in the entire Bauhaus; it was the hub around which all other departments were oriented.
4. Meyer revised the financial basis of the workshops and reorganized internal activities, so that student revenues were raised and Bauhaus returns also grew. There was an overall expansion of productive operations.
5. Meyer now opened the school's doors even to apparently untalented students. 'The Bauhaus ... does not want to specialize in the talented.. but simply wants to attract as many people as possible, to then correctly integrate them into society.' Meyer saw this integration into society as the only acceptable purpose of Bauhaus education: 'Every student should be a lay member of a symbiosis.'[107] In the winter semester of 1929/30 the number of students indeed rose from about 150 to some 190-200. It was only then that Meyer realised his mistake. The Bauhaus and its workshops clearly reached the limits of their capacity. It was announced in the press that the maximum number of students was to be limited to 150.
Gropius' departure was accompanied by that of three other Masters: Herbert Bayer, Marcel Breuer and Moholy-Nagy. Meyer used this as an excuse to reorganize the workshops in the following year.
The metal, joinery and mural-painting workshops were amalgamated into one large interior design workshop and placed under the direction of Alfred Arndt, whom Meyer had specially appointed to the Bauhaus for the purpose. This precipitated the resignation of Marianne Brandt, who had previously been deputizing as head of the metal workshop; Meyer subse-

Gymnastics at the Bauhaus, around 1930.

quently suggested resignation to Hinnerk Scheper, head of the mural-painting workshop, who had been granted a year's sabbatical leave to go to Russia (15 July 1929-1930). Meyer offered the following explanation for his amalgamation of the workshops: 'Under a united management, the joinery, metal and mural-painting workshops may seek to produce results more in the spirit of popular household goods.'[108]
The advertising workshop embraced printing, publicity, exhibitions, photography and plastic design. 'By expanding the advertising workshop (addition of a photographic studio under the direction of the well-known Berlin photographer, Peterhans)...the productive options open to the Bauhaus are to be further improved.'
The 'junge menschen kommt ans Bauhaus' (young people come to the bauhaus) Bauhaus brochure (ill., p. 166), compiled by Meyer himself during the summer holidays of 1929 and printed in a run of 500, carried the most recent version of the revised curriculum, although still not showing the newly-organized interior design workshop.
At the start of 1930 Meyer drew up two plans – probably for the Bauhaus exhibition '10 Years of Bauhaus' which had opened in Dessau (which had already been shown in Basle and Breslau and was to go on to Essen, Mannheim and Zürich) – illustrating the new structure of the school (ill., pp.168-169) and – for the first time – the relationship between the school and the municipal authorities and other organizations. Meyer planned even further-reaching reforms for the winter semester of 1930/31, their headings noted by Albers: 1. 'Expansion of teaching'... / 2. 'Elimination of painters' / 3. 'Exclusively materialistic teaching'.[109] 'We wanted to change and replace the entire pedagogical basis of the Institute with a foundation in sociology, economics and psychology'[110], summarized Meyer, shortly after his dismissal. Klee informed Meyer no later than May 1930 of his decision to resign from the Bauhaus to take up a teaching post in Düsseldorf. This offered other possibilities of reform. A year earlier, in May 1929, Meyer had declared: 'Sociological and biological lectures and courses by prominent figures should allow these sciences greater representation at the Bauhaus.'[111] In October and November 1929 Meyer wrote to J.J.P.

View of the metal workshop and desks with Marianne Brandt and Hin Bredendieck, around 1930.

Josef Pohl: Bachelor's wardrobe on castors, around 1929.

Oud, Willi Baumeister, Karel Teige and Piet Zwaart to ask if they would accept appointments at the Bauhaus. But his long-schemed dismissal on 1 August 1930 prevented Meyer's reforms from becoming reality.

Reorganization of the workshops

On 1 November 1928, and thus before the launch of the new workshop for interior design on 1 July 1929, Hannes Meyer had already published a set of workshop guidelines. Three major themes can be identified: 'greatest possible cost-efficiency', 'self-administration of each cell' and 'productive teaching principles'.

Each workshop was composed of a workshop head, a (technical) Master of Craft, students and 'assistants'. Assistants were students who were required to work an eight-hour day in the workshop, were paid a wage and did not have to pay school fees. Marianne Brandt and Hin Bredendieck were assistants in the metal workshop for a while. These newly-created assistants undoubtedly helped to increase efficiency. The joinery and metal workshops each had two assistants, the mural-painting and weaving workshops one. Workshop and students had their own share in turnover and licences. This enabled many students to finance their studies.

Meyer also injected new inspiration into workshop philosophy. In his 'Principles of Bauhaus Production', Gropius had declared the main goal of the Bauhaus to be the development of models for industrial goods. Meyer went a step further. The Bauhaus was to design models which suited 'the needs of the people', the 'proletariat'. Meyer thus assigned Bauhaus work a social aim which was soon to be condensed into the phrase 'Volksbedarf statt Luxusbedarf' – popular necessities before elitist luxuries. The word 'standard' become a touchstone for workshop activities. Meyer wanted to create just a small number of universally-valid standard products which, thanks to mass-production, would be within the reach of the broadest possible public and which would be anonymously absorbed into everyday life.

But had Gropius not made similar demands in his 'Principles of Bauhaus Production' back in 1925?

'An object is determined by its nature. In order to design it so that it functions correctly – a container, a chair, a house – it is first necessary to study its nature.'

Gustav Hassenpflug: Folding table in three different positions, 1928. The fully-collapsed table is 9 cm wide.

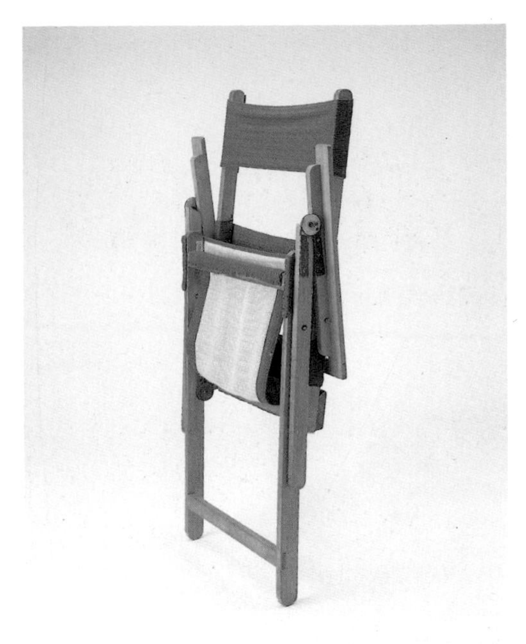

But while Gropius assumed that every object has a 'valid' nature, and furthermore demanded that its design be restricted to 'typical, universally-comprehensible primary forms and colours', Meyer held a different view. His starting-point for design was not this study of natures but the systematic consideration of needs. He thus placed the design process on a completely new footing.

Workshop for interior design – joinery

The consequences of this reorientation were seen most clearly in furniture workshop production. The joinery had, in October 1928, already produced a brochure advertising six of its chairs (by Decker, Bücking, Hassenpflug and Breuer); these were to remain typical of later production.
Its inexpensiveness made plywood (later often in combination with metal) one of the most important workshop materials. Its elasticity was also exploited. A new leg design for tables and chairs further helped cut costs; legs were no longer made of a single wooden post, but of two battens joined at right angles, first pinned and later screwed together. As well as saving materials, this measure meant lighter, frequently dismountable furniture. Legs were rounded off towards the bottom to ensure stability despite their only small area of floor contact.
The furniture and metal products of the Meyer period made greater use of organoid forms. This reflected both the conscious turning-away from Breuer's 'Constructivist' furniture and the assimilation of the results of systematic research.
Almost all the furniture of this period is extraordinarily flexible; it can be folded, collapsed, adjusted and assembled in a number of different stages (ills., p. 174 and 175).
The most significant achievements of the joinery workshop included the furnishing of the General German Trades Union school (ill., p.194), the Dessau labour exchange built by Gropius and the People's Apartment of 1929. The standard products developed for the People's Apartment could have gone straight into mass-production; it thus represented a practical illustration of the socially-oriented design ideal. The chair by Josef Albers in the apartment deserves particular mention. Collapsible and made of shaped laminated wood, it numbers among the most typical and at the same time, pioneering examples of Bauhaus design.

Anonymous: Folding chair in three positions, 1929. This chair stood in the People's Apartment furnished by the Bauhaus.

Many of the new furniture designs were characterized by a high degree of 'specialization'. Examples included the folding stool for the Busch quartet, which was also suitable for camping, a working stool, a factory chair for assembly line work (height-adjustable, sprung, rotatable, with foot support) which was developed for the Dresden Museum of Hygiene, and a wardrobe on castors (accessible from two sides).

Workshop for interior design – meta

While still under the direction of Moholy-Nagy, and chiefly organized by the metal workshop's outstandingly talented Marianne Brandt (ill., p. 172), a contract was signed in the summer semester of 1928 between the Bauhaus and lamp manufacturers Schwintzer and Gräff. The company subsequently manufactured 53 Bauhaus designs, including a number of model variations. Precise details about the nature and length of the contract have not survived, but it was terminated – apparently on the part of the Bauhaus – and expired at the end of 1930.

This decision probably stemmed from Meyer, who later prided himself on having replaced an excessively wide range of products with a small number of standardized models. A new contract was now drawn up with the Leipzig lamp company of Körting and Mathiesen, who further developed many of the Bauhaus lamps and continued the production of certain models right into the fifties. Here, too, it was Marianne Brandt who established the initial contact in the summer semester of 1928. Together with Hin Bredendieck, she was solely responsible for the design of the standard lamps which were to prove such a commercial success.

These standard lamps – a desk lamp and a bedside lamp (ill., p. 176) – represented the first time the metal workshop had taken an already existing model – the desk lamp – and revised its design. This lamp was produced

Opposite page: Aluminium desk lamp with adjustable shade (anonymous). Height 53 cm.

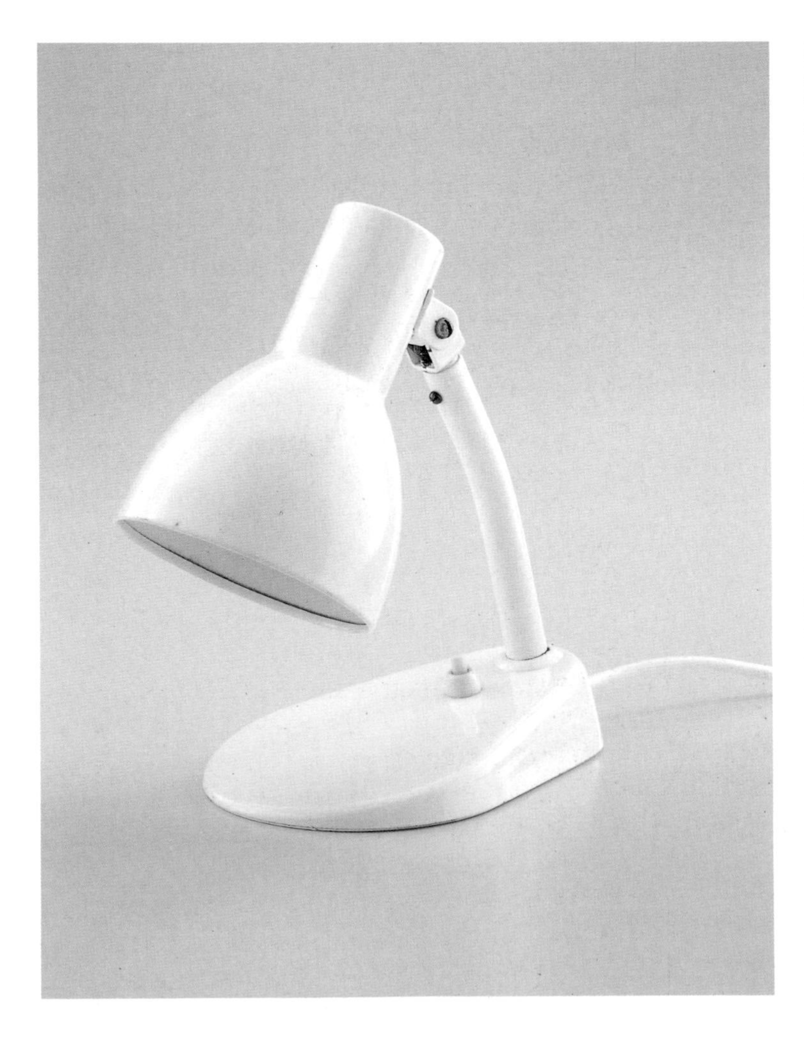

In 1929 Marianne Brandt and Hin Bredendieck revised the design of a bedside light (left) and a desk lamp (right) for the Kandem company. Both models were later mass-produced on a large scale.

with only a few modifications into the thirties. In a similar way, the bedside lamp developed jointly by Brandt and Bredendieck was produced by the thousands and frequently copied. The use of aluminium for lamps was itself an innovation. 'People in those days thought aluminium was dreadful and we therefore sometimes painted the shades. They were designed for everywhere, for living rooms, restaurants, workshops', Marianne Brandt remembered later.

Workshop for interior design – mural-painting

The mural-painting workshop's most important achievement was its Bauhaus wallpaper (ills., p. 178 and 179), launched onto the market by the Rasch company from Hanover in 1930. Licences for this product soon provided the Bauhaus with one of its richest sources of income. As in the case of every successful Bauhaus product, there were several claims to authorship – including, in this case, both Hannes Meyer and Hinnerk Scheper, head of the mural-painting workshop until June 1929.

It was Scheper who organized the first meeting between Meyer and wallpaper manufacturer Emil Rasch; Scheper knew Rasch's daughter Maria, who was studying at the Bauhaus. After initial hesitation Meyer agreed to Rasch's proposals, seeing here the chance to create a standard product.

Students were invited to submit designs, and there were entries from every workshop. The Bauhaus had committed itself 'to supply a set of twelve design samples, each in about five different colour shades'. A four-man

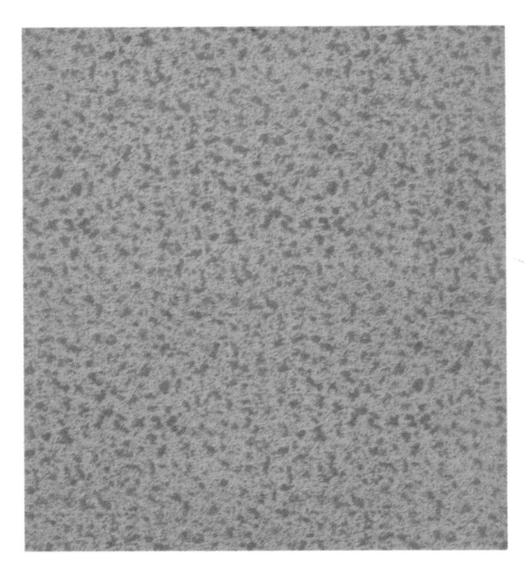

Kurt Stolp: Advert for Bauhaus wallpaper, 1930.

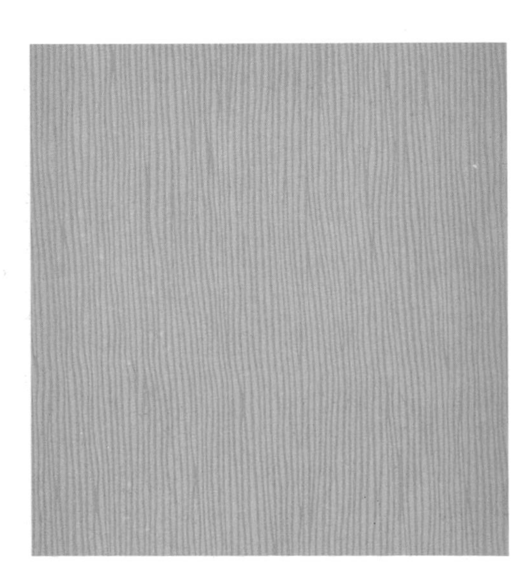

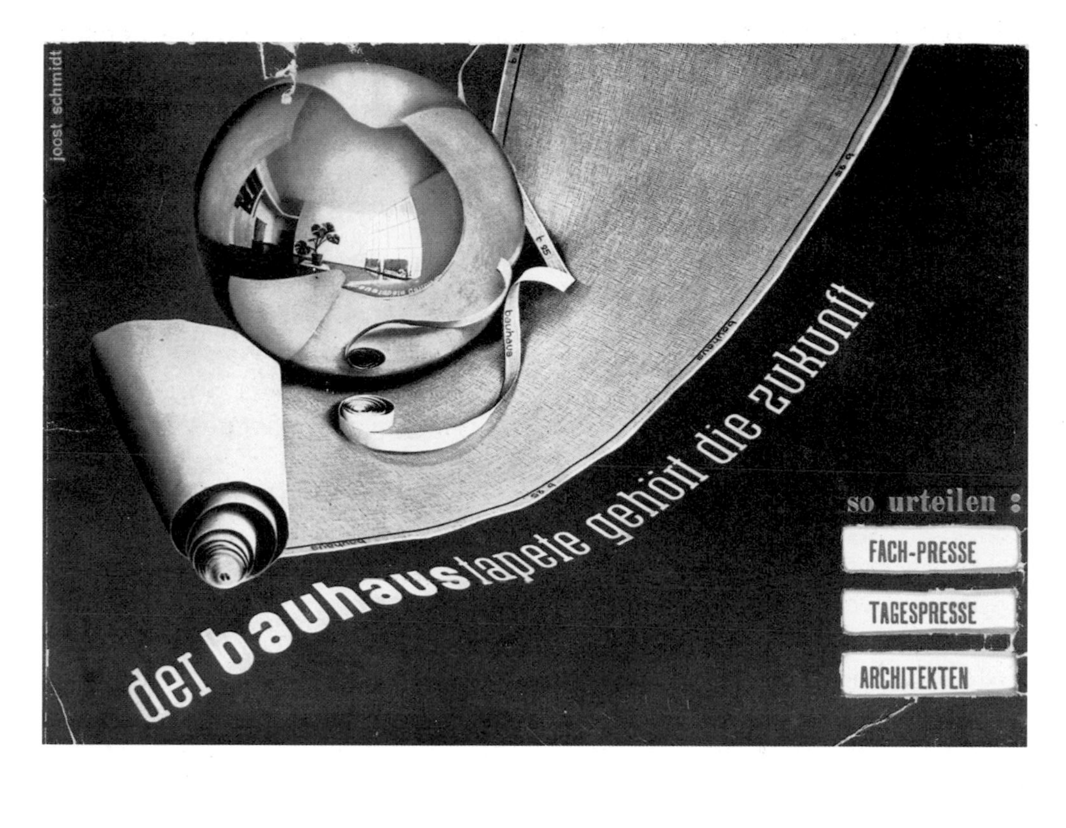

Joost Schmidt: 'The future belongs to Bauhaus wallpaper' catalogue, 1931.

Bauhaus wallpaper, here illustrated in samples from 1929 and 1930, proved the most successful of all Bauhaus products. A fine structuring of lines, grids or flecks is usually combined with two shades of the same colour. With their matt surfaces, these barely-noticeable designs make a room appear bigger – quite the opposite of colourful floral patterns. Colours ranged from relatively clear, bright colours to shades of brown. Outside the Bauhaus, similar ideas resulted at about the same time in the first rough-textured wallpaper. After 1933 the manufacturer continued production in the somewhat darker shades then fashionable. Regularly revised, Bauhaus wallpapers are still being produced today.

commission made the final selection. Bauhaus wallpaper became the school's most successful standard product. It was the first time wallpapers had been produced without a printed pattern and in one colour alone. Their quiet patterning resulted purely from the texture of the paper. They could thus be hung without wastage and were suitable even for smaller rooms.

The advertising workshop

When Herbert Bayer, head of the Bauhaus printing workshop from 1925-28, left the school in April 1928, Meyer transferred the running of the workshop to Joost Schmidt, who was also in charge of the ineffective free sculpture workshop. The name 'advertising workshop' (ill., p.180) had already been introduced in 1927 and was retained under Meyer. The scope of the former printing workshop was thus expanded to incorporate a field in which it was currently impossible to train. In 1929 Meyer succeeded in obtaining municipal funding for the additional appointment of the photographer Walter Peterhans. Peterhans was to work alongside Schmidt as head of a photography department and take a share in the teaching of advertising.

Even more than the other workshops, Meyer considered it the task of 'advertising' to earn money from commissions for advertising and exhibitions. This workshop was to carry out preliminary work for other workshops and, for example, executed the advertising commissions written into the wallpaper licensing agreements with Rasch (ills., p.178 and 179) (as from 1929) and Polytex (as from 1930).

The majority of activities fell within the scope of exhibition design. Franz Ehrlich listed the most important exhibition projects: 'As assistant, I was required to carry out Bauhaus commissions such as the design and mounting of the Junkers' display of gas, water and heating equipment at the "Gas and Water" exhibition and subsequently at the advertising show in Berlin, the Bauhaus stand at the Werkbund exhibition in Breslau, the stand of the German Canned Goods Industry at the Hygiene Exhibition in Dresden, the "Bauhaus People's Apartment" exhibition in Dessau, Leipzig and other cities, and the Bauhaus trade fair exhibition in Leipzig with the first steel windows by the English company "Venestra".'[112]

One of the most important Bauhaus achievements, and one which has been

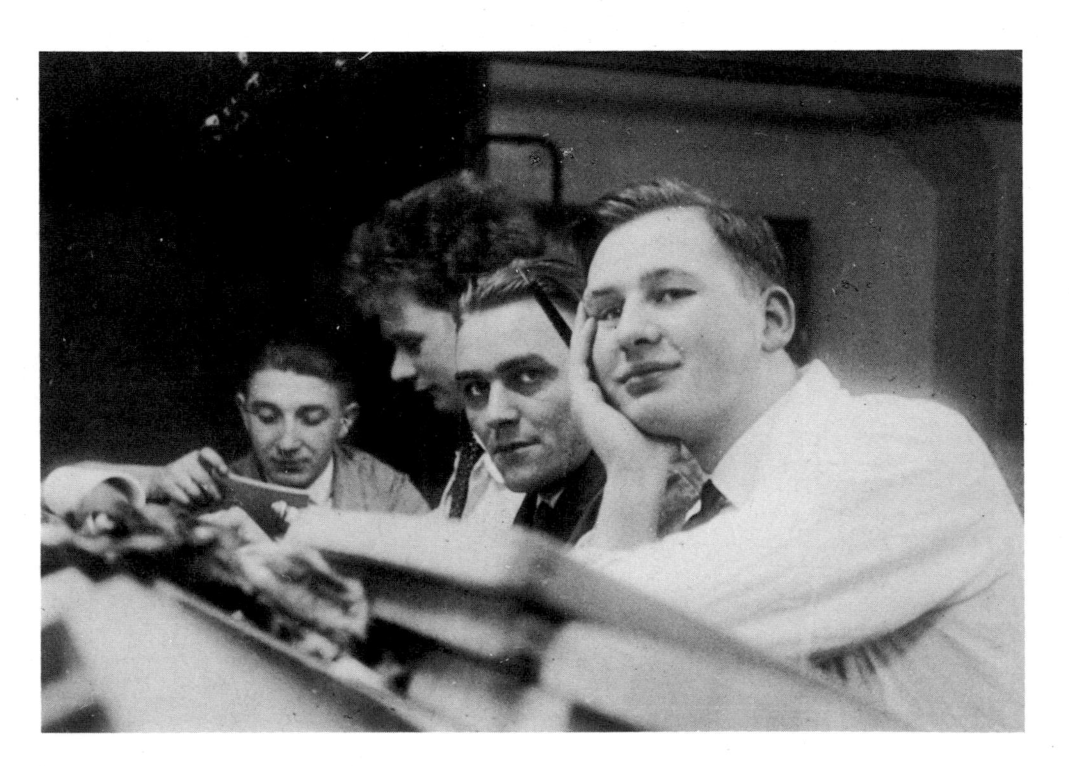

In the Bauhaus composition department, 1931. From left to right: Fiedler, Hajo Rose, Willy Hauswald, Kurt Schmidt.

Opposite page: Poster for the Bauhaus touring exhibition in Basle, 1929.

graph. anstalt
w. wassermann
basel

bauhaus

dessau

im gewerbemuseum
basel

mo.	14-19 uhr
di.	14-19 uhr
mi.	14-19 uhr
do.	14-19 uhr
fr.	14-19 uhr
sa.	14-19 uhr
so.	10-12, 14-19 uhr

eintritt frei

21. IV. - 20. V. 1929

Photographs from the Bauhaus touring exhibition in Basle and Mannheim (below left). All four pictures show only products created during Hannes Meyer's directorship of the Bauhaus.

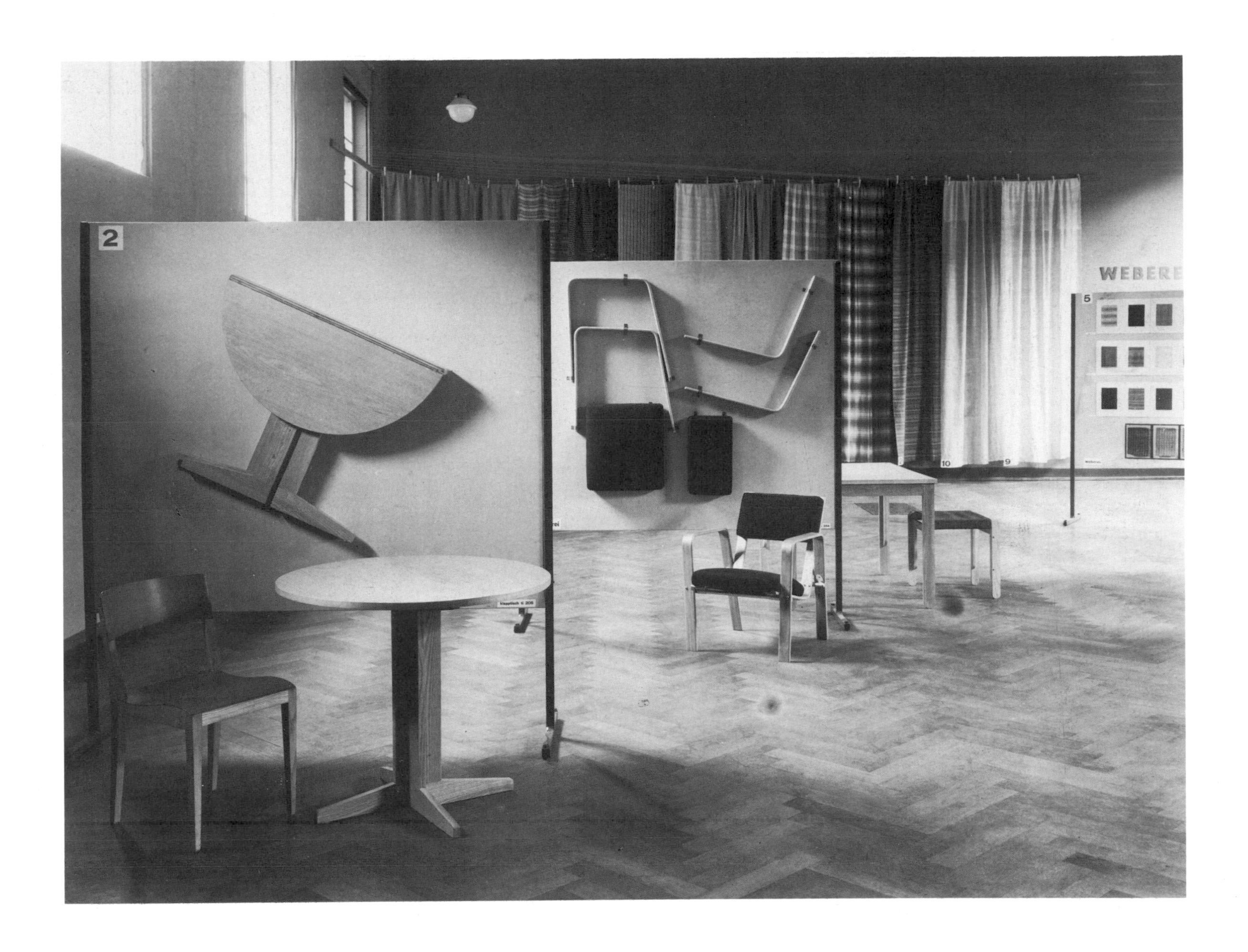
2
WEBERE
5
10
9

WEBEREI

Paul Klee: Measured Fields, 1929. Mies van der Rohe purchased this picture in 1938.

Opposite page: *Lena Meyer-Bergner:* Design for a chaise-longue blanket, 1928.

previously neglected, was the '10 Years of Bauhaus' touring exhibition (ill., p.181). It was shown with great success in Basle, Zürich, Dessau, Essen, Breslau, and Mannheim (ills., p.182 and 183) over the course of a year. The exhibition was not as representative as its title – 'The Dessau Bauhaus' – suggested. It only showed products and exercises from the Meyer era, and thus became an exhibition of Bauhaus achievements under Meyer.

The weaving workshop

In the weaving workshop, too, students were coming to terms with Meyer's new social aims. Instead of 'carpets', the idea was now to produce 'floor coverings', with the emphasis on 'utility materials'. Otti Berger, one of the most talented weavers, spoke impersonally of 'materials in space'. Analysis was assigned first priority, with the words 'aesthetic' and 'art' being carefully avoided.

The women increased their scientific experimentation. They developed seating materials for tubular steel furniture, wall fabrics and translucent curtain materials. Systematic experiments with new materials – cellophane, artificial silk, chenille, for example – had already been started before Meyer's time, however.

One of the most impressive achievements came from Anni Albers, who developed a furnishing fabric whose two sides had different properties. One side absorbed sound while the other reflected light. Anni Albers created this material to improve the acoustics of the auditorium of the German Trade Union school designed by Meyer.

A number of the best students now spent sandwich semesters in industry and subsequently brought practical experience into both the teaching and production sides of the workshop.

Georg Muche had equipped the workshop with Jacquard looms in order to intensify productive operations. At first the weavers had rejected these looms, and they were to induce a positive uprising against Muche which ended in his resignation. In reality, however, Muche's decision was both far-sighted and correct.

His successor, Gunta Stölzl, had already re-equipped the Dessau workshop in 1925 and planned a training course. Although her working methods were criticized as 'emphatically aesthetic', she adjusted to the new workshop philosophy and integrated it into her teaching. Some parts of her 1931 publication, 'Development of the Bauhaus Weaving Work-

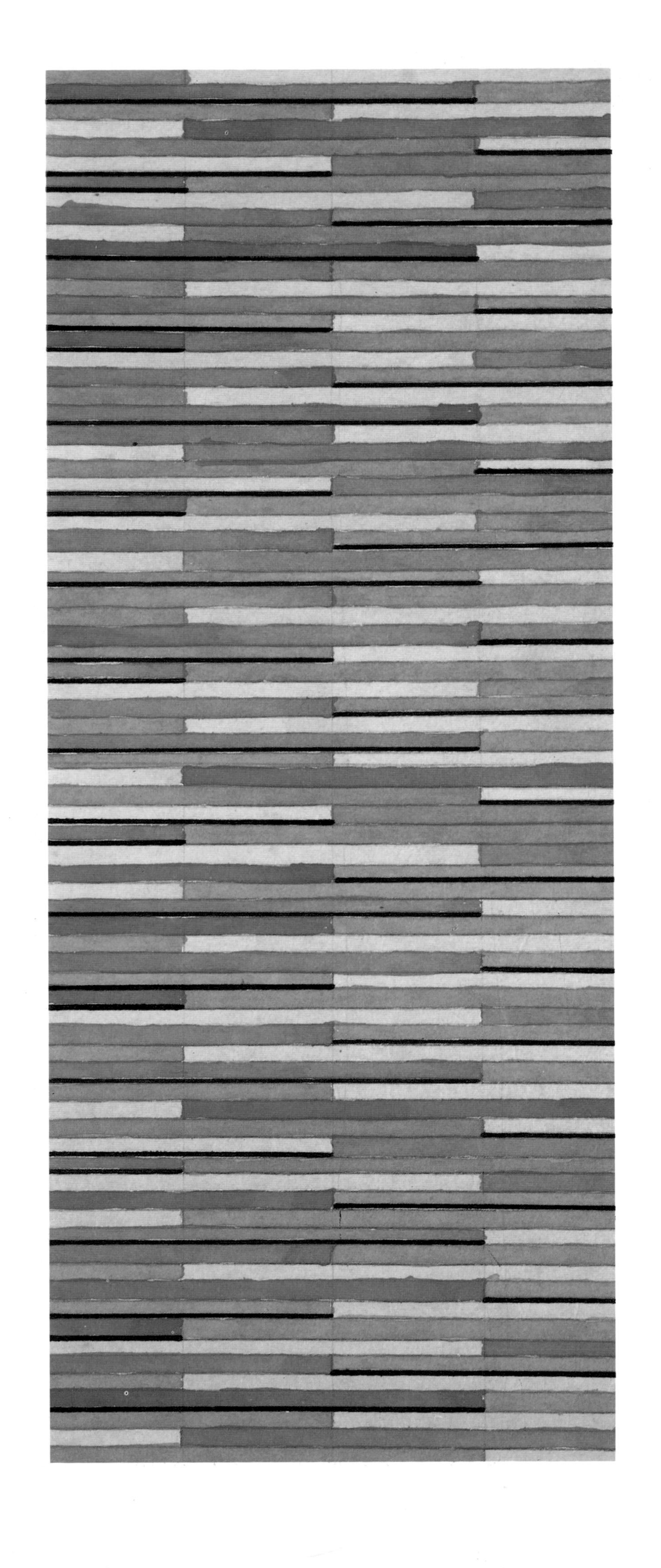

shop', might have been written by Meyer himself: 'Every school ... must be directly linked to the living process ...' – 'Materials in space...have to serve their "function" ... Recognition and understanding of the spiritual problems of building will show us the logical path.'[113]
1930 saw the first joint project with the Berlin Polytex textile company, which wove and sold Bauhaus designs under licence. The Bauhaus based its contract with this company on the contract concluded with the wallpaper manufacturer Rasch. Thus the Bauhaus secured itself both the licences and the advertising for its products.

Theatre under Hannes Meyer

Poster for the Bauhaus theatre workshop tour, 1929.

Although Schlemmer was allowed to remain at the Bauhaus under Meyer's directorship, he had to give up (paid) theatre work since his salary – now brought into line with that of Klee and Kandinsky – was linked to the newly-introduced 'Man' course and his life drawing classes. There was only a small budget available for the theatre workshop. Meyer nevertheless sought to safeguard the theatre workshop and secure its financing when he became director.
The belief that theatre could provide a counterbalance to architecture formed – as at the Weimar Bauhaus – a central part of Schlemmer's thinking. Theatre could be a 'trial balloon' whose 'diameter when fully inflated would equal that of the building department', he wrote in 1928.[114]
In the course of 1928, however, the Bauhaus saw the formation of a 'Young Group' with little interest in Schlemmer-style theatre and its representation of basic stage elements. The 'Young Group' was to produce two pieces with changing casts. It held two things for important – 'collective production' and the confrontation with topical subjects. For this reason – and in contrast to Schlemmer – the spoken word was reincorporated into its work. Its productions were inspired above all by Soviet theatre.
The first piece – 'Sketch No.1', 'Three Against One' – was performed on 17 November 1928, with 'text, production, acting' credited as 'teamwork'. Schlemmer subsequently included it on the first important Bauhaus theatre tour, which he had successfully organized himself.
The second piece was premièred on 22 July 1929 under the title 'bauhaus review' ('collective production by the young theatre') (ill., p.187). Schlemmer described it as: 'A Bauhaus review intended to express the new Bauhaus programme of revolution. Roughly thus: soviet republic of the Bauhaus, the "Masters" are the capitalist kings, who must be deprived of their thrones and their rights ("I'm just leaving") ...'[115]
During these years Schlemmer not only had to make do with an extremely low budget, but had to face student demands – supported by Meyer – for political theatre, a genre which Schlemmer categorically rejected. 'Do not ask me to draw like George Grosz or do (theatre) like Piscator. I believe that we should rightly leave political theatre to the Russians, who do it a lot better; moreover, I also feel that the German problem lies elsewhere!'[116]
Despite his clear refusal to produce political theatre, Schlemmer believed he would be able to continue his stagework at the Bauhaus. Following the successful tour of Germany by the Bauhaus theatre workshop and its programme (ill. p.186), Schlemmer wanted to drop his 'Man' course (which he believed 'finds effectively no resonance, is purely empty talk') and instead devote himself entirely to theatre.
At this point, however, he was offered a post in Breslau which he immediately accepted, having for years been toying with the idea of leaving the Bauhaus.
After the summer semester of 1929, Meyer closed the theatre workshop 'for financial reasons', and no more was heard of the work of the 'Young Theatre'.

Above. The 'Young Theatre at the Bauhaus' in their 'bauhaus revue'.

Below: Bauhaus review entitled 'City Visitor at Professor L's', 1929.

Free painting classes

Upon the Bauhaus move to Dessau in 1925 Klee and Kandinsky had called for the introduction of free painting classes. These classes first appeared in a timetable in 1927 and were subsequently retained by Hannes Meyer. Meyer sought to assign them a new role, however: free art was to provide a sort of balance which, together with increased science teaching, was to nourish workshop activities. The existence of these classes provoked countless discussions at the Bauhaus itself upon the role of art in the design process.
In their 'Bauhaus painting', students employed a dream-visionary, Surrealist style (ill., p.189) usually punctuated by object fragments and often influenced by the techniques of Klee. Gerhard Kadow, a pupil in the

In the years 1929/30 the Bauhaus painters preferred to exhibit as a group, since they felt this brought greater success. Above, the cover of an exhibition catalogue from 1929.

Alexander Schawinsky: Flowing Architecture, 1927.

Monotype by Fritz Winter, around 1929.

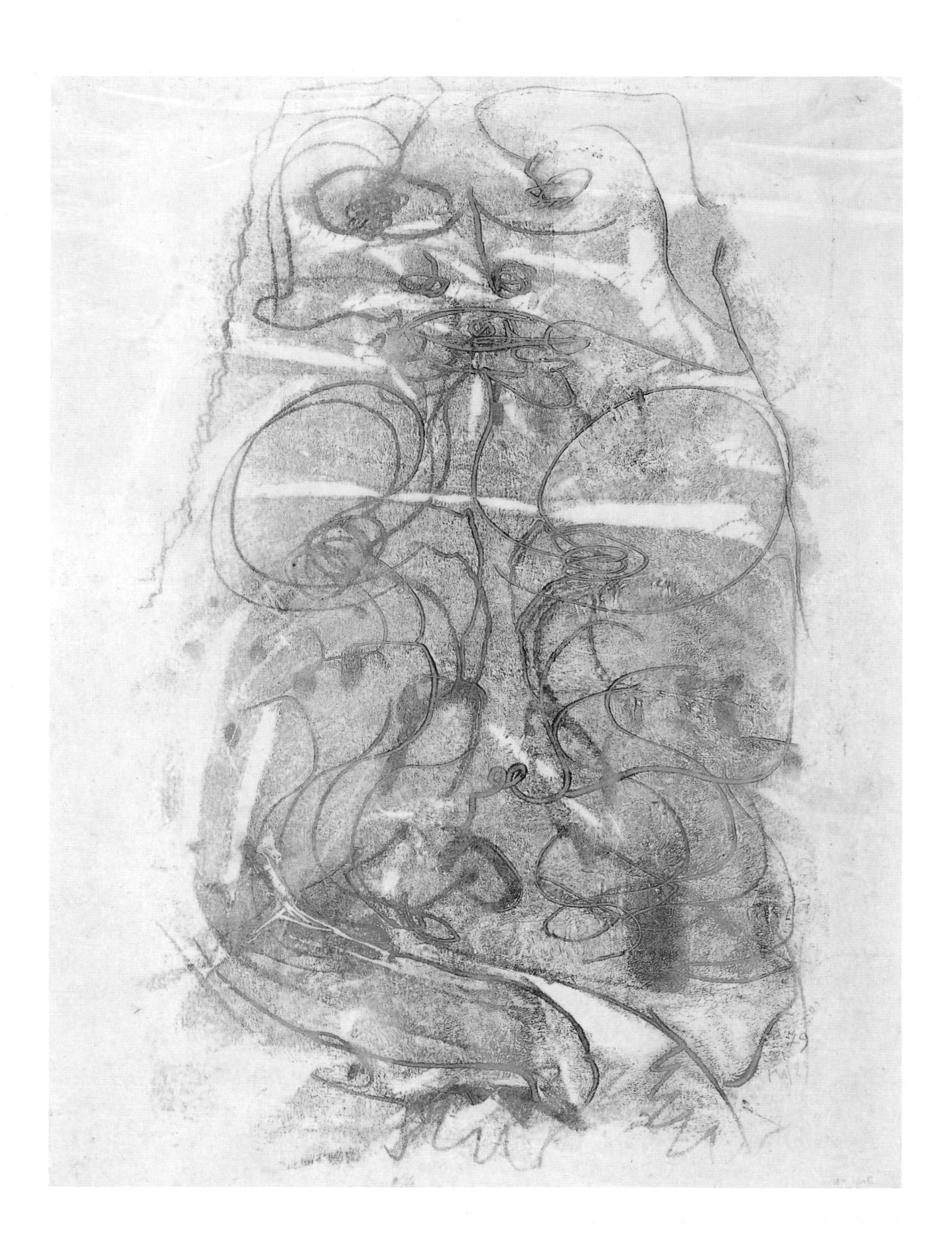

weaving workshop and a participant in Klee's classes, remembered: '... Klee examined the works for a while in absolute silence, and then suddenly began talking...not about the quality or faults of a piece of work, but about artistic problems which struck him in our pictures. '
Both Neue Sachlichkeit – New Objectivity – and the Constructivist style of Moholy-Nagy were strictly rejected.
The relationship between Klee and Hannes Meyer is usually described as poor. At a personal level, however, they got on well, each accepting the other's differences.
Klee refused to take part in the intrigues leading up to Meyer's resignation and was the only Master to write a letter of farewell to him after his resignation. Klee also supported Meyer's teaching aims, but realised that the burden of combining his classroom commitments with a personal artistic career was becoming too much for him. When the Düsseldorf Academy offered him a post involving fewer teaching hours he therefore terminated his contract with the Bauhaus. This step was not the protest against Meyer's directorship it is often called, but rather the result of Klee's need to be able to redevote himself to his own art.

Architecture teaching under Hannes Meyer

The architecture classes given by Hannes Meyer were based on his thorough understanding of building. For Meyer, building was an 'elementary process' which reflected biological, intellectual, spiritual and physical needs and thereby made 'living' possible. It was thus necessary to take into consideration the entire totality of human existence. The aim of such architecture was the welfare of the people. Architecture was to bring the requirements of both individual and community into mutual harmony.
How did Meyer's teaching reflect these aims? Students (ill., p.191) had extremely varied preparatory backgrounds. Some already had architectural training; the majority had completed Bauhaus apprenticeships and now wanted to move on to the *Bau,* the building which was the declared aim of Bauhaus education. Meyer's first step was to divide the variously-qualified students into an architectural theory class ('Baulehre') and a building department ('Bauabteilung'). In the winter semester of 1927/28, eight students were listed in the theory class and thirteen in the building department.

Hans Volger in the Bauhaus building office. The plans for the Dessau Törten estate can be seen in the background.

Architectural theory was taught over four semesters and covered heating, statics, ventilation, building design, materials, sunshine calculations and technical drawing. These subjects were generally taught by engineers. Meyer's partner, Hans Wittwer, also gave classes. When, after about one year, Wittwer gave up his Bauhaus teaching to go and be an architect in Halle, Meyer appointed in his place the Berlin architect Ludwig Hilberseimer, whose systematic classes in apartment building and town planning soon became a central part of the architecture curriculum.
Meyer's theory classes discussed broad-ranging architectural problems as well as examining questions of detail.
Activities in the building department can be divided into three areas:
1. The systematic processing of small, specific building projects.
2. Work in 'co-operative cells' on large projects such as the German Trades Union school and Törten estate.
3. Diploma projects and independent activities by students.

Smaller assignments included, for example, Heiner Knaub's designs for the Klein Köries weekend colony near Berlin. Although based on a concrete contract, it appears that the project was never finally executed.
A contract for a detached house for the Garavagno family in Mentone (Italy) led to the drafting of a family development plan, topographical study of the residence, house plan and function plan and their subsequent architectural solution.
In a guest course given by Mart Stam, students compiled an entry for the competition for the Haselhorst housing estate in Berlin. Although the entry was not submitted, it introduced the students to competition work.
The many areas which students had to investigate are reflected in their drawings, which overflow with the analyses, tables and individual results whose evaluation would produce the final building. Architecture was thus taught as the more or less automatic result of careful analysis.
Meyer's definition was radical: 'Building is not an aesthetic process' and 'Building is only organization: social, technical, economic, psychical organization.'[117]
Meyer had decided right from the start to involve students in the building commissions awarded him by the municipal authorities and in any other private contracts. The first commission in which Meyer's students were able to participate was the school for the General German Trades Union in Bernau. For the planning and execution of the project, the students were organized into 'co-operative cells' which, as 'vertical work gangs', incorporated seniors and juniors, experts and novices into a single team. 'Practising co-operation' was what Hannes Meyer called it.

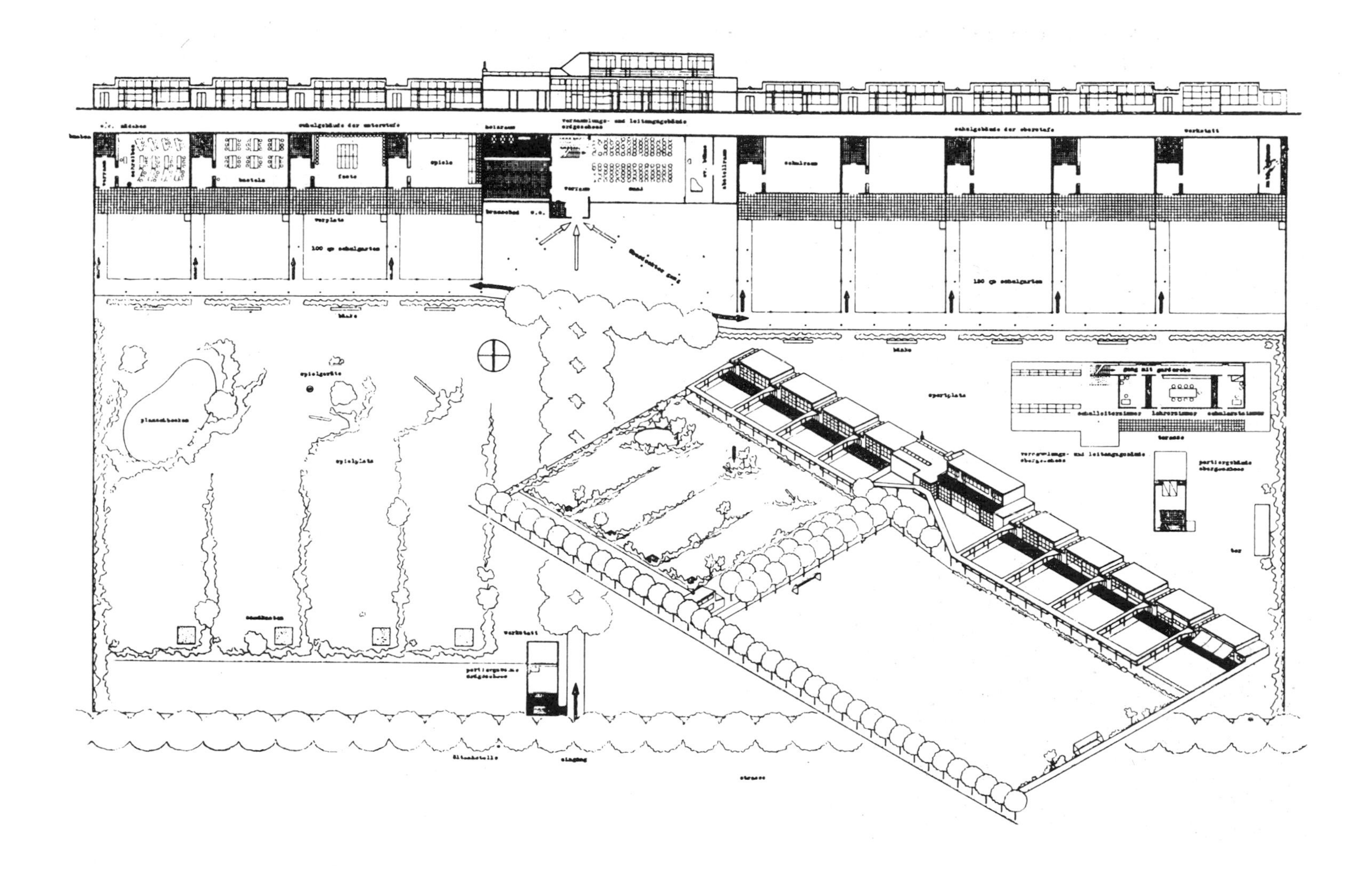

Design for a housing-estate elementary school by Ernst Göhl, 1928. The pavilion-style school with its low building system faces south onto garden and playground areas. The design refers clearly to the Trades Union school at that time being planned by Meyer, Wittwer and the Bauhaus building department.

Students from the building department. From left to right: Hermann Bunzel, Erich Consemüller, Hubert Hoffmann, Ernst Göhl.

Hannes Meyer, Hans Wittwer and the Dessau Bauhaus building department: General German Trades Union school in Bernau, near Berlin, 1928-30. Meyer and Wittwer made the three chimneys of the oil-firing system the dominant motif of the school's entrance, leading one pupil to describe it as an 'education factory'. On the right, a loading ramp; left, garages.

This group model was intended to replace the traditional architect. 'My architecture students will not be architects', 'The "architect" is dead', announced Meyer in a lecture. Instead, he wanted to train a series of specialists to be a creative team. 'The building materials expert, the small-town master builder, the colourist – each an instrument of co-operation.'[118]
Meyer was thereby fixing his sights on a new professional dimension for architects, too.
The promotion of the Bauhaus to Insitute of Design which Gropius had achieved gave the school the right to award diplomas to mark the completion of studies. Meyer was the first director able to graduate Bauhaus students. A total of 133 diplomas had been awarded by the end of the Bauhaus in 1933. Dissertations could discuss real or fictitious projects and often consisted of a set of plans complete with explanatory report.
In one dissertation, for example, Konrad Püschel discussed the Vogelgesang manor estate in its small-farm layout with suggestions for converting it into a co-operative estate.
Vera Meyer-Waldeck submitted a design for an elementary school with eight classes and a child day centre for 60 children which had been built within the framework of a scheme oriented towards real Dessau requirements as a large-scale community project.
Students Tibor Weiner and Philipp Tolziner wrote a thesis entitled 'Attempt to create a typical communal residential block for the workers of a factory of the socialized State with uniform working hours.'

View of the Trades Union school accommodation wing, photographed in June 1931.

Meyer's most significant achievements as an architecture teacher at the Bauhaus remain the systematic and scientific bases upon which he placed the design process and its implementation in practical and theoretical teaching. A new breed of architect was to understand the determining of social needs and his own social responsibility as central to his profession. The teamwork model would enable him to better respond to the growing complexity of many building tasks.

The Bernau Trades Union School

The most important project to be executed by Hannes Meyer, his partner Wittwer and the Bauhaus building department was the Trades Union school in Bernau (ills., p.192 and 193).
Meyer and Wittwer's design had been selected the winner in a restricted competition. The General German Trades Union wanted not a 'school barracks' but an 'example of modern building culture' in which 120 male and female union functionaries could be trained in four-week courses and at the same time find rest and relaxation.
On a prespecified site – a pinewood glade with a small lake – Meyer and Wittwer designed a complex in which teaching operations, daily routines and relaxation facilities were integrated as smoothly and naturally as possible. Students were accommodated in double rooms in four residential blocks arranged in stepped succession. Five double rooms were treated as one unit whose residents were kept together throughout their four-week stay for meals, games and study. There were three such groups of ten

The gymnasium, with windows opening onto parkland. There are further classrooms above this hall.

Desk by Vera Meyer-Waldeck for the school's rooms. For practical reasons the desktop is slightly sloping. The writing surface is covered with black linoleum to avoid reflection. The side drawer is designed to hold DIN-format paper. The desk lamp was also developed at the Bauhaus; the chair was made by the Thonet company.

View of the connecting glass corridor of the Trades Union school which linked the accommodation pavilions. Photograph by Walter Peterhans.

people on each of the three floors of all four residential blocks. The architects had thus not merely planned a pattern of community living but had found an architectural form corresponding to its social relationships. In order to avoid anonymous, hotel-style corridors, Meyer and Wittwer ran a glass walkway past the accommodation pavilions, offering a view of the countryside outside and encouraging communication. The entire interior furnishing of the Bernau school (ill., p.194) was executed by the Bauhaus workshops.
Meyer claimed that the Trades Union school was the result of a scientific analysis of needs. In fact it can be seen that he was equally concerned with aspects of design. In addition to the four stepped residential student blocks, for example, he built a fifth for the staff. Theoretically speaking, this building – having a different function – should have been differently organized. But for design reasons its exterior was fully harmonized with the buildings next door.
'The harmoniously-balanced rhythm of the Z-shaped complex with its stepped central section and two laterally offset end sections clearly determined the composition.' The three chimneys of the school's entrance motif (ill., p.192) – suggesting an 'education factory' to one student – are probably also symbolic in nature: 'In trade union circles they are called the three pillars of the workers' movement: Co-operative, Union and Party.'[119]
The Trades Union school was to influence a number of plans for schools produced by students over the following years (ill., p.191). Mutually offset pavilions reappeared in many of these designs. Students made repeated

Opposite page: *Lux Feininger:* 'bauhäusler', around 1928. From left to right: Georg Hartmann, Naftaly Rubinstein, Miriam Manuckiam (koko), Albert Mentzel.

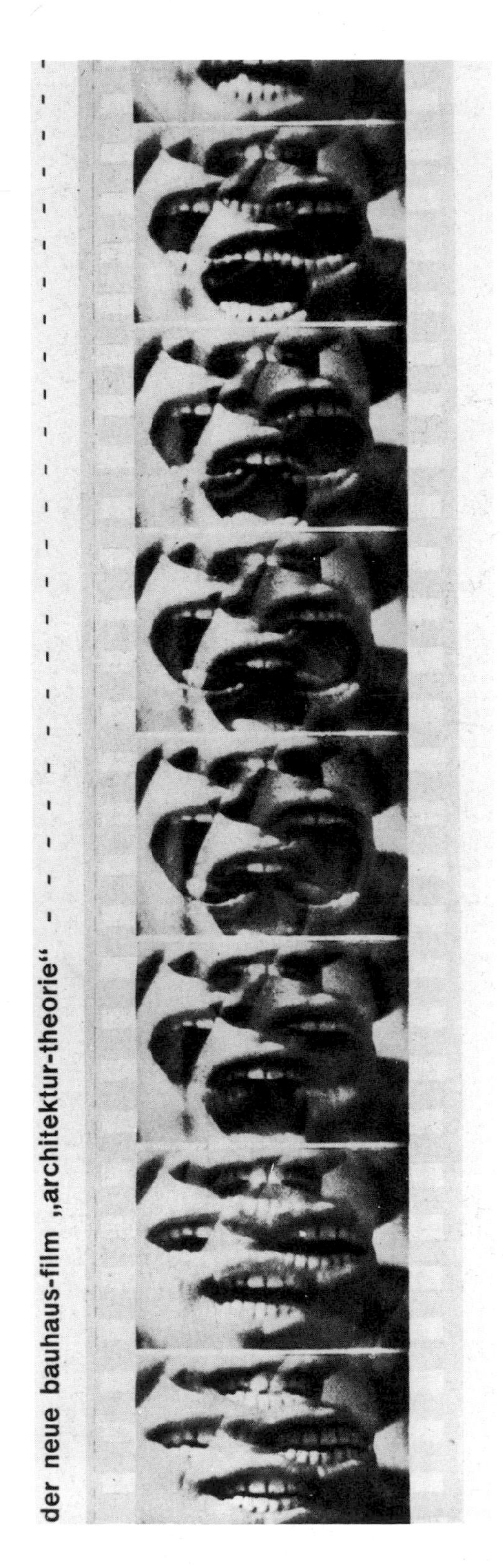

In February 1930 the Carnival edition of the Munich newspaper 'Baukunst' published this film strip as the new Bauhaus film, 'Architecture Theory'.

Hesse (and later Grote) used political necessity to justify his actions. Only an unpolitical Bauhaus such as that run by Gropius – and such as Mies promised to run – could expect to last. But just two years later even the 'purged' Dessau Bauhaus was closed at the insistence of the National Socialists, whereby the Social Democrats abstained in the final vote. The Communist representatives were alone in voting for the Bauhaus.

A significant role in the events leading up to Meyer's dismissal was played by Meyer's opponents within the Bauhaus itself, led by Kandinsky and Albers. They saw their positions threatened by the entire restructuring of the artistic part of the *Vorkurs* which Meyer envisaged. Kandinsky also harboured a profound mistrust of every form of Communism. Outside the Bauhaus, the head of the State Department for Cultural Conservation, Dr. Ludwig Grote, had wanted Meyer's removal since May 1930 if not earlier. He shared the misgivings of Albers and Kandinsky. Gropius followed developments at the Bauhaus from Berlin. He found it particularly hard to accept Meyer's repeated criticism of the 'Gropius Bauhaus'.

In 1928 Meyer (and Kallái) published a portrayal of a three-stage history of the Bauhaus: first, the Weimar phase, born out of chaos, second, a Dessau phase, trapped in formalism and, as the school's final blossoming, a third phase – the Meyer age – in which the Bauhaus had turned to problems of life and society. Although Gropius did not publicly contradict this repeatedly expressed – and hurtful – criticism, he approved its condemnation as 'a falsification of history' by Bauhaus student Xanti Schawinsky.

In May, this circle of opponents agreed that there was no point in removing Meyer from office without first arranging for a successor to take over. Grote would have liked to see Gropius return as director, but Gropius expressed no interest. Gropius himself approached the architect Otto Haesler, who quickly refused. Negotiations were then begun with Ludwig Mies van der Rohe, who indicated his provisional acceptance. This enabled the mayor to announce both Meyer's dismissal and, at the same time, Mies' willingness to succeed him.

Students protested against Meyer's dismissal for several weeks and succeeded in mobilizing the left-wing press. The architect Heiberg, newly appointed to the Bauhaus, resigned in protest, as did secretary Margret Mengel. But there was little other criticism of Meyer's removal from office. No German architects protested. The municipal authorities only received complaints from Eastern Europe, Denmark and a number of guest lecturers.

In the same year, Meyer and a 'red Bauhaus brigade' moved to Moscow to help in the spread of Socialism.

Ludwig Mies van der Rohe:
The Bauhaus Becomes a School of Architecture

Facing, previous page: The Bauhaus building in Dessau, view from the east, around 1930.

Mies van der Rohe (ill., p.205) was already seen as one of the most prominent members of the German architectural avant-garde. Like Gropius he had worked in Peter Behrens' office, and had made a name for himself in the twenties with pioneering designs for glass skyscrapers. In 1923/4 he was among the forces behind the radical newspaper 'G' (for 'Gestaltung' – design). In 1926/7 he was in charge of planning the Stuttgart Weissenhof estate, a project which involved virtually every modern architect of the day and which became a comprehensive exhibition of new building and living philosophies. In 1929 he was commissioned by the German Reich to build the German Pavilion at the Barcelona World Exhibition. Here Mies freed his architecture from all functionalism and designed the building as a spatial work of art: flowing, harmoniously-proportioned rooms decorated with costly materials and expensive furnishings.
'His tall, weighty figure', remembered mayor Hesse, 'and expressive head gave the impression of great inner confidence and stability... No doubt about it: he was the person who could be expected to give back to the Bauhaus leadership what it had recently increasingly lost – authority.'[126]

The new course at the Bauhaus

Mies van der Rohe's directorship began with a provocation. Students felt the removal of Meyer and the smooth selection of Mies had left them without a voice, and called for a strike at the start of the new semester. They demanded 'discussions about the future work of the Bauhaus, and in particular the continuation of the development, begun under former director Hannes Meyer, of a systematic design course on a scientific basis and the abolishment of outmoded art teaching.'[127]
In response, the Council of Masters called upon the students to supply the names of those who, in the Communist student paper 'bauhaus 3' (ill., p.205), had sharply criticized Meyer's dismissal and the involvement of a number of professors. The students refused.
Mies took charge of the situation with an authoritarian style of leadership and with the help of the mayor: 'Under the chairmanship of the new director, Mies van der Rohe, in the presence of the mayor, Hesse, and with the exclusion of student representatives, the Council of Masters decreed on 9.9.1930 the immediate closure of the Institute. The previous Bauhaus statutes were declared null and void, and were replaced by other statutes to safeguard the "new course" at the Bauhaus. In the coming winter semester, which began on 21 October, each of the 170 students were to undergo "readmission". Finally, the residents of the 26 student studio apartments in the Bauhaus were given immediate notice to quit.'[128]
Furthermore, following a magistrate's ruling, 'five of the most active foreign Bauhaus students belonging to Meyer's closest circle of assistants were expelled by the police with no reason within 24 hours'. Their fellow students carried them to the railway station in a triumphal procession (ills., p. 206 and 207).
The new constitution came into force on 21 October, together with 'Amendments to the Constitution' which the students had to sign. Both Gropius and Meyer had placed the work of the Bauhaus within a broad social framework. Mies van der Rohe narrowed the sights, naming the 'purpose of the Bauhaus' the 'handicraft, technical and artistic training of students'. Final decision-making authority now rested chiefly with the director himself. It was no longer necessary to hear the views of the students and students were no longer represented on the Council of Masters, now renamed the Conference. Political activity of all kind was prohibited, a fact criticized by the students as a restriction of their traditional freedom to form a coalition. The constitution even prohibited smoking.
A simple brochure, without illustrations and revised once more in the spring

Ludwig Mies van der Rohe, photographed by Werner Rohde in February 1933.

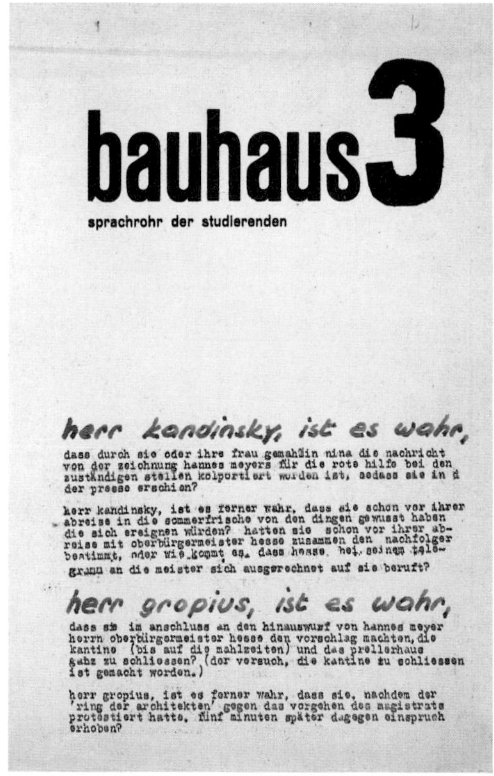

bauhaus 3

sprachrohr der studierenden

herr kandinsky, ist es wahr,

dass durch sie oder ihre frau gemahlin nina die nachricht von der zeichnung hannes meyers für die rote hilfe bei den zuständigen stellen kolportiert worden ist, sodass sie in d der presse erschien?

herr kandinsky, ist es ferner wahr, dass sie schon vor ihrer abreise in die sommerfrische von den dingen gewusst haben die sich ereignen würden? hatten sie schon vor ihrer abreise mit oberbürgermeister hesse zusammen den nachfolger bestimmt, oder wie kommt es, dass hesse bei seinem telegramm an die meister sich ausgerechnet auf sie beruft?

herr gropius, ist es wahr,

dass sie im anschluss an den hinauswurf von hannes meyer herrn oberbürgermeister hesse den vorschlag machten, die kantine (bis auf die mahlzeiten) und das prellerhaus ganz zu schliessen? (der versuch, die kantine zu schliessen ist gemacht worden.)

herr gropius, ist es ferner wahr, dass sie, nachdem der 'ring der architekten' gegen das vorgehen des magistrats protestiert hatte, fünf minuten später dagegen einspruch erhoben?

The radicality assumed by the conflicts within the school can be seen in this cover of the Communist student paper 'bauhaus 3' of autumn 1930. Harsh criticism is directed against the intrigues of the Kandinskys and at Gropius' role in the dismissal of Hannes Meyer.

of 1932, published a now very different curriculum (ill., pp. 208-209). Studies were reduced to six semesters. Architecture was made even more important than under Meyer.

Whereas, under Meyer, work and training in one of the workshops formed a sort of intermediate station on the road to architecture – and here Meyer was essentially following Gropius' original concept –, Mies had different priorities. As the timetable reveals, every student could now take classes in the technical principles of building as from the second stage of the curriculum without having to bother with the remaining workshops at all. A fundamental lever was thus thrown which set Bauhaus educational philosophy in a new direction. The Bauhaus was turned into a school of architecture to which a small number of workshops were attached.

Students expelled by Mies van der Rohe are accompanied to the station by their friends. Left: Bela Scheffler.

Opposite page: Antonin Urban, giving the 'Red Front' sign.

The interior design ('ausbau') workshop introduced by Meyer, which incorporated the metal, joinery and mural-painting workshops, was retained. The weaving ('weberei') and advertising ('reklame') workshops continued to function independently as under Meyer. Photography, however, which under Meyer had formed part of the advertising department, was now a separate area ('foto'). 'Free' art was also made a field in its own right ('bildende kunst').
The *Vorkurs,* a previously compulsory element of Bauhaus education, was now only obligatory for some. Those with sufficient previous training could 'cut in' at the Bauhaus to finish their studies, particularly in architecture. At the end of every semester it was decided whether or not students could continue their studies on the basis of their completed and exhibited works. Articles of apprenticeship were dropped once and for all. Overall, teaching became more school-like; daily routines were regimented and students were expected to gain practical experience during the holidays.
This new authority extended even into Bauhaus language. One brochure for example stated that, in the first stage of the curriculum, 'heterogeneous pupil material' was to be shaped into 'homogeneous attitude'. The building and advertising departments saw the most radical innovations in their teaching and products.
One fundamental change affected the workshops' previously thriving productive activities. Mies abolished them, deciding the workshops were now to produce industrial models alone. The Bauhaus was thus no longer to act as manufacturer or contractor. Although Mies' decision pleased local craftsmen, who had long seen the Bauhaus as competition, it left students with no means of earning extra money during their studies or of financing their studies through their work. Many students criticized this as a form of social cruelty, particularly since the studio apartments remained closed while the school fees had gone up considerably.

Financial difficulties – political struggles

Although Mies took radical steps to depoliticize the Bauhaus, he could not escape the pressures of the political situation in Dessau, as the financial situation at the Bauhaus clearly revealed.
Although Bauhaus subsidies in the years 1930 and 1931 had fallen below the level of 1929, truly drastic cuts were not introduced until 1932. Munici-

pal funding now totalled only 92,000 Marks, in contrast to 162,500 Marks in 1929. The administration sought to cut another 30,000 Marks (10,000 having already been cut at the start of the semester). The reasons behind the economy measures which Mies subsequently had to implement were first and foremost political. The voices of the political opposition, and in particular the National Socialists, could only be silenced by a Bauhaus which demanded less and less public funding and supported itself more and more from its own product licences. This was the argument put forward by mayor Hesse in defence of his budgetary cuts. The Bauhaus was thus forced to rely for its survival on increased school fees and licensing fees collected from outside companies manufacturing Bauhaus products. Figures given for these revenues fluctuate between 21,000 and 30,000 Marks.

A 1931 diary kept by the Bauhaus administration offices is full of appointments for compiling sets of samples of printed materials, glass and wallpapers. Numerous patents – in part for furniture developed under Meyer's directorship – were provisionally registered, although never subsequently exploited. Diary entries include 'Patent application Pohl elastic chair back' and 'Foreign patent Alder chair and Bormann glass holder not to be registered'[129]. The Bauhaus bought other designs from students so that it would have the rights to their future commercial utilization. These sources of income were vital for the survival of the Bauhaus and were in part used to pay the Masters. Ten percent of revenues went to the student self-help association. This distribution of income from licensing fees sparked off a serious confrontation between Mies and the students. Student representatives Cornelius van der Linden and Heinz Schwerin called for cuts in Masters' salaries and more scholarships. They demanded that the student self-help organization should receive a higher percentage of licensing income since the products concerned had been developed by the students themselves. Mies banned a meeting which had been called in the canteen to discuss these demands and had the room cleared by the police. He immediately expelled some fifteen students from the Bauhaus, including the two student representatives. When Budkow, one of those expelled, subsequently resurfaced at the Bauhaus, the police were informed and he was imprisoned for four weeks.

bauhaus dessau
hochschule für gestaltung

september 1930

I. lehr- und arbeits-gebiete

die ausbildung der bauhaus-studierenden erfolgt in theoretischen und praktischen lehrkursen und in den werkstätten des bauhauses.

1. allgemein

werklehre
gegenständliches zeichnen
darstellende geometrie
schrift
mathematik
physik
mechanik
chemie
materialkunde
normenlehre
einführung in die künstlerische gestaltung

vorträge über

psychologie
psychotechnik
wirtschafts- und betriebslehre
farbenlehre
kunstgeschichte
soziologie

2. bau und ausbau

rohbau-konstruktion
ausbau-konstruktion
konstruktives entwerfen
heizung und lüftung
installationslehre
beleuchtungs-technik
veranschlagen
festigkeitslehre
statik
eisen- und eisenbetonkonstruktion
gebäudelehre und entwerfen
städtebau
ausbau-seminar
praktische werkstatt-arbeit in der tischlerei, metall-werkstatt und wandmalerei

3. reklame

typografie
druck- und reproduktionsverfahren
schrift, farbe und fläche
kalkulation von drucksachen
fotografie
werbegrafische darstellung
werbevorgänge und werbsachengestaltung
werbsachen-entwurf
werbe-plastik
praktische werkstattarbeit in druckerei und reklame-werktatt

4. foto

belichtungs-entwicklungs-nachbehandlungstechnik
abbildungsvermittlung
tonwertwiedergabe und tonfälschungen
farbwiedergabe
struktur-wiedergabe
das sehen, helligkeitsdetails und schärfendetails
materialuntersuchungen
spezifische anforderungen der reklame u. reportage

5. weberei

bindungslehre
materialkunde
webtechniken auf schaftstuhl
schaftmaschine
jaquardmaschine
teppichknüpfstuhl
gobelinstuhl
kalkulation
dekomposition
patronieren
stoffveredelung
entwurfszeichnen
warenkunde und warenprüfung
färberei
praktische arbeit in der weberei

6. bildende kunst

freie malklasse
plastische werkstatt

Mies van der Rohe's first curriculum of September 1930. Mies continued the courses dating from the 1927 timetable. Workshops related to building were linked even more closely to architecture. The general ('allgemein') part of the curriculum was dominated by the technical sciences; artistic design is only a subordinate heading. In addition to building and interior design ('bau und ausbau'), there were departments for weaving ('weberei'), advertising ('reklame'), photography ('foto') and art ('bildende kunst'). These, too, concentrated chiefly upon technical knowledge and skills. For the first time, the preliminary course – previously the basis of all Bauhaus activity – was no longer obligatory. The programme marks a decline in Bauhaus Utopianism, since it ignores the social dimension of design. The more regimented structuring of the curriculum produced competent professionals but suppressed artistic individual creativity.

Although the left-wing students at the Bauhaus were weakened by this second round of expulsions, it did not leave them powerless. This was revealed during the elections held to choose new student representatives. Following the expulsion of the fifteen students in March 1932, moderate and left-wing students blocked each other for almost three months before two new student representatives were finally elected at the third attempt. Those elected were the Communist party representative Ernst Mittag and the Moderate Hermann Fischer.
In November 1931, the newly-arrived student Hans Kessler wrote that all but a minority of students were Communists; one year later, from the Berlin Bauhaus, he spoke of 'the three or four Communists we still have'. A confidential letter of August 1932 announced that the Meyer inheritance was now liquidated. The group of Communist students nevertheless continued to act anonymously right up until the closure of the Berlin Bauhaus, publishing the journal 'Kostufra' (Communist student faction), which later called itself the 'Bauhaus Students Organ'.
Mies van der Rohe was not only concerned with 'cleaning up' the Bauhaus through expulsions, but also compiled a programme of lectures and events for 1931 'under the sign of this intellectual struggle'[130]. The Bauhaus 'Society of Friends', together with Ludwig Grote, the mayor and most of the teachers, agreed upon the need for such a programme. It was harshly criticized by the Bauhaus' Communist journal, however: 'Apolitical teaching was... organized so that the Bauhaus invited guest teachers from the right-wing to the central bourgeois parties, who carried out their anaes-

II. lehrkörper

ludwig mies van der rohe, architekt, direktor des bauhauses
josef albers, werklehre, gegenständliches zeichnen
alfred arndt, ausbau-werkstatt
otto büttner, herrengymnastik und herrensport
friedrich engemann, gewerbe-oberlehrer, darstellende geometrie, berufs-fachzeichnen, technische mechanik
carla grosch, damengymnastik und damensport
wassily kandinsky, professor, künstlerische gestaltung, freie malklasse
paul klee, professor, freie malklasse
wilhelm müller, studienrat, chemie, technologie, baustofflehre
walter peterhans, fotografie, mathematik
hans riedel, dr. ing., psychotechnik, betriebswissenschaft, mathematik
alcar rudelt, bauingenieur, bauwissenschaft, festigkeitslehre, höhere mathematik, eisenbau, eisenbetonbau.
hinnerk scheper, wandmalerei, (z. zt. beurlaubt).
joost schmidt, schrift, reklame, plastische werkstatt.
frau gunta sharon-stölzl, weberei-werkstatt.
ludwig hilberseimer, architekt, baulehre.

III. aufnahmebestimmungen

als ordentlicher studierender kann jeder in das bauhaus aufgenommen werden, dessen begabung und vorbildung vom direktor als ausreichend erachtet wird und der das 18. lebensjahr überschritten hat. je nach dem grad der vorbildung kann aufnahme in ein entsprechend höheres semester erfolgen.

anmeldung.
die anmeldung in das bauhaus muß schriftlich erfolgen.
dem antrag sind folgende anlagen beizufügen:
a. lebenslauf, (vorbildung, staatsangehörigkeit, persönliche verhältnisse und unterhaltsmittel, bei minderjährigen unterhaltserklärung durch eltern oder vormund).
b. polizeiliches leumundszeugnis.
c. ärztliches gesundheitszeugnis (ausländer impfschein).
d. lichtbild.
e. etwaige zeugnisse über handwerkliche oder theoretische ausbildung.
f. selbständige zeichnerische oder handwerkliche arbeiten.

aufnahme.
die aufnahme gilt als vollzogen, wenn
1. das schulgeld und sämtliche gebühren gezahlt,
2. die satzungen, sowie die haus- und studienordnung durch unterschrift anerkannt sind.

gebühren.
an gebühren werden erhoben:
1. einmalige aufnahmegebühr rmk. 10.—
2. lehrgebühren: I. semester „ 80.—
für inländer: II. „ „ 70.—
III. „ „ 60.—
IV. „ „ 50.—
V. „ „ 40.—
VI. „ „ 30.—
ausländer zahlen das eineinhalbfache.
3. allgemeine obligatorische gebühren für unfallversicherung und duschenbenutzung pro semester rmk. 5.—.

IV. studiendauer und -abschluß

die ausbildung dauert normal 6 semester.
der abgang vom bauhaus erfolgt nach beendigung des studiums.
austritt aus dem bauhaus ist der leitung schriftlich mitzuteilen.
studierende, deren leistungen nicht befriedigen, können auf beschluß der konferenz zum austritt aus dem bauhaus veranlaßt werden:
erfolgreicher abschluß der studien wird bestätigt durch das bauhaus-diplom.
teilstudien werden durch zeugnis bestätigt.

---

das wintersemester 1930/31 beginnt am 21. oktober 1930.
schluß des wintersemesters 1930/31 am 31. märz 1931.

---

die studierenden benötigen für den lebensunterhalt in dessau durchschnittlich mindestens rmk. 100.— pro monat.
einfach möblierte zimmer sind in den siedlungen nahe beim bauhaus von rmk. 25.— monatlich an zu haben.
die kantine des bauhauses verabreicht zu selbstkostenpreisen frühstück, mittagessen, nachmittagskaffee, abendessen.
das bauhaus-sekretariat steht für jede spezialauskunft zur verfügung.

thetic work gently and without pain...' The later right-wing conservative sociologist and philosopher Hans Freyer spoke on 'Revolution from the Right'. There was criticism of 'Prinzhorn, who revealed himself to be a Nazi academic... no Marxist was permitted to speak.'[131]
The psychiatrist Hans Prinzhorn, whose original invitation to give two guest lectures at the Bauhaus had come from Hannes Meyer, wrote to the latter even after his dismissal. Two years later he was to orchestrate, with Ludwig Grote, initiatives which sought to win tolerance for the Bauhaus from the National Socialists.
In 1931, in addition to this lecture programme, the Bauhaus administration produced a brochure which stated: 'Bauhaus dedication to the design of modern culture should be assigned no party-political dimension, even in politically turbulent times.' It was a sort of summary of the school's achievements which expressly rejected the politicized nature of the Bauhaus under Hannes Meyer but which, by including the industrial licensing agreements dating from the Meyer era, nevertheless claimed the achievements of that period for itself.

Architecture classes by Hilberseimer and Mies van der Rohe

Architecture teaching was clearly divided into three stages. During the first stage, as under Hannes Meyer, students were taught the technical fundamentals: building law, statics, heating and ventilation, the study of materials, mathematics and physics. These classes were given by engineers and teachers, some of whom were taken over from the Meyer era, and were compulsory even for senior students. The course by architect and town

Mies van der Rohe's seminar, 1931. From left to right: Annemarie Wilke, Heinrich Neuy, Mies, Hermann Klumpp.

planner Ludwig Hilberseimer may be seen as the second stage. In 1930 it was still called 'Baulehre' (architectural theory) as under Meyer, but was subsequently renamed the 'Seminar for Apartment and Town Planning'. This course covered theoretical questions of systematic estate planning, whose solutions were guided by a variety of considerations:

1. If possible, all apartments should be east-west oriented so that they enjoyed both morning and afternoon sun. This led to the replacement of the older style of urban block development by the 'Zeilenbau' style of row housing. This east-west orientation had for a long time been one of the most important demands of the modern generation of architects.

2. Large housing estates should always contain both tall and low buildings. Such a mixture was rarely seen in existing estates, but was considered the essential precondition of a socially-balanced population structure. Meyer, for example, had planned to expand the Törten estate with a mixed development of multi-storey balcony-access houses and detached residences.

3. A wide variety of different designs were developed for both tall and low buildings: detached houses, L-shaped, interlinking detached houses and terraced houses (ill., p. 212). Tall building types included the 'boarding' house (providing service installations and designed for single people), the block of rented flats and the balcony-access house which saved staircases and was therefore considered particularly economical. Many of the exercises set by Hilberseimer were concerned with the relationship between population size and development density (ill., p. 213); others were concerned with individual building types and ground-plan solutions. The 'growing' house was a popular topic since it offered a potential answer to the poverty and housing shortages of the day.

4. The estates thus planned were also to contain the right kind of infrastructure. Worker apartments should be near factories without being too close to sources of contamination and pollution as, for example, in Dessau, where the working-class districts fell within the soot-deposit range of the factories. For children, schools should also be located within easy reach of home.

All of Hilberseimer's exercises fell within the overall intellectual framework

Opposite page: Correction of an exercise done by *Wilhelm Hess.*

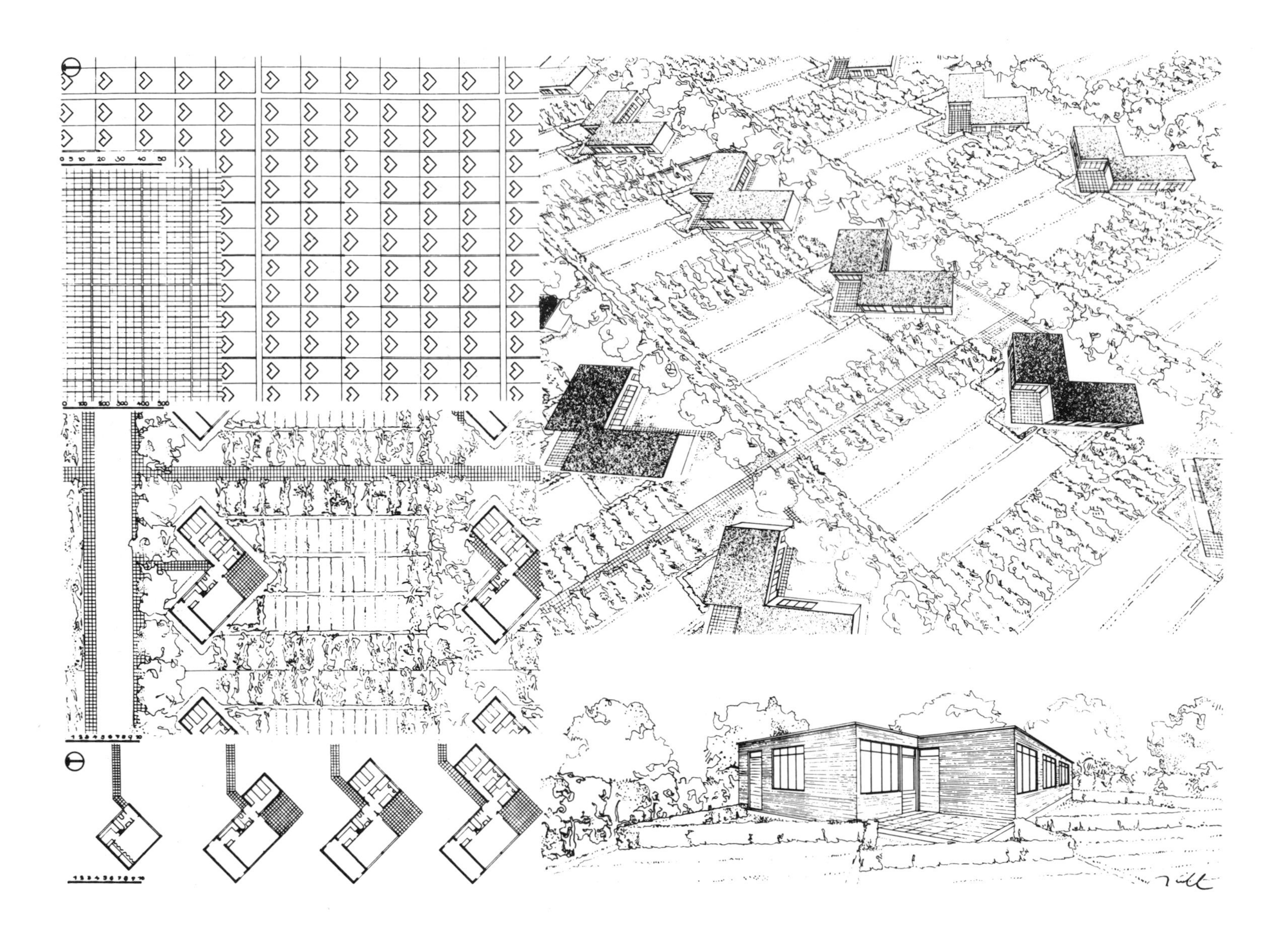

This 1932 drawing of a low-building estate by Pius Pahl matches the theories of Hilberseimer, who used such drawings in his publications. These small houses could be expanded from a sort of basic cell outwards. The main rooms – kitchen, bathroom, living room – were themselves relatively large. Several small bedrooms could then be added to this central complex, a concept employed in many other versions of 'growing' houses around 1930. Each small house, with its south-facing terrace, was to have its own vegetable garden.

of the 'New City', the vision of a city suited to people and traffic in which careful planning appeared to have solved every problem.
Mies only taught students from their fourth semester onwards (ill., p. 210). 'Fifth and sixth semester work with him alone', wrote one student, Kessler, of Mies' *Bauseminar.* Mies considered drawing the central forum for design. His own drawings are both works of art and documents testifying to the intensity of his search for intellectual form. He demanded the same dedication from his students. At his own wish, free-hand drawing was introduced into Albers' preliminary course, enabling students to refine their drawing skills before joining the building seminar. The most important of Mies' regular exercises was to design a 'low building in a residential court', since Mies believed that if you could design a house you could design anything. Solutions also had to be found for the transition between exterior and interior space and the relationship between neighbourhood and privacy.
Three different design types can be distinguished: House A (residential building with studio), House B (two-storey detached house) and House C (single-family bungalow) (ill., p. 215). Kessler described Mies' teaching: 'With Mies ... we are building a small house: 50 m², consisting of a large living room, kitchenette and porch. While the main emphasis of previous tasks had been the functional design of space, we were now to concentrate on pleasing spatial proportions as well as practical factors ... Only a very few people know that – let's say – 90 per cent of architecture is calculation,

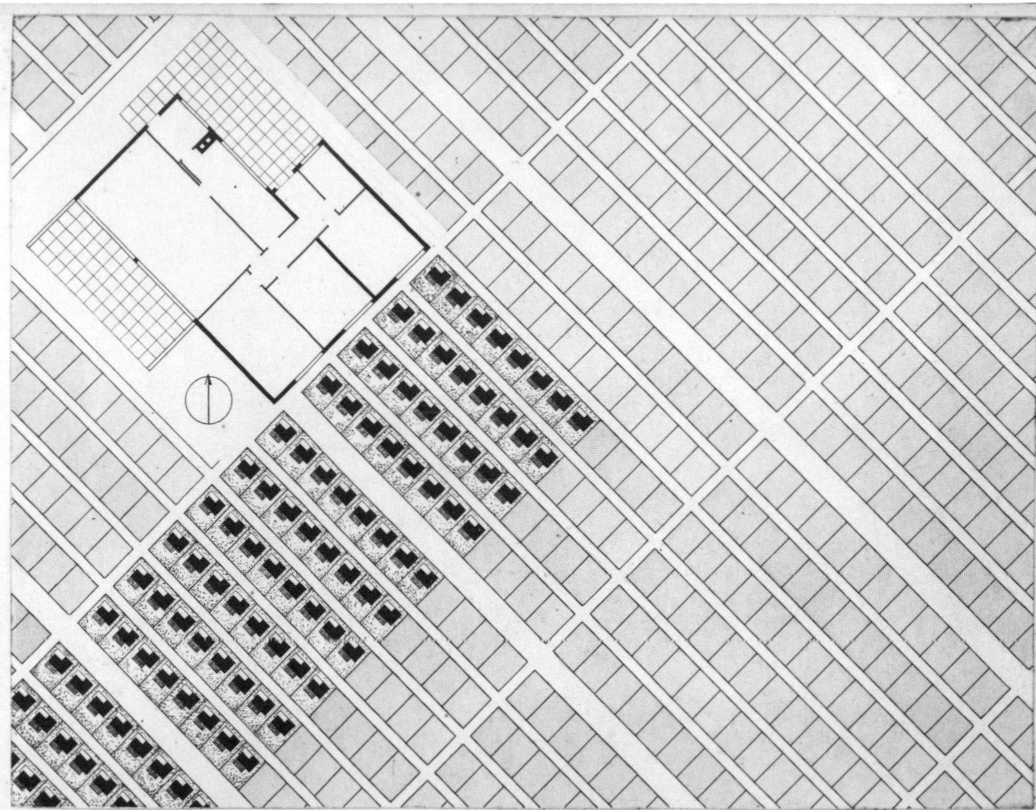

while the remaining ten percent is feeling. Mies is very reluctant to talk about this abstract part, since he hates "intellectual" drivel like the plague.'[132]

Mies' high expectations of his students' designs, and the overwhelming influence of his own architectural achievements, in which material, proportion and space were integrated into a harmonious whole, tempted a whole series of students to design flowing spaces à la Mies and to decorate their interiors with his Barcelona and Weissenhof furniture (ill., p. 215). Mies van der Rohe nevertheless had 'an educational influence during the few years he taught at the Bauhaus.'[133] After 1945, many of his pupils (Herbert Hirche, Wils Ebert, Eduard Ludwig, Gerhard Weber, Georg Neidenberger, Bertrand Goldberg, John Rodgers, Munyo Weinraub) were to promote and pass on – some as college teachers themselves – a philosophy of architecture which was based on Mies' discipline and aesthetics.

They did not teach the essence of Mies' Bauhaus theories, however, but oriented themselves instead towards the architecture which Mies van der Rohe created in the USA in the fifties and sixties.

The differences between Mies and Meyer can be seen in their use of language, too. What Meyer simply called 'Bauen' (building) was, for Mies, 'Baukunst' (the *art* of building). Under Meyer students learned to begin with a systematic assessment of needs, from which constructional solutions would arise almost automatically. By following this principle, 'Training in Building' (the title of a planned book by Meyer) would be applicable to any

Hilberseimer set his students to investigate the relationship between development density and size of population. Different housing types were thereby outlined in principle and on paper, but no individualizing options proposed. In a study of 1931, Wilhelm Jacob Hess proposed three development types, including an eleven-storey balcony-access house, a two-storey terrace and – as illustrated above – detached residences. The text at the side is taken from a publication by Hilberseimer.

Students from the architecture department on the Bauhaus balcony.

task. His pupils accordingly filled every last centimetre of their exercise sheets with calculations and diagrams and thus 'legitimized' their designs at a glance. The sheets surviving from Mies' seminars are empty; extremely delicate designs often 'swim' on outsize pieces of white paper. Mies only set 'ideal tasks' with few specifications.

Exercises from the classes of Meyer and Mies can thus be distinguished on the basis of visual criteria alone. Mies dropped a fundamental aspect of the Bauhaus curriculum: the integration of theory and practice. But this was precisely what had always made the Bauhaus programme so remarkable, and had been respected by Meyer. Now theory triumphed. Even the commissions from the Dessau municipal authorities promised in Mies' contract of employment failed to materialize. Mies and his students were only actually to build one small drinks pavilion.

There was no longer any trace of the social orientation which had characterized Bauhaus activities under Meyer. Mies was more or less indifferent to the burning social questions of the day. For him architecture was art, a confrontation with space, proportion and material. This was demonstrated in, among other things, the model house he designed for the Berlin Architecture Exhibition of 1931, which he organized together with Lilly Reich. In contrast to Mies, the Bauhäusler Albers, Volger, Fieger and Breuer exhibited typical small apartments in line with the current discussion on minimum housing solutions. A comparison of these houses clearly reveals that Mies' aesthetic was not as timeless as many of his admirers still

Opposite page: *Günter Conrad:* Ground-plan and view of the living and dining room of an atrium house, 1931. Mies van der Rohe only taught senior-semester students, and his classes – as the highest stage of the curriculum – gave a chiefly aesthetic training in the spirit of his own philosophy of architecture. Major themes included the harmony between open space and its limits. Since many students adopted both forms and materials from Mies, virtually everthing was a copy of the Master. Günter Conrad placed his teacher's Weissenhof chair at the table on the left and his Barcelona chair on the right.

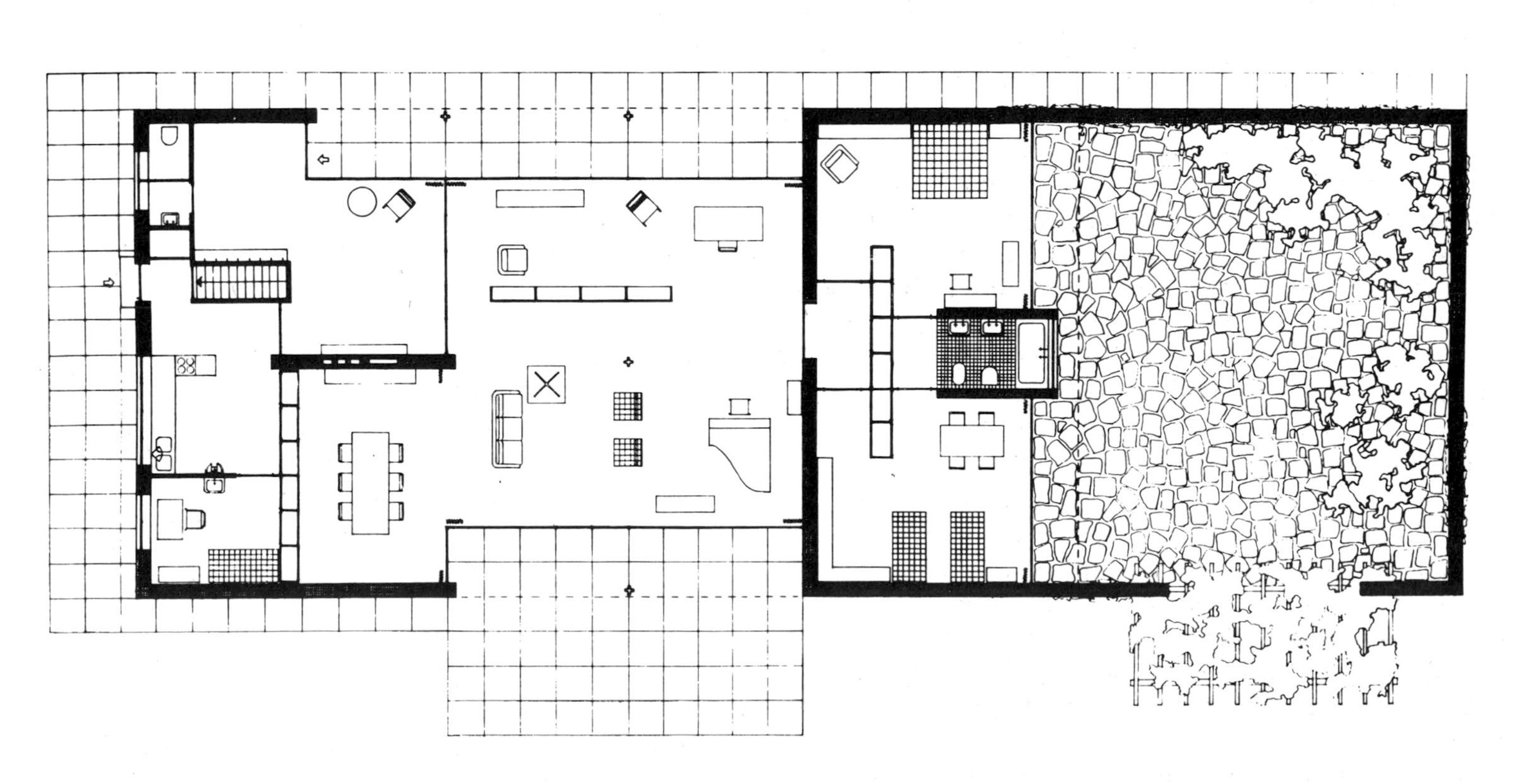

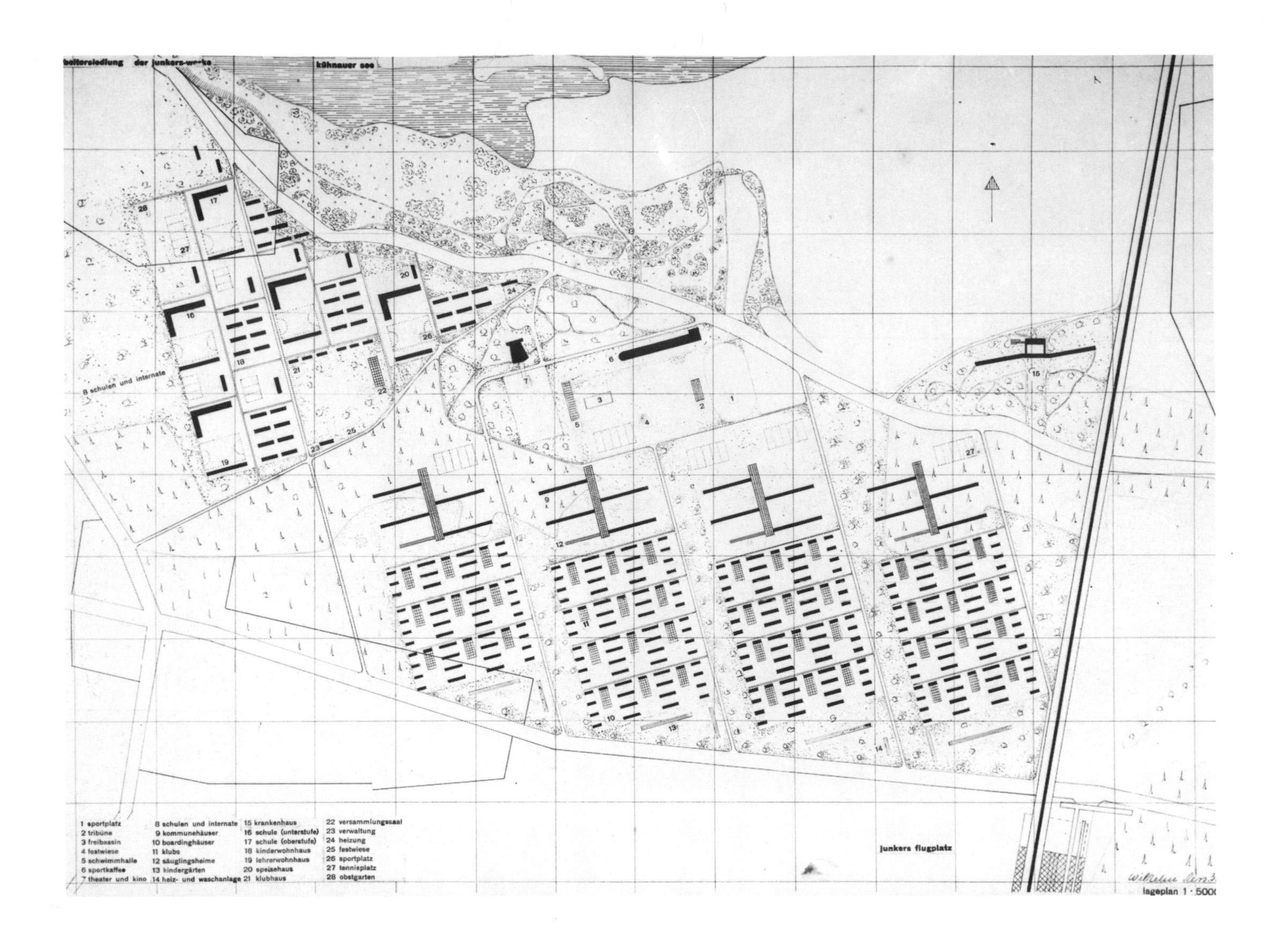

Wilhelm Jacob Hess and Selman Selmanagic: Plan of the Junkers estate, 1932. The lower section of the plan contains the various residential blocks; above these to the left are the schools. In the middle are the sports facilities, cinema and café, and on the right a hospital.

maintain: when viewed alongside the subsistence-level apartment designed to house six persons within 50 square metres, the wastefulness of Mies's own design simply reinforced the point that space was a luxury which only the rich could afford.

Junkers estate

One of the most impressive planning achievements of the Bauhaus architecture department was the 1932 workers' housing estate for the Junkers factory. Originally a fictitious planning exercise set by Hilberseimer (now teaching the 'Seminar for Apartment and Town Planning'), it was executed by a seven-strong collective (including two women) as a seminar project (ill., p.216). The project had little to do with Mies' teaching since the plan and its subject were broadly speaking political. Some members of the collective were also members of the Communist party, and the estate they were designing could only have been built within a Socialist State.
The entire estate was east-west oriented, and development density and size of population were based on figures for the Dessau working classes. The centre of the 20,000-resident estate was occupied by leisure facilities including a sports ground, spectator stands, indoor and outdoor swimming-pools, a sports café and tennis courts. Residents were to be housed in 'communes or boarding houses' (for singles). Clubs (ill., p.217) were available for communal leisure activities. There were crèches and nursery schools near the apartments and even a works hospital was planned.

Wilhelm Jacob Hess: Colour scheme for an interior in a Junkers estate apartment block, 1932.

Schools and boarding schools were concentrated within a separate area in park-like surroundings.
'The advantages of the collective' were to be realized through careful planning; individual budgeting was to be abandoned and the entire complex run on a communal house-keeping basis. Women with children would have their workload relieved by nurseries. Even meals were to be provided centrally, the majority of flats therefore only containing a kitchenette. Planning ideals were applied to traffic, too; 'Road traffic is kept well away from pedestrian areas. Bypasses and feeder routes relieve the inner zones within the groups of apartment blocks.'[134]
In this large-scale project, social Utopias were once more transformed into design realities as the Bauhaus concept came alive for one last time. The project can, however, no longer be described as a combined achievement in the traditional Bauhaus sense since it represented a clear socio-political alternative to the aesthetic character of Mies van der Rohe's architecture teaching.

The back cover of the brochure which Joost Schmidt designed for the City of Dessau in 1931 is an outstanding example of design media employed in spatial perspective. Dessau's attractions float above an aerial view of the city – everything from the latest giant Junkers aircraft to the Wörlitz park.

Opposite page:
Exercise by Eugen Batz from the advertising course, around 1930. Joost Schmidt's classes covered chiefly the representation of object, plane and space, using such means as lettering, three-dimensional bodies and photographs. This study by Eugen Batz is the simplest stage on the path to a sophisticated combination of levels of illustration, such as achieved by Joost Schmidt in his own brochure of 1931 (ill., this page). Like other Bauhaus Masters, Schmidt taught the formal bases of his own work. By limiting himself to visual means of illustration, it is clear that his subject is more graphic art than modern advertising, which was already starting to include marketing concepts.

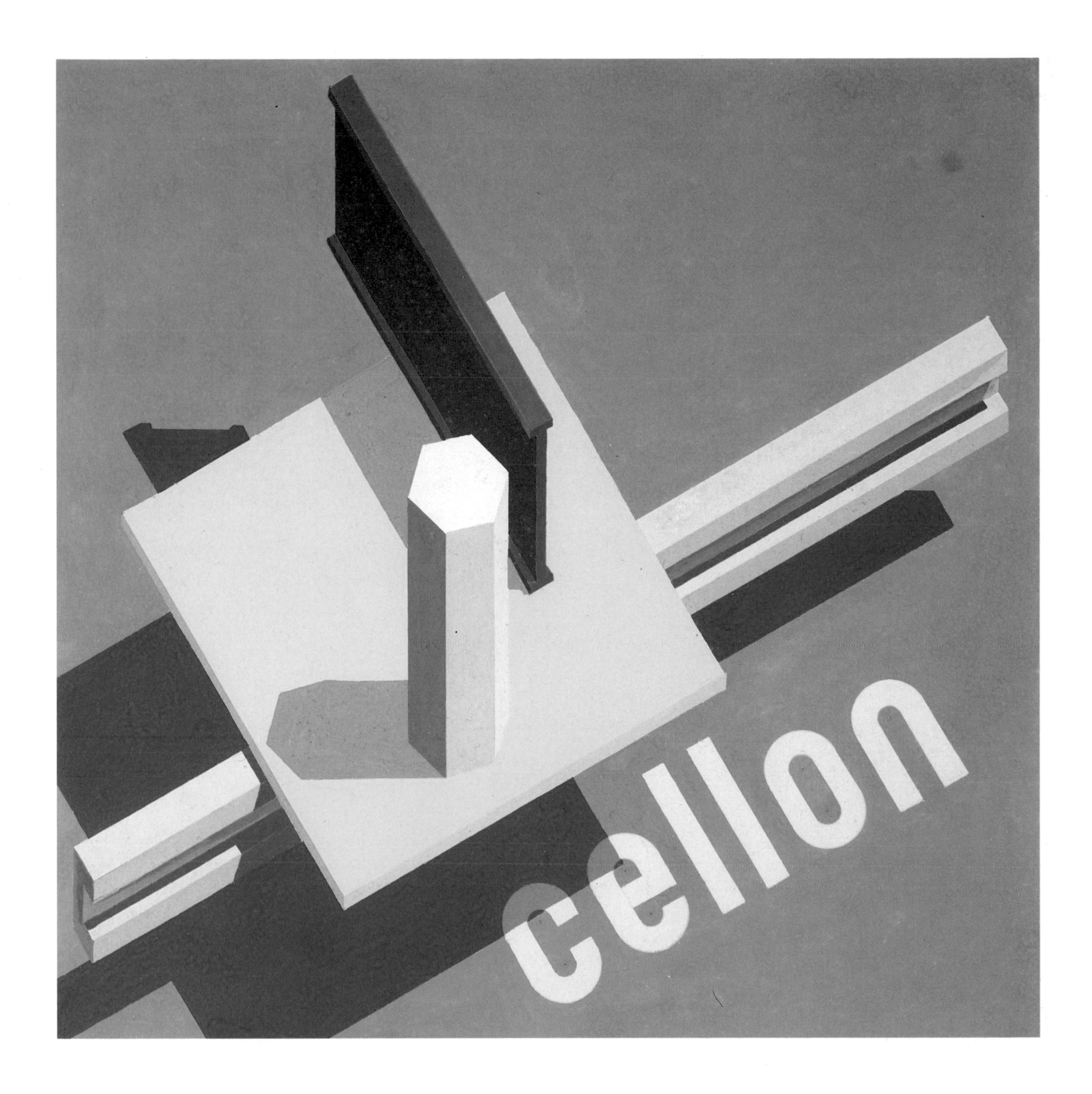

The workshops for advertising and photography

In the Meyer era the advertising workshop had been predominantly concerned with designing and creating exhibitions. Joost Schmidt was only able to develop a more regular advertising curriculum when Mies van der Rohe stopped all practical and exhibition activities.
In the winter semester of 1930/31 Schmidt introduced a systematic advertising class (ills., p. 220 and 221). He was only able to run the course for a year, however, since Mies was not to take the suspiciously left-wing Schmidt with him when the Bauhaus moved to Berlin. Schmidt taught students from four different semesters concurrently, but their training was to remain incomplete. The exercises which have survived from these courses reveal two very different areas of focus. On one hand there was systematic practice in the combination of photographs and texts. Students often had to find contrasting elements, perhaps as many as six or nine, for specific

Erich Mrozek: Exercise from Joost Schmidt's advertising class employing lettering and perspective, 1929.

forms such as a circle, a letter of the alphabet or a photograph. On the other hand there was accurate, three-dimensional perspective drawing. This enabled real space to be created on the image plane, which could be used, e.g. to present an item of merchandise (ill., p. 219). Schmidt's students thus had to concentrate equally intensively on planar design and three-dimensional space. After such preliminary exercises they then drew designs for posters. 'Work must be handed in by a certain deadline; all the drawings are then pinned up on the walls – without names – and, as almost the most important part of the whole lesson, discussed by the teacher.'[135]
The final goal of the course was a job in the advertising or exhibition industry. Schmidt also saw advertising as a source of information. It was to 'convince through its clear presentation of facts, of economic, scientific data' rather than through propaganda or persuasion. Also part of the advertising course was the lettering class which Joost Schmidt had given since 1925 and which counted as part of the preliminary course for students from other disciplines.
Photography was originally conceived as a subsection of the advertising workshop, since photographs were now becoming automatic components of every advertisement. But since photography teacher Walter Peterhans was uninterested in supplying 'tools' for the typographic department, no co-operation between him and Joost Schmidt took place. Peterhans concentrated above all on teaching his students the principles of taking technically perfect photographs. A number of already qualified photographers came to him for supplementary training. Some sixteen students were

Joost Schmidt's students were regularly required to contrast different photomontages. In this work from 1930 Irene Hoffmann contrasts elements from the fields of politics/society and sport/leisure.

Walter Peterhans: Dead Hare, around 1929. This photograph, clearly lit from the left, shows carefully-arranged objects on an almost square wooden background; a piece of reflecting metal foil, a glittering Christmas-tree ornament, a prism lens with a scrap of carbonized paper beneath it and a piece of feather down or fur. Peterhans called this photograph 'Dead Hare' and thus encouraged the viewer to explore the associations called forth by the contrasts of hard and soft, organic and metallic-geometric objects.

trained altogether. In his view of himself as photographer Peterhans was radically different to Moholy-Nagy, and rejected the latter's conception of productive photography and light design. 'The photographic technique is a process of precise detailing in halftones', he wrote. But those who explored the methodic 'development of the technical singularity of photography' would experience 'a delicate nearness and certainness of the subject'[136].
While Moholy-Nagy's interpretation of photography fascinated countless artists and scientists and inspired many amateurs, Peterhans' photography has only recently attracted a response.
The majority of his photographs are still-lifes in the tradition of trompe-l'oeil painting. Peterhans composed carefully balanced pictures and captured with his camera even the most delicate contrasts in materials and shading. Associative titles, such as the 'Dead Hare' of 1929 (ill., p. 222) were used to 'cryptify' these still-lifes.

Above: Bella Ullmann and Willi Jungmittag learning photography, around 1930.

Below: Snapshot from the photo album of the Japanese couple Iwao and Mityko Yamawaki, who studied at the Bauhaus.

The workshops for weaving and interior design

After many years as head of the weaving workshop, Gunta Stölzl resigned in autumn 1931. Mies replaced her with the Berlin interior designer Lilly Reich, with whom he had shared an office since 1925. The exhibitions and interiors they developed together (the Weissenhof estate, the Tugendhat house, the Barcelona pavilion) still rank among the most revolutionary designs of their age.
Although Lilly Reich had devoted intense study to the effect of textiles in space, in which field her achievements have yet to be surpassed, she had no technical knowledge of weaving. The new course introduced into the 1932 weaving workshop timetable, entitled 'Combination exercises in material and colour', clearly carried her own signature.
As far as can be deduced from surviving records, the workshop concentrated upon designing patterns for cloth prints (ill., p. 225) and upon compiling sets of samples for companies, often by students who had already completed their training. These prints were soon marketed commercially together with the Bauhaus wallpaper patterns.
Heinrich König, one of the general agents for Bauhaus products, recalled the sales of Bauhaus materials: 'These prints were very cheap even in those days: 2.25 Reichsmarks per metre. They were produced on M. van Delden's looms in Gronau; a whole series of Bauhaus wallpaper designs were also used for the cloth prints. These prints were sold in large quantities not only for decoration purposes as curtain material but also for children's clothes, for example. There was an equally fat catalogue of Bauhaus cloth designs for furnishings and curtains. These pattern books, like the Bauhaus wallpaper catalogues, could be found in every modern architecture office as from about 1930 onwards.'
The interior design workshop, with its metal and furniture departments, was run by Alfred Arndt until the end of 1931, when he had to hand it over to Lilly Reich. Work on the standardized furniture programme of the Meyer period thus continued unbroken until this juncture. For 1931 there were, e.g., three 'einfach' ('simple') standardized furniture programmes of varying degrees of sophistication, some of which were submitted in competitions. Arndt subsequently only taught 'interior design, design drawing and perspective', and that only for about a year, since he – like Schmidt – was considered too left-wing to be taken to the Berlin Bauhaus.

The Japanese student Mityko Yamawaki in the weaving workshop; next to her, technical drawing teacher Friedrich Köhn, 1930.

Opposite page: This cloth print design by Hajo Rose, later likewise manufactured, was produced on a typewriter in 1932.

00000 00000 00000 00000 00000 00000 00000 00000 00000
00 00000 00000 00000 00000 00000 00000 00000 00000 00000
000 00000 00000 00000 00000 00000 00000 00000 00000 0000
0000 00000 00000 00000 00000 00000 00000 00000 00000 000
00000 00000 00000 00000 00000 00000 00000 00000 00000
00000 00000 00000 00000 00000 00000 00000 00000 00000
00000 00000 00000 00000 000000 00000 00000 00000 00000
00000 00000 00000 00000 00000 00000 00000 00000 00000 0
00000 00000 00000 00000 00000 00000 00000 00000 00000
00000 00000 00000 00000 00000 00000 00000 00000 00000
00 00000 00000 00000 00000 00000 00000 00000 00000 00000
0000 00000 00000 00000 00000 00000 00000 00000 00000 0000
00000 00000 00000 00000 00000 00000 00000 00000 00000 000
00000 00000 00000 00000 00000 00000 00000 00000 00000
00000 00000 00000 00000 00000 00000 00000 00000 00000
0 00000 00000 00000 00000 00000 00000 00000 000000 00000
00000 00000 00000 00000 00000 00000 00000 000000 00000
00000 00000 000000 00000 00000 00000 00000 00000 000000
00000 00000 00000 00000 00000 00000 00000 00000 00000
000 00000 00000 00000 00000 00000 00000 000000 00000 0000
0000 00000 00000 00000 00000 00000 00000 00000 00000 000
00000 00000 00000 00000 00000 00000 00000 00000 00000 00
00000 00000 00000 00000 00000 00000 00000 00000 00000
0 00000 00000 00000 00000 00000 00000 00000 00000 00000
00 00000 00000 00000 00000 00000 00000 00000 00000 00000
00000 00000 00000 00000 00000 00000 00000 00000 00000
00000 00000 00000 00000 00000 00000 00000 00000 00000
00000 00000 00000 00000 00000 00000 00000 00000 00000
0000 00000 00000 00000 00000 00000 00000 00000 00000 000
00000 00000 00000 00000 00000 00000 000000 00000 00000 00
00000 00000 00000 00000 00000 00000 00000 00000 00000 0
0 00000 00000 00000 00000 00000 000000 000000 00000 00000
00 00000 00000 00000 00000 00000 00000 00000 00000 00000
000 00000 00000 00000 00000 00000 00000 00000 00000 0000
000000 00000 00000 00000 00000 00000 00000 00000 00000
000000 00000 00000 00000 00000 00000 00000 00000 00000
00000 00000 00000 00000 00000 00000 00000 00000 00000
00000 00000 00000 00000 00000 00000 000000 00000 000000 00
000000 00000 00000 00000 00000 00000 00000 00000 00000 0
00000 00000 00000 00000 00000 00000 00000 00000 00000
0 00000 00000 00000 00000 00000 00000 00000 00000 00000
00 00000 00000 00000 00000 00000 00000 00000 00000 0000
000 00000 0 000000 00000 0000000 00000 00000 00000 00000 000
000000 00000 00000 00000 00000 00000 00000 00000 00000
00000 00000 00000 00000 00000 00000 00000 00000 00000
00000 00000 00000 00000 00000 00000 00000 00000 00000
_00000 ___00000 ___00000 ___00000 ___00000 ___00000 ___00000 ___00000 ___00000 ___0
_00000 ___00000 ___00000 ___00000 ___00000 ___00000 ___00000 ___00000 ___00000 ___
00000 00000 00000 00000 00000 00000 00000 00000 00000
000 ___00000 ___00000 ___00000 ___00000 ___00000 ___00000 ___00000 ___00000 ___0000
0000 ___00000 ___00000 ___00000 ___00000 ___00000 ___00000 ___00000 ___00000 ___000
00000 00000 00000 00000 00000 00000 00000 00000 00000 00
___00000 ___00000 ___00000 ___00000 ___00000 ___00000 ___00000 ___00000 ___00000 _
0 ___00000 ___00000 ___00000 ___000000 ___00000 ___00000 ___00000 ___00000 ___00000
00 00000 00000 00000 00000 00000 00000 00000 00000 00000
_00000 ___00000 ___00000 ___00000 ___00000 ___00000 ___00000 ___00000 ___00000 ___
_00000 ___00000 ___00000 ___00000 ___00000 ___00000 ___00000 ___00000 ___00000 ___
00000 00000 00000 00000 00000 00000 00000 00000 00000 00000
000 ___00000 ___00000 ___00000 ___00000 ___00000 ___00000 ___00000 ___00000 ___000
0000 /// 00000 //// 00000 /// 00000 /// 00000 /// 00000 /// 00000 /// 000000 /// 00000 //// 00
00000 00000 00000 00000 00000 00000 00000 00000 00000 0
___00000 ___00000 ___00000 ___00000 ___00000 ___00000 ___00000 ___00000 ___00000
0 00000 00000 00000 00000 00000 00000 00000 00000 ___00000
00 00000 00000 00000 00000 00000 00000 00000 00000 0000

Wähler und Wählerinnen Dessaus!

Der 25. Oktober gibt in Anhalt dem schaffenden Volke die Möglichkeit, den Grundstein zur Neugestaltung der politischen und wirtschaftlichen Verhältnisse zu legen. Die Not der Gemeinden ist eine Not des Volkes, entstanden aus den ungeheuren Fehlschlägen einer marxistisch-demokratisch-pazifistischen Außen- und Innenpolitik. Dem Elend und der Not durch eigene Kraft restlos zu steuern, wird den Gemeinden so lange eine Unmöglichkeit sein, so lange in Reich und Ländern nicht die letzten Vertreter der sterbenden Welt der Demokratie aus ihren Machtpositionen verschwunden und an ihre Stellen Vertreter des Volkes berufen sind, die es als ihre heilige und ernste Aufgabe ansehen, die nationalen und sozialen Belange des schaffenden Volkes zu vertreten und durchzusetzen.

Am 25. Oktober treten auch in Dessau zur Gemeindewahl erstmalig nationalsozialistische Kämpfer vor das schaffende Volk Dessaus und rufen ihm zu:

Wählt Nationalsozialisten!

Was wir Nationalsozialisten in der Gemeindevertretung wollen ist **Arbeit und Brot** für unsere Mitbürger zu schaffen. Wir stehen grundsätzlich auf dem Standpunkte, daß diese Aufgabe nur durch eigene Kraft gelöst werden muß und nicht durch Aufnahme von Krediten, die das Gemeindevermögen aufzehren und durch eine drückende Zinslast die weitere Aufbauarbeit unmöglich machen.

Wir fordern deshalb größte Sparsamkeit im Gemeindehaushalt und sofortige Streichung sämtlicher Ausgaben, die nicht lebensnotwendig für unsere Mitbürger sind.

Wir fordern:

Sofortige Streichung sämtlicher Ausgaben für das Bauhaus.

Ausländische Lehrkräfte sind fristlos zu kündigen, da es unvereinbar ist mit der Verantwortung, die eine gute Gemeindeführung gegenüber ihren Bürgern zu tragen hat, daß deutsche Volksgenossen hungern, während Ausländer in überreichlichem Maße aus den Steuergroschen des darbenden Volkes besoldet werden. Deutsche Lehrkräfte sind durch Vermittlung der Gemeinde in Dessau oder anderwärts unterzubringen.

Für die im Bauhaus befindlichen Handwerkerschulen ist Unterkunft andernorts zu schaffen.

Der Abbruch des Bauhauses ist sofort in die Wege zu leiten.

Wir fordern:

Abbau der Stadtratsstelle Sinsel.

Die dieser Stadtratsstelle bisher obliegenden Aufgaben sind den einzelnen Ressorts zuzuteilen.

Wir fordern:

Streichung sämtlicher Aufwandsentschädigungen für städtische Beamte und Bedienstete.

Festsetzung des Oberbürgermeistergehaltes auf höchstens 9000.— RM jährlich.

Kürzung sämtlicher städtischer Gehälter über 6000.— RM jährlich um 25—30%.

Wir fordern:

Sofortige Einführung einer Filial- und Sondersteuer für Konsumgenossenschaften, Warenhäuser und Einheitspreisgeschäfte.

Wir fordern:

Laufende Winterhilfe für Kleinrentner, Kriegsbeschädigte, Kriegshinterbliebene, kinderreiche Familien und Wohlfahrtsempfänger.

Wir fordern:

Errichtung guter und billigster Kleinwohnungen für Minderbemittelte, dazu **Rückführung der Hauszinssteuer zu ihrem eigentlichen Zweck,** auch zur Instandsetzung der vielen alten baufälligen Häuser.

Wir fordern:

Unbedingten Mieterschutz, so lange die Wohnungsnot nicht behoben und ausreichende und billige Wohnmöglichkeiten geschaffen sind.

Wir fordern:

Zurückführung der Städtischen Sparkasse auf den ihr zukommenden Zweck, nämlich die Bereitstellung langfristiger Darlehen zu niedrigen Zinssätzen an Handel- und Gewerbetreibende.

Wir betrachten diese Forderungen als Mindestforderungen und erklären, daß wir bei unserer Arbeit im Stadtparlament alle weiteren Wege rücksichtslos aufzeigen und ausschöpfen werden, die geeignet sind, Arbeit und Brot zu schaffen.

Unsere Arbeit wird unter der Losung des erwachenden Deutschlands stehen:

Gemeinnutz geht vor Eigennutz!

Wer diesen Grundsatz zur Tat umgesetzt wissen will, der

Wählt Liste 5

Liste **Nationalsozialisten.** N.S.D.A.P. Ortsgruppe Dessau.

The political end in Dessau

The increasing politicization of the late twenties was not to escape the Bauhaus, and proved fateful for the school's continuing existence.
Following the world depression of 1929, the Reichstag parliamentary elections of September 1930 gave the National Socialists their first major breakthrough. Hitler was styled – with pseudo-religious exaggeration – the 'Führer' of future Germany. The Communists also attracted a larger number of votes in the 1930 Reichstag elections.
This polarization of right and left-wing opinion at the expense of the moderate centre was repeated in the Thuringian Landtag elections and in the municipal elections in Dessau itself.
Left-wing forces grouped at the Bauhaus and, despite Mies' numerous expulsions, survived until the beginning of 1933. Right-wing – in other words, Nazi – students only appeared during the school's last few weeks in Berlin.
The first state in which the National Socialists won a share in government was Thuringia, of which Weimar was also a part.
The National Socialist Minister of the Interior and Education Wilhelm Frick, who took office in January 1930, was the first to exercise his administrative powers to move against modern art and culture. In Weimar, following the departure of the Bauhaus, the government had set up a sort of successor school in the same van de Velde buildings – an 'Academy of Architecture and Handicrafts' headed by the architect Otto Bartning. Frick closed down the school, sacked 29 teachers and commissioned the conservative, Nazi-approved architect and author Paul Schultze-Naumburg with the reorganization of the school. It reopened a few months laters as the 'State School for Architecture, Fine Art and Handicraft'. A newspaper article gave its motto as the 'Avowal of the supreme German!' It was now a question of 'placing value on the representation of the heroic' and of creating 'art appropriate to race'. [137]
Frick had initiated the first of the Nazis' iconoclastic programmes even before opening this new school. The modern pictures in the Weimar Landesmuseum – whose director, Otto Koehler, had purchased works by Bauhaus artists from very early on and had exhibited many others as loans – had to be taken down and older paintings hung in their place. Despite noisy protests from all over the country, this measure was not reversed.
At the same time Schultze-Naumburg had the murals by Oskar Schlemmer in the van de Velde stairwell stripped and painted over. The first Schlemmer knew of this was in the papers, and he was thus given no chance to view or photograph his work one last time.
The Nazis repeated their election successes in 1931 and 1932. In the October 1931 elections in Dessau they won 19 of 36 seats. P. Hofmann became chief city councillor and deputy gauleiter. The Nazis now had the majority in the Landtag, and the government – which, according to Hesse, had 'previously always held a protective hand over the Bauhaus'[138] – was toppled. 'In both the municipal elections in Dessau and now the regional parliament elections the National Socialist party has campaigned against the "Bolshevist" Bauhaus.'[139]
The Dessau Nazis had been demanding the closure of the Bauhaus even before their election victory (ill., p. 226). 'Immediate stoppage of all Bauhaus funding. Foreign teachers must be dismissed without notice, for it is irreconcilable with the responsibility of worthy municipal leadership towards its citizens that German comrades go hungry while foreigners are handsomely paid from the taxes of a starving nation.'[140]
Directly after their election success the Nazis proposed a number of motions against the Bauhaus, none of which was approved with a majority. Even the budget for the following year was approved in March, albeit with

Opposite page: Handbill printed by the Dessau National Socialists for the municipal elections of 25 October 1931. The stoppage of all funds to the Bauhaus is at the top of their list of campaigns, together with the demand that the Bauhaus building should be demolished.

precautionary notice of termination for 1 October 1932. Soon afterwards, the new National Socialist Minister-President Freyberg visited the Bauhaus accompanied by Schultze-Naumburg, who subsequently compiled a thoroughly negative report on the school. The regional government also replaced two municipal councillors with Nazis and thus guaranteed themselves a majority in the next divisions. On 22 August 1932 Hesse was once again obliged to include a Nazi petition for the closure of the Bauhaus on the day's agenda. Only Hesse and the four Communists voted against the motion. The Social Democrats abstained from the vote, arguing that their traditional support for the Bauhaus had cost them an increasing number of popular votes. The Nazi motion was thus passed and the Bauhaus forced to close. 'The Masters launched a legal appeal against the winding-up order, based... on an edict by the President of the German Reich, since it breached a number of valid contracts (with Hilberseimer, Arndt, Rudelt, Peterhans, Joost Schmidt, Albers, Kandinsky, Mies himself and others). In a settlement, the City of Dessau agreed to continue to pay salaries, to allow the Bauhaus to keep furniture and inventory on a loan basis and to transfer the patents and registered designs awarded to the Bauhaus and all rights from licensing agreements to the last Bauhaus director.'[141]

A German Bauhaus? End of the Bauhaus

There are still no sources to suggest that the Bauhaus under Mies van der Rohe organized any own political activities during these final months. Mies trusted that people would simply recognize the quality of Bauhaus work and accept its unpolitical character. Another leading Dessau figure felt called upon to take more active steps in defence of the Bauhaus – Grote, then head of the Dessau cultural conservation department and director of the local art gallery, for which he had already purchased works by Bauhaus Masters. In 1925 he had been involved in fetching the Bauhaus from Weimar to Dessau; in 1930 he had played a key role in Hannes Meyer's dismissal.

After the Landtag elections in May 1932, Grote wrote to the neurologist Dr. Prinzhorn: 'I am approaching you in particular in response to your last Dessau lecture and the article in the "Ring" on the National Socialist movement, of which Mies van der Rohe has sent me a copy... I see Mies van der Rohe at the Bauhaus as a projection of the fate of Germany.' He hoped Prinzhorn would answer his question of whether it was possible 'to enlighten the cultural policy-making departments of the National Socialist party about the situation at the Bauhaus... If people like Schultze-Naumburg still hold sway, naturally the situation is hopeless.'[142] In conclusion, he emphasized that he was writing without the knowledge of Mies van der Rohe.

Grote was clearly unaware that Mies and Prinzhorn were friends. Mies' wife, Ada, had gone to the same school in Hellerau as Prinzhorn's wife. Prinz immediately declared his willingness to help and two strategies were adopted. Prinzhorn organized a declaration of confidence in Mies van der Rohe which was sent to the mayor, Hesse, who in turn used it as an argument in his last speech before the final vote on the Nazi motion to close the Bauhaus. This declaration stated: 'In his character, in his intellectual stance, in his professional convictions and powers of design as expressed in his buildings and work, we see in Mies van der Rohe an exemplary German architect. It is our conviction that, under his direction, young people are educated in honest, artist design and responsible working. We would consider it regrettable should Mies van der Rohe be deprived, through the closure of the Bauhaus, of the opportunity to educate young people according to his convictions. This declaration of confidence is

Opposite page: Article on the closure of the Dessau Bauhaus in the Berliner Tageblatt of autumn 1932.

Es ist, wenn kein Wunder geschieht, wieder mal soweit: die Schüler und Schülerinnen des Bauhauses müssen ihre sieben Sachen zusammensuchen und auswandern. Die Schulglocke holt zum letzten Zeichen aus! Die Jungen und Mädel, verbunden durch den Geist produktiver Studienarbeit, müssen sich trennen und auf Wanderschaft gehen. Wohin? Es wird ein hoffnungsloser Aufbruch werden — ein Aufbruch ohne Ziel. Als vor Jahren die Gemeinschaft der Bauhaus-Schüler und Bauhaus-Lehrer Weimar verlassen musste, verfolgt von einem zusammengelaufenen Haufen nationalistischer Spiessbürger, war es noch ein Aufbruch mit einem Ziel. Das Ziel hiess Dessau. Heute hat sich in demselben Dessau eine Gruppe spiessbürgerlicher Nationalisten zusammengefunden, um die früher freudig begrüssten Emigranten aus Weimar auszutreiben. Mit brutalen Schritten und höhnischem Lachen sind diese Leute in die Bezirke einer freiheitlichen Jugend und eines modernen Studiums eingedrungen. Sie wollen ganze Arbeit machen! Nicht nur die Schüler und Lehrer sollen vertrieben werden — das Schulgebäude soll dem Erdboden gleichgemacht werden. Jungen und Mädchen und Lehrer werden sich in alle vier Winde zerstreuen und vielleicht anderswo lernen und lehren — das Studium des Kunstgewerbes, der Architektur und des Kunsthandwerks aber wird in Deutschland an einer Schule weniger möglich sein: am Bauhaus in Dessau. Wir haben in Deutschland an modernen Kunstgewerbeschulen keinen Ueberfluss. Der Verlust des Bauhauses ist nicht zu verschmerzen.

Vier Etagen Balkone des Atelierhauses

Eine Studie auf dem Balkon der Malklasse

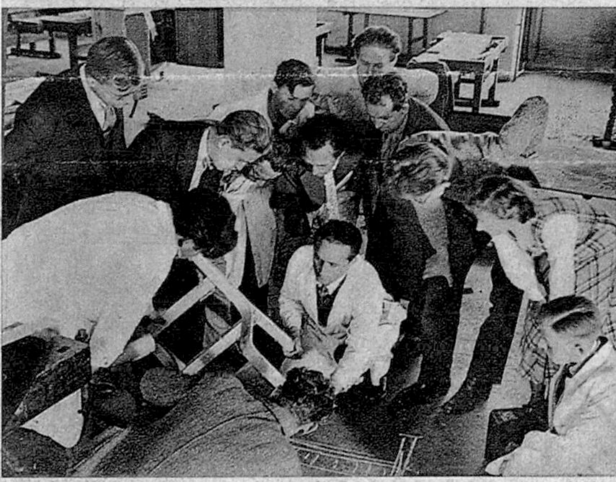

Unterricht in Möbelkonstruktion

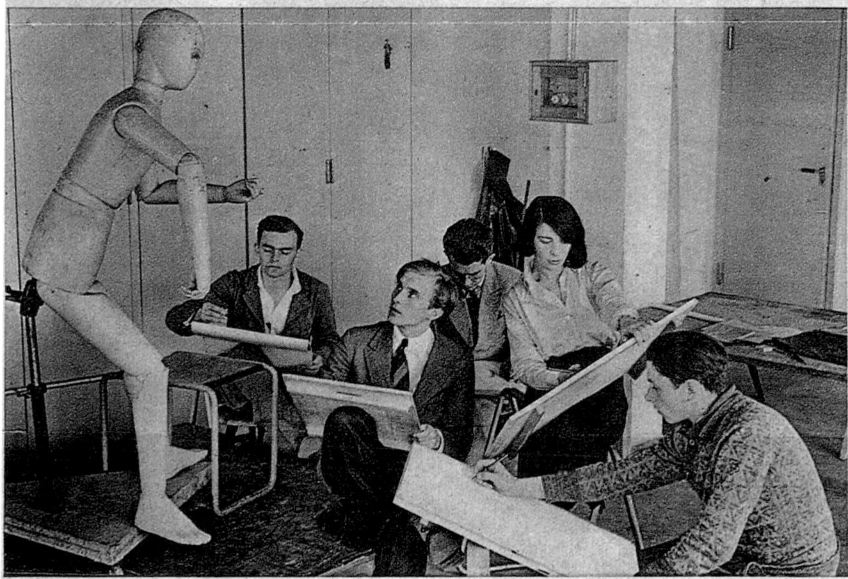

Zeichenunterricht nach einem beweglichen Modell

Aufnahmen A. P.
Alfred Eisenstaedt

DESSAU

signed by Peter Behrens, Paul Bonatz – Stuttgart, Adolf Busch, Count von Dürckheim, Professor Emge – Weimar, Edwin Fischer, Privy Councillor Theodor Fischer, Professor H. Freyer – Leipzig, H. von Gleichen, Eduard Hanfstaengl – Munich, Josef Hoffmann – Vienna, Georg Kolbe, Wilhelm Kreis, Professor Krüger – Leipzig, Mrs. Möller van den Bruck, Professor Pinder, H. Prinzhorn, Heinrich Hereditary Prince Reuss, R. Riemerschmid, Chief Director of Building F. Schumacher – Hamburg and Heinrich Tessenow.'[143]
Prinzhorn apparently also helped establish communications between Grote and Hugo Bruckmann in Munich, who was closely connected with the national leadership of the 'Kampfbund für deutsche Kultur' (an association dedicated to the 'fight' for German culture). The 'Kampfbund' was at that time the centre of Nazi cultural policy-making. Grote was able to visit Bruckmann and ply him with information materials on the Bauhaus. With Bruckmann's help, it was sought to influence the two most powerful National Socialists: Minister-President Freyberg and chief city councillor Hoffmann.[144]
'Bruckmann told me that Rosenberg had written to Freyberg to the effect that he should "allow Mies van der Rohe's school to carry on – but abandon the name and concept of the D[essauer] Bauhaus, with its ominous associations".'[145] Reference was also made to 'the conversion of the "Deutsche Werkstätten" in Hellerau, near Dresden, into a National Socialist school of arts and crafts under Mies'[146]. But neither the declaration of confidence nor such alternative future 'prospects' were to influence Hoffmann's decision. The 'Marxist' Bauhaus was closed down by order of the city council. The cultural policy-makers in Munich lost to Dessau's local and regional politicians. The argumentation which was employed ranged across a variety of themes. Grote presented Mies as a 'German' architect. 'Among young architects today he is generally seen as a Fascist, because he stresses in architecture the spiritual values which Moscow Marxism condemns; for Mies v.d. Rohe, the ideal is not objectivity but beauty.'[147] He embodied 'Germanness and Classicism'. This view was obviously shared by the 'Kampfbund'. Bruckmann planned an article about him and was ready to support him. Mies did not oppose his interpretation as a 'German architect', but nor did he request it. He hoped in vain that, in the 'Third Reich', this classification would bring him larger building commissions.

1932 New Year greetings card from the advertising workshop.

Opinions on the value of the Bauhaus differed. Grote sought to present the modernity which the Bauhaus embodied as a German style: 'The new style may be Marxist-Communist, but it may also be German and Classical.'[148] The Nazis ought to support the Bauhaus in order to attract young people. The 'Kampfbund' appeared to be against retaining the Bauhaus as it was. While Alfred Rosenberg apparently wanted a modified Bauhaus, 'Kampfbund' member Schultze-Naumburg was fundamentally opposed to the Bauhaus, and it was his argument that won the day.
Today it seems astonishing that members of the National Socialist 'Kampfbund' should have even given the Bauhaus a second thought. There were at that time, however, numerous efforts among National Socialist cultural politicians to promote modern art and architecture and Expressionism, as 'German' currents, to the status of national art. It was not until 1934 that the Nazis finally condemned modern art as fundamentally 'un-German', 'alien' and 'Bolshevist'.

Opposite page: The Attack on the Bauhaus. Collage by Iwao Yamawaki, 1932.

DAS BAUHAUS IN BERLIN

Wegweiser auf dem Fabrikhof

Schüler der Textilklasse bringen die Webstühle in den Lehrsaal

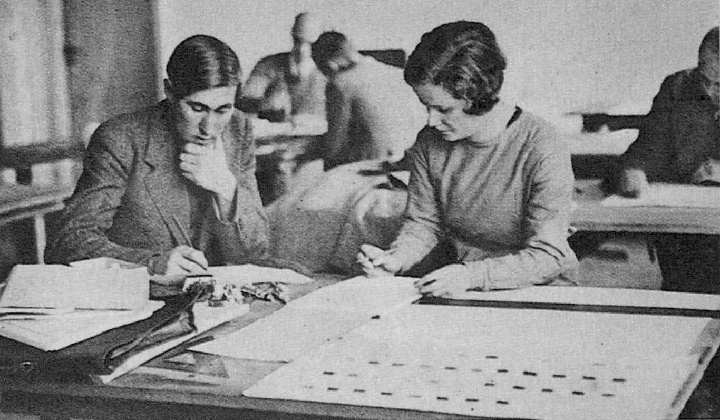
. . . und inmitten des Einzugs beginnt schon der Unterricht

Aufnahmen Reinke-Degephot

Die Kunstschule auf dem Fabrikhof

Die Bitte der ordnungsliebenden Polizei

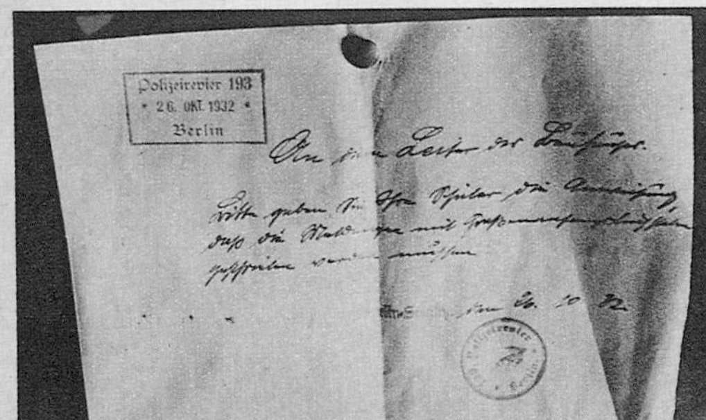
Polizeirevier 193
26. OKT. 1932
Berlin

Der Hauptlehrsaal drei Tage vor Beginn des Unterrichts

Eine amerikanische Bauhaus-Schülerin beim Anstreichen der Wände ihres neuen Lehrsaals in Berlin. Hier hat sich das aus Dessau vertriebene Bauhaus in einer stillgelegten Fabrik eingerichtet

The Bauhaus in Berlin

Following its closure in Dessau, the Bauhaus was offered a home by two Social Democrat cities, Magdeburg and Leipzig. However, Mies had already decided – several months before it finally shut – to continue the Bauhaus in Berlin as a private school. The former Institute of Design was now subtitled 'Independent Teaching and Research Institute'. Mies quickly found new premises; he rented – at first in his own name – a disused telephone factory in the Birkbuschstrasse in Steglitz (ills., p. 232 and 233). Students were informed of the new arrangements in a circular. The curriculum was changed yet again: courses were now to last seven semesters and the fees were increased. In Berlin, Mies explained his pragmatic intentions: 'It is our aim to train architects so that they master every last area of architecture, from small apartments to town planning – not merely the actual building, but the entire interior design right down to textiles.'[149] Since Mies did not take with him to Berlin the Dessau Masters Alfred Arndt and Joost Schmidt, the advertising course was left without a teacher. Four Communist students who protested about the situation were promptly expelled. Mies had two financial pillars on which to base this new start in Berlin: product licensing fees of around 30,000 Marks, and the teacher salaries which Dessau had agreed to pay until 1935.
But politics soon caught up with the Bauhaus here, too. Soon after the Nazis seized power, the Dessau public prosecutor's office appointed an investigative committee to gather incriminating evidence to be used in a trial against the mayor for his funding of the Bauhaus. The trial eventually dragged on till 1935 and ended in salary and pension cuts for Hesse. But the new ruling powers first needed to 'prove' the Bauhaus had been a 'Bolshevist' institution, since this was the only juridical line of attack open to them. The Dessau public prosecutor's office therefore sent a public prosecutor to the Berlin Bauhaus to secure such 'evidence'. Shortly beforehand the former Bauhaus library had been sent on to Berlin by the Dessau authorities, and in its packing cases were now 'discovered' a number of 'Communist' journals. But these 'incriminating materials' were probably planted in the cases in Dessau prior to their dispatch.[150] On 11 April, the Bauhaus was searched and placed under seal by the Gestapo in a move stage-managed from Dessau. A number of photographs were taken (ill., p. 236) a clear indication that the Press were notified in advance. In the following few months Mies – and the students – made numerous approaches to state authorities in attempts to have the school reopened. But where did ultimate responsibility really lie? The answer is still unclear.

The new Bauhaus building in the Birkbuschstrasse in the Steglitz district of Berlin was a disused telephone factory, photographed at the end of 1932 by Howard Dearstyne.

Opposite page: Photographic report on the Berlin Bauhaus from the Berliner Tageblatt, October 1932.

Students inspect the new Berlin premises, 25 October 1932.

Weeks went by as one authority simply used another as a pretext for not lifting the seal. There appear to have been four departments involved in the closing of the school: the secret police (Gestapo), the Arts Ministry (Minister Bernhard Rust, with Principal Winfried Wendland responsible for this particular case), the Provincial School Council and Rosenberg as the head of the 'Kampfbund für deutsche Kultur'. As a fifth authority, students even wrote to Goebbels in his capacity as Minister of Public Information and Propaganda.

Mies had talks with Rosenberg on the day after the school's closure, but these proved fruitless. Although Rosenberg promised to do what he could to have the school reopened, still nothing happened. All hopes were nevertheless pinned on the 'Kampfbund'. Right-wing students were asking for membership just four days after the closure, offering their 'positive contribution to the new Germany'. Both Lilly Reich and Kandinsky recommended joining the 'Kampfbund'. Appointing a state commissioner who was acceptable to the regime represented another possible solution. Engemann, a teacher who was already a Party member, was willing to accept such a post. Students sent a memorandum to the Minister of Arts requesting a commissioner as a means of getting the school reopened.

Meanwhile, a new law had come into force which placed all private schools under the jurisdiction of the Provincial School Council.[151] This enabled the new ruling power to apply the 'Permanent Civil Service' law to persons working in this field, too, and to demand proof of Aryan ancestry.

Moving into the Berlin Bauhaus, October 1932.

At the end of May Mies applied to this authority for permission to run a private art school. Some six weeks later he received in reply the promise that the Gestapo would agree to approve the reopening of the Bauhaus on certain conditions. These conditions were formulated by Arts Ministry representative Wendland. A short while later Mies received an almost identical version of these conditions from the Gestapo, sent by post and marked 'Strictly Confidential'. Wendland wrote: 'I do not wish to conceal from you, however, that I have no choice but to insist that both Mr. KANDINSKY and Mr. HILBERSEIMER do not continue teaching at the school.'[152] It was also to be determined if there were any Jewish members of staff. 'That would also, in my opinion, prohibit any further Bauhaus activity.' It was further recommended that some of the teachers should join the Party. The Gestapo also demanded a timetable with Nationalist Socialist orientation. By the time these letters reached the Bauhaus (15 June and 21 July), the Dessau municipal authorities had already delivered a final blow to the Bauhaus. The law on the 'Restoration of the Permanent Civil Service' in force since April was invoked to terminate the salary payments which had previously been contractually guaranteed. 'Support for and action on behalf of the Bauhaus, which presented itself as a Bolshevist cell', now constituted a political action. Mies' protest 'that the closure of the Bauhaus affected people with almost exclusively nationalist beliefs' was ineffective. The school's closure had meant the additional loss of tuition fees, and income from product licences was also stagnating. The Kandem company

Haussuchung im „Bauhaus Steglitz"

Kommunistisches Material gefunden.

Auf Veranlassung der Dessauer Staatsanwaltschaft wurde gestern nachmittag eine größere Aktion im „Bauhaus Steglitz", dem früheren Dessauer Bauhaus, in der Birkbuschstraße in Steglitz durchgeführt. Von einem Aufgebot Schutzpolizei und Hilfspolizisten wurde das Grundstück besetzt und systematisch durchsucht. Mehrere Kisten mit illegalen Druckschriften wurden beschlagnahmt. Die Aktion stand unter Leitung von Polizeimajor Schmahel.

Das „Bauhaus Dessau" war vor etwa Jahresfrist nach Berlin übergesiedelt. Damals waren bereits von der Dessauer Polizei zahlreiche verbotene Schriften beschlagnahmt worden. Ein Teil der von der Polizei versiegelten Kisten war jedoch verschwunden, und man vermutete, daß sie von der Bauhausleitung mit nach Berlin genommen worden waren. Die Dessauer Staatsanwaltschaft setzte sich jetzt mit der Berliner Polizei in Verbindung und bat um Durchsuchung des Gebäudes. Das Bauhaus, das früher unter Leitung von Professor Gropius stand, der sich jetzt in Rußland aufhält, hat in einer leerstehenden Fabrikbaracke in der Birkbuschstraße in Steglitz Quartier genommen. Der augenblickliche Leiter hat es aber vor wenigen Tagen vorgezogen, nach Paris überzusiedeln. Bei der gestrigen Haussuchung wurde zahlreiches illegales Propagandamaterial der KPD. gefunden und beschlagnahmt.

Alle Anwesenden, die sich nicht ausweisen konnten, wurden zur Feststellung ihrer Personalien ins Polizeipräsidium gebracht.

On 12 April 1933 the Berliner Lokalanzeiger carried a photograph and article on the house search at the Bauhaus.

Opposite page: Conference in the courtyard following the school's closure on 12 April 1933.

had already terminated its contract with the Bauhaus at the end of 1932. The lucrative contract with the Rasch wallpaper company was cancelled on 27 April. Who was behind this cancellation is unclear.

On 19 July, following Wendland's announcement of the conditions under which the school might reopen, the Masters gathered in Lilly Reich's studio. Mies gave an account of the financial and political situation and then proposed dissolving the Bauhaus. This was approved by all present (ill., p. 238). Albeit taken in a context of extreme political and financial tribulation, this decision nevertheless represented one final exercise in the intellectual freedom of choice.

Student Pius Pahl photographed this conference held following the closure of the Bauhaus in April 1933.

Opposite page: Student Ernst Louis Beck in front of the Berlin Bauhaus.

bauhaus

Notes

1 Heinrich Waentig: Wirtschaft und Kunst. Jena 1909, p. 47
2 Ibid. p. 292
3 See: Winfried Nerdinger: Walter Gropius. Bauhaus-Archiv exhibition catalogue, Berlin 1985, pp. 11, 40
4 Walter Gropius, letters to Karl Ernst Osthaus of 24.4.1917 and 23.12.1918. In: Karl Ernst Osthaus. Leben und Werk. Recklinghausen 1971, pp. 469, 471
5 Walter Gropius, letter to State Representative Paulsen of 3.3.1919. Bauhaus-Archiv
6 See: I.B.Whyte: Bruno Taut. Baumeister einer neuen Welt. Stuttgart 1981, p. 51 ff.
7 Hans M.Wingler: Das Bauhaus. 1919–1933 Weimar Dessau Berlin und die Nachfolge in Chicago seit 1937. Bramsche, 3rd ed. 1975, p. 13
8 Tut Schlemmer: ...vom lebendigen Bauhaus und seiner Bühne. In: Bauhaus und Bauhäusler. Eckhard Neumann (ed.). Bern and Stuttgart 1971, p. 124
9 Walter Gropius, letter to Ernst Hardt of 14.4.1919. In: Reginald R. Isaacs: Walter Gropius. Der Mensch und sein Werk. Vol.1. Berlin 1983, p. 208
10 Johannes Itten, letter to Josef Matthias Hauer of 5.11.1919. In: Johannes Itten. Werke und Schriften. Willy Rotzler (ed.). Zürich 1972, p. 68
11 Alfred Arndt: wie ich an das bauhaus in weimar kam...
In: Bauhaus and Bauhäusler 1971 (note 8), p. 41
12 Ibid.
13 Oskar Schlemmer, letter to Otto Meyer-Amden of 16.5.1921. In: Oskar Schlemmer. Briefe und Tagebücher. Tut Schlemmer (ed.). Munich 1958, p. 112
14 Paul Klee, letter to Lilly Klee of 16.1.1921. In: Paul Klee. Briefe an die Familie. Vol. 2. 1907–1940. Felix Klee (ed.). Cologne 1979, p. 970
15 Paul Citroen: Mazdaznan am Bauhaus. In: Bauhaus and Bauhäusler 1971 (note 8), p. 29, the following quotations ibid. and p. 34
16 Bruno Adler: Das Weimarer Bauhaus. Darmstadt 1963
17 Excerpt from an unidentifiable publication from Verlag Diederich, Jena 1920. Property of Bauhäusler Hildegard Hesse-Kube, copy in Bauhaus-Archiv
18 Statutes of the Weimar State Bauhaus. July 1922, p. 3
19 Winfried Nerdinger: Von der Stilschule zum Creative Design – Walter Gropius als Lehrer. In: Ist die Bauhaus-Pädogogik aktuell? Rainer Wick (ed.). Cologne 1985, p. 35
20 Schlemmer 1971 (note 8), p.124
21 Christian Schädlich: Bauhaus Weimar 1919–1925. Weimar, Tradition und Gegenwart. No. 35, 2nd ed. 1980, p. 23
22 Helmut von Erffa: Das frühe Bauhaus: Jahre der Entwicklung 1919–1924. In: Wallraf-Richartz-Jahrbuch. Vol. 24. Cologne 1962, p. 413.
23 Gunta Stölzl: In der Textilwerkstatt des Bauhauses 1919 bis 1931. In: Werk. 1968. No.11, p. 745. The following quotation ibid.
24 Walter Scheidig: Die Bauhaus-Siedlungsgenossenschaft in Weimar 1920–1925. In: Dezennium II. Dresden 1972, p. 249
25 Walter Gropius, letter to Eckart (Adolf Behne) of 2.6.1920. Quoted from: Nerdinger 1985 (note 3), p. 58
26 Walter Gropius: Raumkunde. Undated (1922). Manuscript in the Bauhaus-Archiv, p. 9
27 Walter Gropius: Die Tragfähigkeit der Bauhaus-Idee. Notes of 3.2.1922. In: Wingler 1975 (note 7), p. 62
28 W. Gropius: Die Notwendigkeit der Auftragsarbeit für das Bauhaus. Notes of 9.12.1921. In: Wingler 1975 (note 7), p. 61
29 Oskar Schlemmer, letter to Otto Meyer-Amden of 7.12.1921. In: Karl-Heinz Hüter: Das Bauhaus in Weimar. Berlin 3rd ed. 1983, p. 186
30 Hüter 1982 (note 29), p.15
31 Walter Gropius – Kampf um neue Erziehungsgrundlagen. In: Bauhaus und Bauhäusler 1971 (note 8), p.10
32 Schädlich 1980 (note 21), p.104
33 Walter Gropius, letter to Ferdinand Kramer of 15.10.1919. In: Bauhaus und Bauhäusler 1971 (note 8), p. 64
34 Vilmos Huszár: Das Staatliche Bauhaus in Weimar. In: De Stijl, 5.1922. No.9, p. 136
35 Theo van Doesburg: Der Wille zum Stil. In: Theo van Doesburg 1883–1931. Van Abbemuseum exh. cat. Eindhoven 1968, p. 49
36 Theo van Doesburg: Stijl-Kursus 1. In: Theo van Doesburg 1883–1931 (note 35), p. 46
37 Theo van Doesburg to Walter Dexel, 24.3.1922. Quoted from: Volker Wahl: Jena als Kunststadt. Leipzig 1988, p. 244
38 Peter Röhl: Die Ausmalung des Residenz-Theaters in Weimar. In: De Stijl.4.1921. No.9, p.144
39 Werner Graeff: Mit der Avantgarde. In: Kunstverein für die Rheinlande und Westfalen exh. cat. Düsseldorf 1962
40 Werner Graeff: Bemerkungen eines Bauhäuslers. In: Werner Graeff. Ein Pionier der Zwanziger Jahre. Skulpturenmuseum der Stadt Marl exh. cat. 1979, p. 7
41 Bauhaus-Drucke – Neue europäische Graphik. Brochure of 1921. In: Wingler 1975 (note 7), p. 57
42 Gerhard Marcks, letter to Walter Gropius of 23.3.1923. In: Hüter 1982 (note 29), p. 213
43 L. Feininger, letter to Julia Feininger of 5.10.1922. In: Wingler 1975 (note 7), p. 68
44 Minutes of a meeting of the Council of Masters of 18.8.1923. In: Claudine Humblet: Le Bauhaus. Lausanne 1980, p. 325
45 Sibyl Moholy-Nagy: László Moholy-Nagy, ein Totalexperiment. Mainz and Berlin 1973, p. 47
46 Paul Klee, letter to Lilly Klee of 16.4.1921. In: Paul Klee Briefe 1979 (note 14), p. 975
47 W. Kersten: Paul Klee. 'Zerstörung, der Konstruktion zuliebe?' Marburg 1987, p. 108
48 Paul Klee. Beiträge zur bildnerischen Formlehre. Facsimile of original manuscript. Jürgen Glaesemer (ed.) Basle 1979, p. 150
49 O.K.Werckmeister: Versuche über Paul Klee. Frankfurt 1981, p. 155
50 Gerhard Marcks, letter to Gerhard Fromme of 12.3.1919. In: Gerhard Marcks 1889–1981. Briefe und Werke. Munich 1988, p. 34
51 Minutes of a meeting of the Council of Masters of 20.9.1920. Quoted from: Klaus Weber: Die keramische Werkstatt. In: Experiment Bauhaus. Das Bauhaus-Archiv, Berlin (West) zu Gast im Bauhaus Dessau. Bauhaus-Archiv exhibition catalogue, Berlin 1988, p. 58
52 Gerhard Marcks on the Bauhaus pottery. In: Gerhard Marcks 1988 (note 50), p. 37
53 Gropius, letter to Marcks of 5.4.1923. Quoted from: Weber 1988 (note 51), p. 58
54 Gerhard Marcks to the State Bauhaus, 2.1.1924. In: Hüter 1982 (note 29), p. 219
55 Weber 1988 (note 51), p. 59
56 László Moholy-Nagy: Das Bauhaus in Dessau. In: Qualität. 4.1925. No. 5–6, p. 85
57 Stölzl 1968 (note 23), p. 746
58 Ibid.
59 W.Wagenfeld: Zu den Arbeiten der Metallwerkstatt. In: Junge Menschen. 5.1924. No. 8, p. 187
60 Marcel Breuer: Die Möbelabteilung des Staatlichen Bauhauses in Weimar. In: Fachblatt für Holzarbeiter. 20.1925, p. 18
61 Wolfgang Pfleiderer: Introduction. In: Die Form ohne Ornament. Werkbund Exhibition. Berlin 1924
62 Oskar Schlemmer, letter to the Bauhaus Council of Masters of 22.11.1922. In: Wingler 1975 (note 7), p. 72
63 Alma Buscher: Kind Märchen Spiel Spielzeug. In: Junge Menschen. 5.1924. No. 8, Special Weimar Bauhaus issue, p. 189
64 Hans M. Wingler: Die Mappenwerke 'Neue europäische Graphik.' Mainz and Berlin 1965, p. 10f.
65 Statutes of the Weimar State Bauhaus, Appendix 3, Verlag Bühne. July 1922
66 Lothar Schreyer: Kreuzigung. 1920. No. 158, sheet II. Quoted from: Dirk Scheper: Oskar Schlemmer – Das triadische Ballett und die Bauhausbühne. Schriftenreihe der Akademie der Künste vol. 20. Berlin 1989, p. 67
67 Lothar Schreyer: Das Bühnenkunstwerk. 1918. No. 345, p. 93. Quoted from: Scheper 1989 (note 66), p. 66
68 Karin von Maur: Oskar Schlemmer. Munich 1982, p. 198
69 Kurt Schmidt: Das mechanische Ballett – eine Bauhaus-Arbeit. In: Bauhaus und Bauhäusler 1971 (note 8), p. 56

70 Hans Heinz Stuckenschmidt: Musik am Bauhaus. Berlin 1978/79, p. 6f.
71 Eric Michaud: Das abstrakte Theater der zwanziger Jahre: Von der Tragik erlöste Figuren. In: Die Maler und das Theater im 20. Jahrhundert. Schirn Kunsthalle exh. cat. Frankfurt 1986, p. 104
72 Bühnenarbeit am Bauhaus. In: Junge Menschen, 1924 (note 59), p. 189
73 Sigfried Giedion: Bauhaus und Bauhaus-Woche zu Weimar. In: Pressestimmen für das Staatliche Bauhaus Weimar. Weimar 1924, p. 43
74 Volker Wahl: Jena und das Bauhaus. In: Wissenschaftliche Zeitschrift der Hochschule für Architektur und Bauwesen. Weimar. 26.1979. No. 4–5, p. 344
75 Nerdinger 1985 (note 3), p. 54
76 Walter Gropius, letter to Lange of 22.6.1922. In: Humblet 1980 (note 44), p. 320f.
77 Fréd Forbát: Erinnerungen eines Architekten aus vier Ländern. Quoted from: Nerdinger 1985 (note 3), p. 58 and Forbát p. 66
78 Nerdinger 1985 (note 3), p. 60
79 Scheidig 1972 (note 24), p. 258
80 Max Greil: Die Erdrosselung des Bauhauses. In: Das Volk. 3.1.1925
81 Walter Gropius: Report on the economic prospects of the Bauhaus. 19.10.1924. Manuscript. Bauhaus Archiv
82 Moholy-Nagy 1925 (note 56), p. 84
83 Ibid.
84 Nerdinger 1985 (note 3), p. 74
85 Ibid.
86 Nelly Schwalacher: Das neue Bauhaus. In: Evening edition of the Frankfurter Zeitung. 31.10.1927
87 Ibid.
88 Nerdinger 1985 (note 3), p. 76
89 Nina Kandinsky: Kandinsky und ich. Bergisch Gladbach 1978, p. 121
90 Fannina W. Halle: Dessau: Burgkuhnauer Allee 6–7. In: Das Kunstblatt. 13.1929. No. 7, p. 203
91 Max Osborn: Das neue 'Bauhaus'. In: Vossische Zeitung. 4.12.1926. In: Wingler 1975 (note 7), p. 134
92 Walter Gropius: Bauhaus-Produktion. In: Qualität. 7.1925. No. 7–8, p. 127
93 Hannes Beckmann: Die Gründerjahre. In: Bauhaus und Bauhäusler 1971 (note 8), p. 159f.
94 Paul Klee to Felix Klee, of 11.9.1929. In: Paul Klee Briefe 1979 (note 14), pp. 1079f., 1050, 1102, 1098
95 Max Gebhard: Arbeit in der Reklamewerkstatt. In: form + zweck. 11.1979. No. 3, p. 73
96 Ute Brüning: Die Druck- und Reklamewerkstatt: Von Typographie zur Werbung. In: Experiment Bauhaus 1988 (note 51), p. 154
97 Oskar Schlemmer: Die Bühnenwerkstatt des Staatlichen Bauhauses in Weimar. 1.4.1925. In: Wingler 1975 (note 7), p. 73
98 Dirk Scheper: Die Bauhausbühne. In: Experiment Bauhaus 1988 (note 51), p. 256
99 Karin von Maur: In: Oskar Schlemmer. Staatsgalerie Stuttgart exh. cat. 1977, p. 200
100 Georg Muche: bildende kunst und industrieform. In: Bauhaus. 1.1926. No. 1, p. 6
101 Ise Gropius' diary, entry of 3.2.1927. Bauhaus-Archiv
102 Fritz Hesse: Von der Residenz zur Bauhausstadt. Bad Pyrmont, undated (1963), p. 227
103 Ise Gropius' diary, entry of 1.2.1927. Bauhaus-Archiv
104 Hannes Meyer, letter to Walter Gropius of 3.1.1927. Following quotation: letter of 16.2.1927. In: Hannes Meyer. Bauen und Gesellschaft. Lena Meyer-Bergner (ed.). Dresden 1980, pp. 42, 44
105 Meyer, letter to Behne of 24.12.1927. In: Bauwelt. 68.1977. No. 33, p. 1096
106 Hannes Meyer, letter to Adolf Behne of 12.1.1928. In: Magdalena Droste: Unterrichtsstruktur und Werkstattarbeit am Bauhaus unter Hannes Meyer. In: Hannes Meyer 1889–1954. Architekt Urbanist Lehrer. Bauhaus-Archiv and Deutsches Architekturmuseum exh. cat. Berlin 1989, p. 134
107 Anhalter Rundschau. 23.11.1928. Quoted from: Droste 1989 (note 106), p. 135
108 Anhalter Anzeiger. 26.5.1929. Quoted from: Droste 1989 (note 106), p.136. The following quotation ibid., p. 136f.
109 Josef Albers, letter to Otti Berger of 26.3.1930. Quoted from: Droste 1989 (note 106), p. 137
110 Hannes Meyer, letter to the CA architecture group of 2.9.1930. Quoted from: Droste 1989 (note 106), p. 137
111 Anhalter Anzeiger. 26.5.1929
112 Franz Ehrlich. die frühen jahre. Galerie am Sachsenplatz exh. cat. Leipzig 1980, p. 8f.
113 Gunta Sharon-Stölzl: die entwicklung der bauhausweberei. In: bauhaus. 1931. No. 2
114 Scheper 1989 (note 66), p. 177
115 Ibid., p. 215
116 Ibid., p. 179
117 Hannes Meyer: bauen. In: bauhaus 2.1928. No. 4, p. 12f.
118 Hannes Meyer: Vorträge in Wien und Basel 1929. In: Hannes Meyer 1980 (note 104), p. 60
119 Winfried Nerdinger: 'Anstößiges Rot'. Hannes Meyer und der linke Baufunktionalismus – ein verdrängtes Kapitel Architekturgeschichte. In: Hannes Meyer 1989 (note 106), p. 21. The preceding quotation ibid.
120 Die Laubenganghäuser bezugsfertig. In: Volksblatt. 25.7.1930. Quoted from: Klaus-Jürgen Winkler: Der Architekt Hannes Meyer. Anschauungen und Werk. Berlin 1989, p. 91
121 Hannes Meyer, letter to Edwin Redslob of 11.8.1930. Quoted from: Droste 1989 (note 106), p. 160
122 Katja and Hajo Rose: Manuscript of 1932 for the Weltbühne (in which unpublished). Quoted from: Droste 1989 (note 106), p. 161
123 Court of arbitration minutes of 12.8.1930. Quoted from: Droste 1989 (note 106), p. 162
124 Hannes Meyer, letter to Edwin Redslob of 11.8.1930. Quoted from: Droste 1989 (note 106), p. 162
125 Hannes Meyer, letter to Edwin Redslob of 15.8.1930. Quoted from: Droste 1989 (note 106), p. 163
126 Hesse 1963 (note 102), p. 247
127 Nochmals der Fall Bauhaus. In: Stein Holz Eisen. 44.1930. No. 19 of 6.10.1930, p. 417
128 Ibid. The following quotation ibid., p. 418
129 Bauhaus diary, entries for 30.11.1931 and 11.1.1932. In: bauhaus berlin. Peter Hahn (ed.). Weingarten 1985, pp. 33, 35
130 Ludwig Grote, letter to Hans Prinzhorn of 23.5.1932. Archiv für Bildende Kunst im Germanischen Nationalmuseum Nürnberg. Grote estate, sheet 213
131 Politik am Bauhaus. In: bauhaus 11 (1932). In: bauhaus berlin 1985 (note 129), p. 48
132 Hans Kessler, letter to his mother of 12.11.1932. In: bauhaus berlin 1985 (note 129), p. 168
133 Wingler 1975 (note 7), p. 508
134 Experiment Bauhaus 1988 (note 51), p. 340
135 Helene Nonne-Schmidt: Reklame-Unterricht 1930–1932. In: Joost Schmidt. Lehre und Arbeit am Bauhaus 1919–32. Düsseldorf 1984, p. 96
136 Walter Peterhans: über fotografie. In: junge menschen kommt ans bauhaus (brochure). Dessau 1929
137 Eröffung der umgestalteten Weimarer Lehranstalten. In: Deutschland (Weimar). 10.11.1930
138 Hesse 1963 (note 102), p. 251
139 Ludwig Grote, letter to Hans Prinzhorn of 23.5.1932. Archiv Nürnberg (note 130)
140 Wähler und Wählerinnen Dessaus! 1932 election handbill from the Dessau branch of the National Socialist German Workers' Party. In: bauhaus berlin 1985 (note 129), p. 41
141 Peter Hahn: Die Schließung des Bauhauses 1933 und seine amerikanischen Nachfolgeinstitutionen. In: 100 Jahre Walter Gropius. Schließung des Bauhauses 1933. Berlin 1983, p. 66
142 Grote, letter to Prinzhorn 1932 (note 139)
143 Hans Prinzhorn: Vertrauenskundgebung für Mies van der Rohe. Archiv Nürnberg (note 130). Grote estate, sheet 242
144 See correspondence between Ludwig Grote and Hugo Bruckmann from August to December 1932. Archiv Nürnberg (note 130), Grote estate, sheet 213
145 Ludwig Grote, letter to W.A. Fahrenholtz of 16.8.1932. Archiv Nürnberg, Grote estate, sheet 213
146 W.A. Fahrenholtz, letter to Hoffmann of 18.8.1932. Archiv Nürnberg (note 130), Grote estate, sheet 213
147 Ludwig Grote, letter to Hugo Bruckmann of 3.8.1932. Archiv Nürnberg (note 130), Grote estate, sheet 213
148 Ibid.
149 rb: Das Steglizter 'Bauhaus'. In: Steglitzer Anzeiger. October 1932. In: bauhaus berlin 1985 (note 129), p. 93
150 Adalbert Behr: Ludwig Mies van der Rohe und das Jahr 1933. In: Wissenschaftliche Zeitschrift der Hochschule für Architektur und Bauwesen. Weimar. 33.1987. No. 4–6, p. 279f.
151 Ibid., p. 280
152 Ibid.

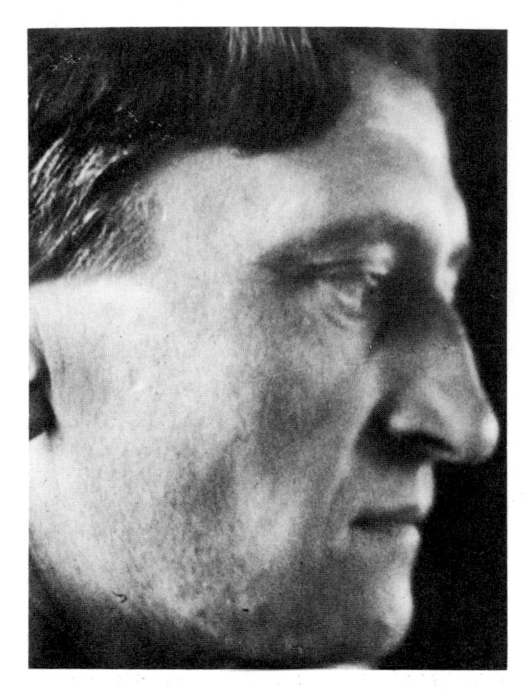

Josef Albers, early thirties

Alfred Arndt, 1929

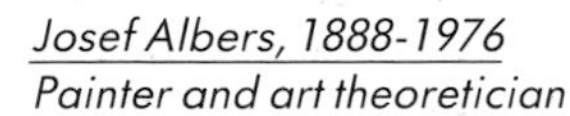

<u>Josef Albers, 1888-1976</u>
Painter and art theoretician
Born 1888 in Bottrop. Trained as an elementary-school teacher from 1905 to 1908 and then taught for eight years. Studied at the Royal Academy of Art in Berlin from 1913 to 1915, graduating as an art teacher. In 1916, began studying at the Essen Arts and Crafts School; part-time teaching. Studied under Franz von Stuck at the Munich Academy, 1919-20. Student at the Bauhaus from 1920 to October 1923; attended Itten's 'Vorkurs', then set up stained-glass workshop. Promoted to journeyman in 1922. Teacher at the Bauhaus from October 1923 to April 1933. His classes on the study of materials for first-semester students were the most important part of the preliminary course, of which he became official head in 1928. Head of the joinery workshop from May 1928 to April 1929. From October 1930, taught representational drawing to senior-semester students. During this period, produced glass montages, glass pictures and designs for typography, furniture and utensils of glass and metal. Emigrated to the United States in 1933, where he taught part of the foundation course at the avant-garde Black Mountain College in Chicago. Director of the Department of Design at Yale University, New Haven/Connecticut from 1950 to 1959, followed by numerous guest professorships at American and European academies, including the Institute of Design in Ulm. Died 1976 in New Haven/Connecticut. At the Bauhaus, Albers examined problems of design and materials and their appearance and representation in his preliminary course; from the forties onwards, however, he devoted his teaching and painting exclusively to the optical effects of colour. He thereby inspired the American avant-garde of the sixties and seventies and was a forerunner of op art. The series 'Homage to the Square', on which he worked from 1950 onwards, represents the summit of his artistic achievement.

<u>Literature:</u> Josef Albers: Interaction of Color. New Haven 1963
Eugen Gomringer: Josef Albers. German ed. Starnberg 1971
Josef Albers: Eine Retrospektive. Staatliche Kunsthalle Baden-Baden und Bauhaus-Archiv exhibition catalogue. Cologne 1988

<u>Alfred Arndt, 1898-1976</u>
Architect
Born 1898 in Elbing/West Prussia. Draftsman's apprenticeship in an architectural and design office in Elbing. 1919-20, handicrafts course at the Elbing School of Trades, then to the Academy in Königsberg. Student at the Bauhaus from October 1921 until 1926; attended Itten's 'Vorkurs' and courses by Kandinsky, Klee and Schlemmer. Trained in the mural-painting workshop. Journeyman's examination. Then free-lance architect in Probstzella; 'House of the People' and other buildings. Master at the Bauhaus from 1929 to September 1932: head of the workshop for interior design (mural-painting, metal and furniture workshops) until 1931, then taught interior design, design drawing and perspective. In 1933, moved to Probstzella; commercial art work. As from 1935, free-lance work for AEG, publication of technical information materials. From 1936, designs for industrial buildings in Thuringia. From 1945 to 1948, head of the City of Jena building and planning department. In 1948, moved to the West. Free-lance work as architect and painter in Darmstadt. Died 1976 in Darmstadt.

<u>Literature:</u> Alfred Arndt. Maler und Architekt. Bauhaus-Archiv exhibition catalogue. Darmstadt 1968
Alfred Arndt: wie ich an das bauhaus in weimar kam. In: Bauhaus und Bauhäusler. Bekenntnisse und Erinnerungen. Eckhard Neumann (ed.). Bern and Stuttgart 1971

Herbert Bayer, 1927

Herbert Bayer, 1900-1985
Graphic designer and painter
Born 1900 in Haag/Upper Austria. 1919-20, apprentice in the office of designer Georg Schmidthammer in Linz; first typographical works. In 1921, worked in the studio of designer Emanuel Margold in Darmstadt. Student at the Bauhaus from October 1921 to July 1923 and from October 1924 to February 1925. Studied mural-painting under Oskar Schlemmer and Kandinsky. Journeyman's examination. Teacher and 'Young Master' at the Bauhaus from April 1925 to April 1928; head of the new printing and advertising workshop, later renamed the workshop for typography and advertisement design. Also designed school's own printed materials. From 1928, head of the Berlin office of the Studio Dorland advertising agency. Exhibition design, including the German section of the 1930 'Exposition de la société des artistes décorateurs' in Paris. Painting and photography in spare time. Emigrated to the USA in 1938, and in the same year designed the 'Bauhaus 1919-1928' exhibition and catalogue for the Museum of Modern Art, then worked in New York as a graphic designer. From 1946, designs at the Aspen Cultural Center, Colorado; painting, graphic design, architecture and landscaping work. From 1946 to 1956, artistic consultant to the Container Corporation of America, and after 1966 for the Atlantic Ritchfield Company. In 1968, designed the '50 Jahre Bauhaus' exhibition and catalogue in Stuttgart. Moved to Montecito/California in 1975. Died 1985 in Santa Barbara. Bayer was the Bauhaus' most talented and innovative designer of advertising and exhibitions. His work from the twenties is characterised by his early use of photography. In the USA, he moved towards comprehensive 'environmental design' from the forties onwards.

Literature: Herbert Bayer. Das künstlerische Werk 1918-1938. Bauhaus-Archiv exhibition catalogue. Berlin 1982
Arthur A. Cohen: Herbert Bayer. The complete work. Cambridge/Mass. and London 1984
Herbert Bayer. Kunst und Design in Amerika. Bauhaus-Archiv exhibition catalogue. Berlin 1986

Marianne Brandt, 1893-1983
Metal designer
Born Marianne Liebe in Chemnitz in 1893. Studied painting and sculpture from 1911 to 1917 at the Grand-Ducal Saxon Academy of Fine Art in Weimar. Student at the Bauhaus from January 1924 to July 1926. Preliminary course under Albers and Moholy-Nagy and courses by Klee and Kandinsky. Studied in the metal workshop, articles of apprenticeship as silversmith. Assistant in the Bauhaus metal workshop as from April 1927 and its acting head from April 1928 to September 1929. In 1929, employed in Gropius' architecture office in Berlin. Furniture and interiors, in particular for the Karlsruhe Dammerstock estate. From 1930 to 1933, employed at the Ruppel metal goods factory in Gotha, where she revised the entire design programme. Unemployed in 1933; return to Chemnitz. Private painting and weaving. From 1949 to 1951, lecturer at the Dresden Academy of Fine Art in the wood, metal and ceramics department. At the Academy of Applied Art in Berlin Weissensee under Mart Stam from 1951 to 1954; work as designer and consultant to industry at the Institute of Applied Art. Re-devoted herself to private work in Chemnitz as from 1954. Died 1983 in Kirchberg/Saxony. Marianne Brandt was one of the most talented members of the Bauhaus metal workshop. Her early, individual pieces, including teapots and silver services, are outstanding examples of design inspired by elementary geometric forms. Even after the school turned to industrial design, her works – above all her lamps – remained among the best of the Bauhaus products.

Literature: Marianne Brandt. Hajo Rose. Kurt

Marianne Brandt, around 1926

Marcel Breuer, around 1928

Lyonel Feininger, 1928

Schmidt. Drei Künstler aus dem Bauhaus. Exhibition catalogue from the Printroom, Staatliche Kunstsammlungen Dresden. Dresden 1978
Ommagio a Marianne Brandt. In: forme. 1985. No.110

Marcel Breuer, 1902-1981
Architect
Born 1902 in Pécs/Hungary. Student at the Bauhaus from 1920 to 1924; trained in the joinery workshop. Journeyman's examination in 1924. Stay in Paris. Master at the Bauhaus from April 1925 to April 1928: head of the furniture workshop. Numerous furniture designs; produced his first tubular steel chair in 1925. Interiors, including the Dessau Bauhaus buildings in 1925/26 and Piscator's flat in Berlin in 1927. Self-employed in Berlin from 1928; furniture, interiors and exhibition design. First building – 'Haus Harnischmacher' – completed in 1932. Architect in London from 1935 to 1937. Collaboration with F.R.S. Yorke. From 1937, Professor of Architecture at Harvard University, Cambridge/Mass., USA. Joint architecture practice with Gropius from 1938 to 1941. Moved his office to New York in 1946. In 1947, built his own house in New Canaan/Connecticut. Many other buildings followed, including the Whitney Museum in New York; participated on the UNESCO building in Paris. In 1956, founded 'Marcel Breuer and Associates' office in New York. Died 1981 in New York. The tubular steel furniture and furnishings which Breuer developed from 1925 onwards were instrumental in shaping a new, modern concept of living. He went on to become one of the 20th century's most important designers of furniture and interiors.

Literature: Marcel Breuer 1921-1962. Introduction: Cranston Jones. Stuttgart 1962
Christopher Wilk: Marcel Breuer. Furniture and Interiors. The Museum of Modern Art exhibition catalogue. New York 1981

Lyonel Feininger, 1871-1956
Painter
Born 1871 in New York to parents of German extraction. Travelled to Hamburg in 1887 to commence studies at the School of Arts and Crafts. Pupil at the Berlin Academy of Art the following year; produced drawings for publishers and newspapers in his spare time. Study trip to Paris in 1892. Finished studies at the Berlin Academy in 1894. His cartoons appeared regularly as from 1896 in magazines such as 'Ulk' and 'Das Narrenschiff'. Earliest lithographs and etchings in 1906. Comic strip series for the Chicago Sunday Tribune. Took up painting in 1907. Lived in Paris and London in 1907-08. In 1913, exhibited five pictures at the 'First German Autumn Salon' in Berlin. In 1917, first one-man show at the Berlin gallery 'Der Sturm'. Master at the Bauhaus from May 1919 to April 1925; head of the graphic printing workshop from the end of 1920. Following the Bauhaus' move to Dessau, and at his own request, he remained a Master without teaching commitments from 1925 to September 1932. Regular summer holidays in Deep/Pomerania on the Baltic Sea between 1924 and 1935. In 1931, exhibition at the Berlin National Gallery in honour of his 60th birthday. In 1933, moved from Dessau to Berlin where he remained until 1936. Left Germany in 1937 and settled in New York. In 1944, retrospective at the Museum of Modern Art, New York. Elected president of the Federation of American Painters and Sculptors in 1947. Died 1956 in New York. Feininger was acknowledged as an important Expressionist painter even during the twenties. His direct artistic influence on the Bauhaus was limited, however, since – unlike Klee and Kandinsky – he neither gave regular courses nor developed a systematic artistic theory.

Literature: Hans Hess: Lyonel Feininger. Stuttgart 1959
Leona E. Prasse: Lyonel Feininger. Karikaturen Comic strips Illustrationen. Museum für Kunst

Walter Gropius, around 1928

und Gewerbe exhibition catalogue. Hamburg 1981
Lyonel Feininger. Gemälde Aquarelle und Zeichnungen Druckgraphik. Kunsthalle zu Kiel exhibition catalogue. Kiel 1982

Walter Gropius, 1883-1969
Architect
Born 1883 in Berlin. Studied architecture in Munich in 1903 and in Berlin from 1905 to 1907. Worked in Peter Behrens' office from 1908 to 1910, then opened his own architecture practice in Berlin. From then until 1925, the majority of his designs were produced jointly with his colleague Adolf Meyer. Fagus factory in Alfeld begun in 1911. Head of the Berlin 'Arbeitsrat für Kunst' in 1919. Appointed head of the art academy in Weimar; on 1.4.1919, took up office at what then became the 'Staatliches Bauhaus in Weimar'. Director of the Bauhaus until April 1928; from March 1921 to April 1925, Master of Form in the joinery workshop. Designed the new Bauhaus buildings in 1925/26, following the move to Dessau. Designed a 'Total Theatre' for Erwin Piscator in 1927. Housing estates commenced in Törten/Dessau in 1926 and Dammerstock/Karlsruhe in 1930. Architect in Berlin from 1928; frequent lectures on aspects of 'New Building' and the Bauhaus. From 1934 to 1937, shared an office in London with Maxwell Fry. In 1937, appointed to the Graduate School of Design in Harvard/USA; made head of the architecture department in 1938. In the same year, organized the 'Bauhaus 1919-1928' exhibition in New York and built his own house in Lincoln/Mass. From 1938 to 1941, shared an architecture practice with Marcel Breuer. In 1946, founded 'The Architects Collaborative' in Cambridge/Mass. In 1964/65, designed a Bauhaus Archiv for Darmstadt which was eventually built in Berlin in 1976-79. Died 1969 in Boston. Gropius remains one of the greatest architects of modern times. His Fagus factory and Bauhaus buildings are key works of an age. Even after his departure, Gropius remained the inspiration and authority behind the Bauhaus. He continued to champion the Bauhaus philosophy even after the school's final closure.

Literature: Reginald R.Isaacs: Walter Gropius. Der Mensch und sein Werk. Vol.1. Berlin 1983. Vol.2. Berlin 1984
Winfried Nerdinger: Walter Gropius. Bauhaus-Archiv exhibition catalogue. Berlin 1985

Gertrud Grunow, 1870-1944
Music teacher
Born 1870 in Berlin. Trained as a musician under Bülow, Scharwenka and Lamperti. Interested in the elementary relationships between sound, colour and movement even before 1914. First lectures in Berlin in 1919. Taught 'Harmonization theory' at the Bauhaus from 1919 to 1923. Continued teaching in Hamburg from 1926 to 1934. In the following years she spent several months at a time in England and Switzerland. Returned to Germany during the War. Died 1944 in Leverkusen.

Literature: Gertrud Grunow: Der Aufbau der lebendigen Form durch Farbe, Form, Ton. In: Staatliches Bauhaus Weimar 1919-1923. Staatliches Bauhaus in Weimar und Karl Nierendorf (eds). Weimar and Munich 1923
Hildegard Nebel-Heitmeyer: Die Grunow-Lehre. Eine Erziehung der Sinne durch Ton und Farbe. In: Bildnerische Erziehung. 1967. No.1

Ludwig Hilberseimer, 1885-1967
Architect and town planner
Born 1885 in Karlsruhe. From 1906 to 1911, studied architecture in Karlsruhe under Friedrich Ostendorf and others. Then moved to Berlin and worked as an architect. Intense spell as art critic from 1919: cultural reports from Berlin in magazines such as 'Das Kunstblatt' and 'Sozialistische Monatshefte'. Resumed architecture and town

Gertrud Grunow, 1917

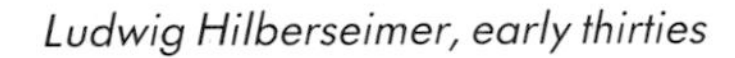

Ludwig Hilberseimer, early thirties

Johannes Itten, around 1921

planning in 1922. Executed several residential buildings and one office building in Berlin, as well as a residential building for the 1927 Stuttgart exhibition 'Die Wohnung' ('The Apartment') (Weissenhof estate). At the same time, publications on modern architecture and town planning, including 'Metropolitan architecture' (1927) and 'Concrete as designer' (1928). At the Bauhaus from spring 1929 to April 1933. First, head of architectural theory and classes in constructional design; later taught the 'Seminar for Apartment and Town Planning'. In 1933, compulsory restriction of his journalistic activities. Work as architect in Berlin. In 1938, emigrated to Chicago/Illinois where he worked under Ludwig Mies van der Rohe as Professor of City and Regional Planning at the Illinois Institute of Technology. Made director of the Department of City and Regional Planning in 1955. Died 1967 in Chicago. Hilberseimer published important essays on modern architecture very early on. In his town-planning work, often criticized as systemized, he was above all a theoretician. He took contemporary, practically-oriented ideas and generalized them into the principles of a very abstract, general theory of town planning.

Literature: Ludwig Hilberseimer 1885-1967. Special issue of the magazine Rassegna. 8.1986. No.27
Der vorbildliche Architekt. Mies van der Rohes Architekturunterricht 1930-1958 am Bauhaus und in Chicago. Bauhaus-Archiv exhibition catalogue. Berlin 1986

Johannes Itten, 1888-1967
Painter and art theoretician
Born 1888 in Süderen-Linden/Switzerland. Teacher training near Bern from 1904 to 1908, then short period as elementary-school teacher. Between 1910 and 1912, studied mathematics and natural sciences in Bern. In 1913, trained under Adolf Hoelzel at the Stuttgart Academy. First one-man show in the Berlin gallery 'Der Sturm' in 1916. Moved to Vienna in the same year and opened an art school. Increasing interest in Eastern philosophies of life. A number of pupils followed him from Vienna to the Bauhaus, where he was a Master from October 1919 to March 1923. As from October 1920 he taught, in the winter semester, his own 'Vorkurs' (preliminary course) plus some form theory classes. He initially shared the running of several workshops with Georg Muche. After 1921 he retained only the metal, mural-painting and stained-glass workshops. From 1920, adopted Eastern Mazdaznan beliefs which he spread at the Bauhaus. In 1923, went to a Mazdaznan centre in Switzerland. Founded a private 'Modern Art School' in Berlin in 1926, called the 'Itten School' after 1929, which survived until 1934. Director of a textiles college in Krefeld from 1932 to 1938. Then director of the Zürich Arts and Crafts Museum and School until 1953. Built up the Rietberg Museum for Non-European Art in Zürich as from 1950, which he then ran from 1952 to 1956. Subsequent revision and publication of theories of art teaching. Died 1967 in Zürich. Itten was the dominant figure at the early Bauhaus and his influence characterized its first phase. The 'Vorkurs' which he developed was fundamental to the school's teaching philosophy. Later continued in modified form, the preliminary course remained a vital element of artist education.

Literature: Johannes Itten. Werke und Schriften. Willy Rotzler (ed.), 2nd rev. ed. Zürich 1978
Johannes Itten: Gemälde Gouachen Aquarelle Tuschen Zeichnungen. Westfälisches Landesmuseum für Kunst und Kulturgeschichte exhibition catalogue. Münster 1980
Johannes Itten. Künstler und Lehrer. Kunstmuseum Bern exhibition catalogue. Bern 1984

Wassily Kandinsky, 1925

Wassily Kandinsky, 1866-1944
Painter
Born 1866 in Moscow. Studied law and economics in Moscow from 1886 to 1892 and then became an assistant at Moscow University. In 1896, moved to Munich, where he studied painting at the Azbè School of Art. Rejected by the Munich Academy in 1898, continued freelance. Studied at the Academy under Franz von Stuck in 1900; subsequently based in Munich as a painter. Lived in Paris in 1906-07, then in Berlin until 1908. Produced his first abstract compositions in 1910. In 1911, Kandinsky published 'Concerning the Spiritual in Art'. Took part in numerous exhibitions in Germany, Paris and Russia during this period. Returned to Russia in 1914; cultural-political work in various institutions after 1918. Moved back to Berlin at the end of 1921. Master at the Bauhaus from June 1922 to April 1933; head of the mural-painting workshop until October 1925; then gave courses in 'Analytical Drawing' and 'Abstract Form Elements' for first-semester students. Free painting classes as from April 1927. Moved to Neuilly-sur-Seine/Paris in 1933. Died in Neuilly in 1944. Kandinsky's philosophy of synthesis in all fields helped shape the Bauhaus programme. His theories of colour and form influenced design in the years around 1923. The painting class he gave as from 1927 was one of the main attractions of the later Bauhaus.

Literature: Clark V. Poling: Kandinsky-Unterricht am Bauhaus. Weingarten 1982
Kandinsky und München. Begegnungen und Wandlungen 1896-1914. Städtische Galerie im Lenbachhaus exhibition catalogue. Munich 1982
Kandinsky. Russische Zeit und Bauhausjahre 1915-1933. Bauhaus-Archiv exhibition catalogue. Berlin 1984
Kandinsky in Paris 1934-1944. Solomon R.Guggenheim Museum exhibition catalogue. New York 1985

Paul Klee, 1879-1940
Painter
Born 1879 in Münchenbuchsee, near Bern. Started an art course in Munich in 1898. At the Munich Academy under Franz von Stuck from 1900 to 1901. Returned to Bern in 1901, and then to Munich in 1906. First one-man show in Bern in 1910. Took part in the second 'Blauer Reiter' exhibition in Munich in 1912. Trip to Tunis with August Macke and Louis Moilliet in 1914. Active service from 1916 to 1918. Master at the Bauhaus from January 1921 to March 1931; head of the stained-glass workshop from October 1922 to 1924. Taught 'Elementary design of the plane' for second-semester students from October 1923, plus some life classes. Free painting classes as from April 1927, and design theory for the weaving workshop after October 1927. Professor at the Düsseldorf Academy of Art from 1931 until his dismissal by the Nazis in 1933. Emigrated to Bern in 1933. Died in Locarno-Muralto in 1940. At the Bauhaus, Klee was both a highly-respected artist and a dominant personality. His design teaching had a direct influence in particular on the formal language of the weaving workshop.

Literature: Jürgen Glaesemer: Paul Klee. Catalogues of the Berner Kunstmuseum collection. Vols. 1-4. Berlin 1973-1984
Paul Klee als Zeichner 1921-1933. Bauhaus-Archiv exhibition catalogue. Berlin 1985
Paul Klee. Leben und Werk. Kunstmuseum Bern exhibition catalogue. Bern 1987

Gerhard Marcks, 1889-1981
Sculptor
Born 1889 in Berlin. First sculptural works in 1907. Workshop co-operative with sculptor Richard Scheibe from 1908 to 1912. In 1914, reliefs for the factory designed by Gropius for the Cologne Werkbund exhibition. Active service in 1914. Master at the Bauhaus from October 1919

Paul Klee, 1927

Gerhard Marcks, around 1924

Hannes Meyer, second half of the twenties

to March 1925; head of the Bauhaus pottery in Dornburg, near Weimar, from October 1920. In 1925, appointed teacher of ceramics at the School of Arts and Crafts in Burg Giebichenstein/Halle; director of the School from 1930 until his dismissal in 1933. Lived in Berlin from 1936; participated in some exhibitions but was also prohibited from others and had sculptures seized. In 1945, accepted appointment at the Regional School of Art in Hamburg. Moved to Cologne in 1950. Numerous exhibitions after the War. In particular in the forties and fifties, worked on memorials and figure sculptures for churches. Died 1981 in Burgbrohl/Eifel.

Literature: Gerhard Marcks. Das plastische Werk. Günter Busch (ed.). Frankfurt, Berlin and Vienna 1977
Gerhard Marcks 1889-1981. Briefe und Werke. Archiv für Bildende Kunst im Germanischen Nationalmuseum Nürnberg (ed.). Munich 1988
Keramik und Bauhaus. Bauhaus-Archiv exhibition catalogue. Berlin 1989

Hannes Meyer, 1889-1954
Architect and town planner
Born 1889 in Basle. Mason's training in 1905, then work in a construction company and study at the Basle School of Arts and Crafts. Worked in Albert Froehlich's architecture practice from 1909 to 1912, then with Emil Schaudt in Berlin. Study trip to England in 1912-13. In 1916, senior clerk in Georg Metzendorf's Munich studio, then department head of the Krupp building administration in Essen until 1918. Architect in Basle from 1919; built the Freidorf estate near Basle from 1919 to 1924. Lived in Belgium in 1924. In 1926, architecture practice with Hans Wittwer; joint designs for the Basle Petersschule (1926) and the Geneva League of Nations building (1926/27). Master of architecture at the Bauhaus from April 1927 to March 1928, then Bauhaus director and head of the building department until July 1930. Appointed Hans Wittwer to the Bauhaus (1928/29). Together with Wittwer and the school's building department, Meyer produced his most important work: the German Trades Union school in Bernau, near Berlin (1928-1930). Following his politically-motivated dismissal, appointed professor at the WASI architectural college in Moscow. Head of the Housing Cabinet at the Academy of Architecture from 1934. In Switzerland again from 1936 to 1939. Built Mümliswil children's home. Worked as an architect and town planner in various institutions in Mexico from 1939 to 1949, and finally as publishing house director. Returned to Switzerland in 1949. Died 1954 in Crocifisso di Savosa/Lugano. Despite producing only a few works, Meyer was one of the most important Functionalists in the architecture of the twenties.

Literature: Hannes Meyer. Bauen und Gesellschaft. Schriften Briefe Projekte. Lena Meyer-Bergner (ed.). Dresden 1980
Klaus-Jürgen Winkler: Der Architekt Hannes Meyer. Anschauungen und Werk. Berlin 1989
Hannes Meyer. Architekt Urbanist Lehrer. Bauhaus-Archiv and Deutsches Architekturmuseum exhibition catalogue. Berlin 1989

Ludwig Mies van der Rohe, 1886-1969
Architect
Born 1886 in Aachen. Four years as stucco and ornament draughtsman in Aachen workshops and offices. Worked under Bruno Paul from 1904 to 1907, at the same time studying at the School of Arts and Crafts. Worked in Peter Behrens' office from 1908 to 1911, then as self-employed architect in Berlin. Between 1921 and 1924, produced four pioneering ideal designs for skyscrapers, villas and office buildings. Built villas and designed exhibition architecture in the twenties. In 1927, organized the Stuttgart Werkbund exhibition 'Die Wohnung' (Weissenhof estate) and built an apartment house. In 1929, built the

Ludwig Mies van der Rohe, 1932

German Pavilion at the Barcelona World Exhibition. Director of the Bauhaus from August 1930 until its final closure in July 1933; taught architecture to senior students. Then architect in Berlin, plus teaching in spare time. Emigrated to Chicago in 1937; from 1938 to 1958, director of the architecture department at the Armour Institute, the later Illinois Institute of Technology. Also ran his own office in Chicago. Numerous influential buildings, above all in Chicago and New York, including the Farnsworth house (Plano/Illinois, 1946-1951), the two high-rise apartment buildings at 860-880 Lake Shore Drive (Chicago, 1948-1951), the Seagram Building (New York, 1956-1959) and the New National Gallery (Berlin, 1962-1967). Died 1969 in Chicago.

Literature: bauhaus berlin. Auflösung Dessau 1932. Schließung Berlin 1933. Bauhäusler und Drittes Reich. Weingarten 1985
Der vorbildliche Architekt. Mies van der Rohes Architekturunterricht 1930-1958 am Bauhaus und in Chicago. Bauhaus-Archiv exhibition catalogue. Berlin 1986
Fritz Neumeyer: Mies van der Rohe. Das kunstlose Wort. Berlin 1986
Franz Schulze: Mies van der Rohe. Leben und Werk. German ed. Berlin 1986

László Moholy-Nagy, 1895-1946
Visual designer
Born 1895 in Bárcbasód/Hungary. Started law studies in Budapest in 1913. Active service from 1914 to 1917; began painting and drawing. Abandoned studies in 1918; continued painting and established contact with the avant-garde group 'MA'. Moved to Vienna in 1919 and to Berlin in 1920. First one-man show in the Berlin gallery 'Der Sturm' in 1922. At the Bauhaus from April 1923 to May 1928. Master of Form of the metal workshop. As head of the preliminary course, taught 'materials and space' class to second-semester students from October 1923. Painting, typography and photography work. Edited the 'Bauhausbücher' and published his own writings on design theory – 'Painting Photography Film' (1925) and 'From material to architecture' (1929). Ran a graphic design studio in Berlin from 1928 to 1934; also designed sets for the Kroll Opera and Piscator theatre and exhibitions in Berlin, Brussels and Paris. Worked on experimental films from 1926; completed his 'Light-Space Modulator', the first ever kinetic sculpture, in 1930. Emigrated to Amsterdam in 1934, and to London in 1935, where he worked as a graphic designer. In 1937, founded the 'new bauhaus' in Chicago. After its closure the following year, founded the School of Design. Development of acrylic sculptures; renewed concentration upon painting from 1944. Died 1946 in Chicago; 'Vision in Motion', his last publication on design theory, appeared in the same year. In his teaching, which emphasized the visual character of each material in the design process, he influenced the development of the Bauhaus as from 1923 towards a modern language of form. In founding the 'new bauhaus', he sought to perpetuate the Bauhaus philosophy in the USA.

Literature: Andreas Haus: Lázsló Moholy-Nagy. Fotos and Fotogramme. Munich 1978
Krisztina Passuth: Moholy-Nagy. German ed. Weingarten 1986
50 Jahre new bauhaus. Bauhausnachfolge in Chicago. Bauhaus-Archiv exhibition catalogue. Berlin 1987

Georg Muche, 1895-1987
Painter and graphic artist
Born 1895 in Querfurt/Saxony. Studied at the Azbè School of Art in Munich from 1913 to 1914. Moved to Berlin in 1915. Contact with circle around the Expressionist gallery 'Der Sturm'; produced his first abstract pictures during this period. Three exhibitions in the 'Sturm' gallery between 1916 and 1919. Active service from 1917 to 1918. Master at the Bauhaus from April

László Moholy-Nagy, around 1927

Georg Muche, around 1924

Walter Peterhans, 1927

1920 until June 1927; taught the 'Vorkurs' in the summers of 1920 and 1921; from October 1920 to April 1921, shared the running of several workshops with Itten. Subsequently in charge of the weaving workshop. Head of the 1923 Bauhaus exhibition committee; designed the experimental Haus am Horn. Study trip to the USA in 1924. Built a steel house in Dessau in 1926 together with Richard Paulick. Teacher at the art school run by Johannes Itten in Berlin from 1927 to 1930. Professor of Painting at the Breslau Academy from 1931 until his dismissal without notice in 1933. Then teacher at the Reimann school in Berlin under Hugo Häring until 1938. Head of the master class in textile art at the Krefeld Engineering College from 1939 to 1958. Moved to Lake Constance in 1958 and to Lindau in 1960. Worked as painter and graphic artist. Died 1987 in Lindau. At the Bauhaus, Muche – who around 1916 had belonged to the avant-garde centred upon Herwarth Walden's Expressionist gallery 'Der Sturm' – returned in about 1922 to representational painting. His work from this period is inconsistent, however. Muche's artistic influence on the weaving workshop under his charge was relatively small.

Literature: Georg Muche. Der Zeichner. Graphische Sammlung der Staatsgalerie Stuttgart exhibition catalogue. Stuttgart 1977
Georg Muche. Das künstlerische Werk 1919-1927. Bauhaus-Archiv exhibition catalogue. Berlin 1980
Georg Muche. Das malerische Werk 1928-1982. Bauhaus-Archiv exhibition catalogue. Berlin 1983

Walter Peterhans, 1897-1960
Photographer
Born 1897 in Frankfurt as the son of the director of Zeiss-Ikon AG, Dresden. Active service from 1916 to 1918. Studied mathematics, philosophy and art history in Munich and Göttingen from 1920 to 1923. Studied process photography from 1925 to 1926 at the State Academy for Graphic Arts and Printing in Leipzig. Master's diploma as photographer in Weimar in 1926. Own photographic studio in Berlin in 1927; commissions from industry. Took part in the 1928 'Pressa' exhibition in Cologne and the 1929 'Film und Foto' exhibition in Stuttgart. From April 1929 to April 1933, head of the newly-introduced photography department at the Bauhaus. From 1933 until its closure in 1934, teacher at Werner Graeff's photography school. From 1935 to 1937, taught photography at the Reimann school in Berlin under Hugo Häring. Free-lance photographer in Berlin; published a number of specialist books on photographic techniques. Through Mies van der Rohe, obtained a post at the Illinois Institute of Technology in Chicago in 1938, where he taught 'Visual Training', analysis and art history until 1960. Also taught philosophy at the University of Chicago between 1945 and 1947. In 1953, guest lecturer at the Institute of Design in Ulm, where he ran the first foundation course. In 1959/60, guest lecturer at the Hamburg Academy of Fine Art. Died 1960 in Stetten, near Stuttgart.

Literature: Walter Peterhans: Zum gegenwärtigen Stand der Fotographie. In: ReD. 3. 1930. No.5
Ute Eskildsen: Walter Peterhans. In: Contemporary Photographers. London 1982
bauhausfotos. Fotografie am Bauhaus 1919-1933. Bauhaus-Archiv exhibition catalogue. Berlin 1990

Lilly Reich, 1885-1947
Interior designer
Born 1885 in Berlin. After finishing school, trained as decorative embroideress. In 1908, worked for Josef Hoffmann in the Wiener Werkstätte. Returned to Berlin in 1911. Joined the Deutscher Werkbund in 1912, and in 1920 was the first woman to become a member of the

Lilly Reich, spring 1933

Werkbund Board. From 1914 to 1924, own studio for interior design, furnishings and fashion in Berlin. Between 1924 and 1926, studio for exhibition design and fashion in Frankfurt; exhibition designer for the Werkbund committee of the Frankfurt Trade Fair Office. From 1927, apartment and studio in Berlin. In the same year, designed exhibition halls and an apartment for the Stuttgart Werkbund exhibition 'Die Wohnung' (Weissenhof estate). In 1929, worked on the German section of the Barcelona World Exhibition; in 1931, designed the materials display and a one-storey house at the German Building Exhibition in Berlin. Head of the interior design workshop at the Bauhaus from January 1932 to April 1933. Some wartime service. After 1945, studio for architecture, design, textiles and fashion in Berlin. Taught at the Berlin Academy of Fine Art in 1945/46. Died 1947 in Berlin.

Literature: bauhaus berlin. Auflösung Dessau 1932. Schließung Berlin 1933. Bauhäusler und Drittes Reich. Peter Hahn (ed.). Weingarten 1985
Sonja Günther: Lilly Reich 1885-1947. Innenarchitektin Designerin Austellungsgestalterin. Stuttgart 1988

Hinnerk Scheper, 1897-1957
Colour designer, painter and curator of monuments
Born 1897 in Wulften/Osnabrück. Training and journeyman's examination as painter. Attended the Düsseldorf School of Arts and Crafts and Art Academy from 1918 to 1919, and the Bremen School of Arts and Crafts in 1919. Student at the Bauhaus from 1919 to 1922; trained in the mural-painting workshop under Itten and Schlemmer, classes with Klee. Master's diploma as painter from the Weimar Chamber of Handicrafts. From 1922 to 1925, self-employed painter and colour designer; colour schemes and decoration of various buildings, including the Weimar Schlossmuseum. At the Bauhaus from 1925 to 1933: head of the mural-painting workshop. In addition, restoration work and colour schemes for the Essen Folkwang Museum and others. Sabbatical leave from the Bauhaus between 1929 and 1931; offered a post in Moscow to set up the Malyarstroy, an information centre and design office for the use of colour in architecture. Series of photographs and reports on the Soviet Union. Collaboration with the Degephot photographic agency in Berlin from 1932, later also with the Kind and Atlaphot agencies. Free-lance artistic activity after 1934, chiefly in Berlin; colour schemes and restoration work. From 1945, Municipal Curator of Berlin and head of the Department for the Preservation of Monuments. Preservation and restoration of works of art and architecture damaged in the War. In addition, taught monument preservation at the Berlin Technical University. Died 1957 in Berlin.

Literature: Larissa A.Shadowa: Hinnerk Scheper und Boris Ender im Maljarstroj. Über Verbindungen von Mitarbeitern des Bauhauses und sowjetischen Künstlern. In: Wissenschaftliche Zeitschrift der Hochschule für Architektur und Bauwesen. Weimar. 26.1979. No.4/5

Oskar Schlemmer, 1888-1943
Painter
Born 1888 in Stuttgart. Apprentice draughtsman in a workshop for inlay work from 1903 to 1905. Then studied at the Stuttgart Academy until 1909. From 1912 to 1914, pupil of Adolf Hoelzel in Stuttgart. Active service from 1914 to 1918, then returned to study with Hoelzel until 1920. As from 1920, worked on costume sketches for his first theatre production, the 'Triadic Ballet', premièred in Stuttgart in 1922. Master at the Bauhaus from 1921 to 1929; head of the mural-painting workshop until 1922, the stone-sculpture workshop as from 1921 and the wood-carving workshop from 1922 to 1925. Head of the theatre workshop from 1923 until its closure in 1929. Life

Hinnerk Scheper, around 1928

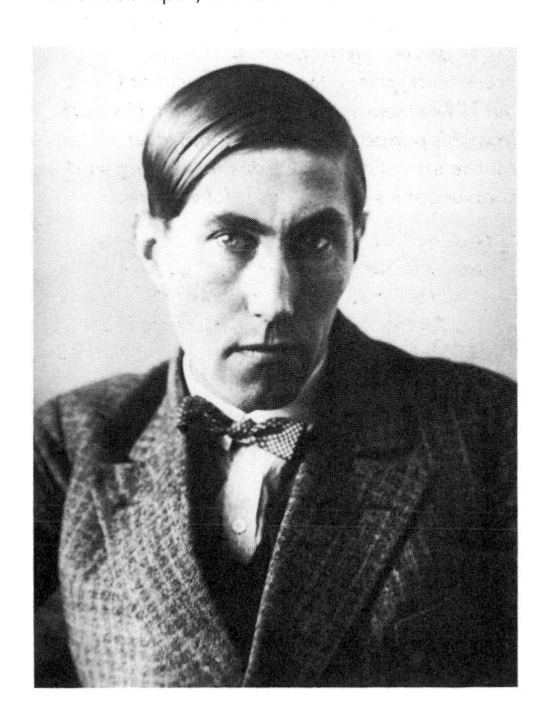

Oskar Schlemmer, 1941/42

Joost Schmidt, around 1930

classes and, in 1928/29, 'Man' course. Toured Germany and Switzerland with the Bauhaus theatre workshop in 1928/29. As well as productions of his 'Bauhaus Dances', activities during this period included painting, mural design and sets for the Berlin Kroll Opera and others. Between 1929 and 1932, professor at the Breslau Academy, head of the theatre class and 'Man and space' course. Then professor at the Combined State Art Schools in Berlin until his dismissal in 1933. Moved to Eichberg, later to Sehringen/Baden. From 1938, earned living from mural decoration; from 1940, worked for the Herberts paint factory in Wuppertal. Died 1943 in Baden-Baden.

Literature: Karin von Maur: Oskar Schlemmer. Œuvrekatalog der Gemälde, Aquarelle, Pastelle und Plastiken. Munich 1979
Karin von Maur: Oskar Schlemmer. Monograph. Munich 1979
Oskar Schlemmer. The Baltimore Museum of Art exhibition catalogue. Baltimore 1986
Dirk Scheper: Oskar Schlemmer – Das triadische Ballett und die Bauhausbühne. Schriftenreihe der Akademie der Künste, vol. 20. Berlin 1989

Joost Schmidt, 1893-1948
Typographer and sculptor
Born 1893 in Wunstorf/Hanover. In 1910, began studying at the Grand-Ducal Saxon Academy of Fine Art in Weimar; as a pupil of Max Thedy, awarded master's diploma for painting. Active service from 1914 to 1918. Student at the Bauhaus from autumn 1919 to April 1925; training in the wood-carving workshop under Itten and Schlemmer. First typographical works from 1923. Teacher at the Bauhaus from 1925 to October 1932. Head of the sculpture workshop from October 1925 until its closure in April 1930; head of the advertising department as from May 1928. Taught 'Lettering' course for first-semester students from 1925, plus life drawing in 1929/30 and 'Nude and figure drawing' for senior students from October 1930. Moved from Dessau to Berlin in 1933. Together with Gropius, designed the Non-Ferrous Metals section of the 'German Nation, German Work' exhibition in Berlin in 1934. Rented a studio in Berlin and worked as a cartographer in a publishing house. In 1935, taught at the Reimann school under Hugo Häring. Subsequently banned from teaching; employed on occasional basis. Charlottenburg studio destroyed in 1943. Active service in 1944/45. In 1945, appointed professor at the Berlin Academy of Fine Art by Max Taut to teach preliminary course for architects. Together with a group of Bauhäusler, designed the exhibition 'Berlin plans' in 1946. In 1947/48, invited by the USA Exhibition Center to design exhibitions. Plans for a Bauhaus exhibition and a Bauhaus book. Died 1948 in Nuremberg.

Literature: Joost Schmidt. Lehre und Arbeit am Bauhaus 1919-1932. Düsseldorf 1984
Bauhaus. Drucksachen Typografie Reklame. Gerd Fleischmann (ed.). Düsseldorf 1984

Lothar Schreyer, 1886-1966
Author, dramaturg, painter
Born 1886 in Blasewitz/Dresden. Studied art history and law at the universities of Heidelberg, Berlin and Leipzig. Doctorate in jurisprudence in 1910. Growing interest in aspects of art and theatre; began painting. From 1911 to 1918, dramaturg and assistant producer at the Deutsches Schauspielhaus in Hamburg. Worked with Herwarth Walden, head of the Berlin gallery 'Der Sturm', from 1914; editor of 'Der Sturm' journal from 1916 to 1928. Founded the 'Sturm-Bühne', an Expressionist experimental theatre, with Walden in 1918. After the War, Schreyer ran this theatre as the 'Kampf-Bühne' in Hamburg. Performances of the stage works 'Crucifixion', 'Man' and 'Infant death'. Appointed Bauhaus Master in 1921, where he ran the theatre work-

Lothar Schreyer

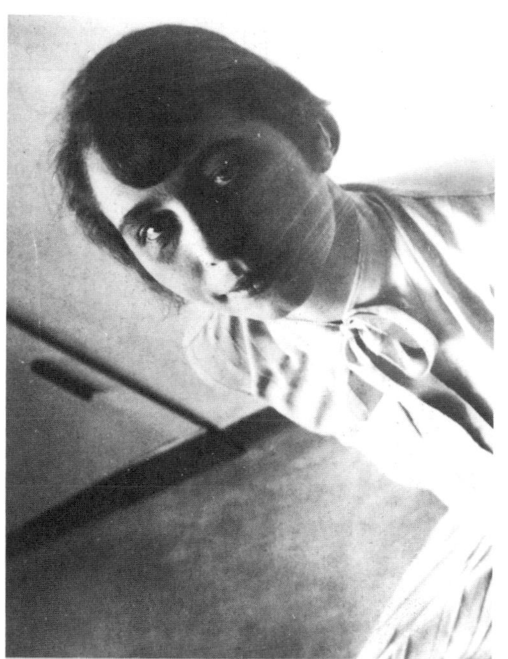

Gunta Stölzl, 1927

shop. Left the school at the beginning of 1923 following the bad reception of his 'Moonplay' production. Between 1924 and 1927, teacher and for a while head of the art school 'Der Weg' in Berlin. From 1928 to 1931, senior reader at the Hanseatic publishing company in Hamburg. In 1933, Schreyer converted to Catholicism and subsequently devoted himself to writing, chiefly addressing aspects of Christian art. Died 1966 in Hamburg. Schreyer's theatre works from the period around 1920 reflected cultic Expressionist beliefs which by 1922/23 were already conflicting with the move at the Bauhaus away from Expressionism towards a supra-individual and objective formal language. With his view of the work of art as an 'annunciation from the spiritual world' of a nation and an age, Schreyer turned in the thirties to Christian mysticism and racial ideas and ultimately came close to National Socialist ideologies.

Literature: Lothar Schreyer: Erinnerungen an Sturm und Bauhaus. Hamburg and Berlin 1956
Lothar Schreyer: Hoffnung auf eine neue Welt. In: Bauhaus und Bauhäusler. Bekenntnisse und Erinnerungen. Eckhard Neumann (ed.). Bern and Stuttgart 1971

Gunta Stölzl, 1897-1983
Weaver
Born 1897 in Munich. Studied at the Munich School of Arts and Crafts from 1914 to 1916. Worked in a field hospital from 1916 to 1918. Resumed studies at the School of Arts and Crafts in 1919. Student at the Bauhaus from October 1919 to 1925; attended Itten's 'Vorkurs' and classes with Klee. Studied in the weaving workshop. Journeyman's examination as weaver in 1922/23. In Herrliberg/Zürich from January to September 1924 to set up and run the Ontos weaving workshops. Teacher at the Bauhaus from October 1925 to September 1931. Master of Craft in the weaving workshop then – as from April 1927 – overall charge of the workshop. Together with fellow Bauhäusler Gertrud Preiswerk and Heinrich-Otto Hürlimann, founded the 'S-P-H-Stoffe' handloom weaving mill in Zürich in 1931; in collaboration with architects, produced furnishing materials and carpets. Weaving mill closed in 1933, and 'S-H-Stoffe' founded in the same year. Following the departure of her partner, Hürlimann, in 1937, she ran the weaving mill single-handedly as 'Sh-Stoffe, Handweberei Flora'. From 1950, renewed concentration upon gobelins. Gave up weaving mill in 1967, continued work on wall tapestries. Died 1983 in Küsnacht/Switzerland. Gunta Stölzl was the most important weaver at the Bauhaus, supporting and influencing the transition from pictorial individual pieces to modern industrial designs. Among her most outstanding works are the wall tapestries in which she translated the forms taught by Itten and Klee into her weaving.

Literature: Gunta Stölzl. Weberei am Bauhaus und aus eigener Werkstatt. Bauhaus-Archiv exhibition catalogue. Berlin 1987

I would like to thank my colleagues Peter Hahn, Klaus Weber and Karsten Hintz, as well as Karin Albers and Manfred Ludewig, for their help and advice.
Particularly warm thanks are due to Winfried Nerdinger for his generous comments, important suggestions and personal support. M.D.

8AB

126 and 127: Photos Lucia Moholy; BHA
128 above: Photo Lucia Moholy; BHA Inv. 6338/3
128 below: Photographer unknown; BHA Inv. 9886-15
129 above: Photographer unknown; BHA
129 below: Photographer unknown; BHA Inv. 10063/3
130 above: Photographer unknown; BHA Inv. F 8221
130 below: Photographer unknown; Centre Pompidou, Paris
131 above: Collection The Josef Albers Foundation
131 below: Photo Lucia Moholy; Felix Klee, Bern
132: Photo Musche, Dessau; BHA Inv. 6010/1
133 above: Photo Musche, Dessau; BHA Inv. 6040/4
133 below: Photo Otto Wedekind, Dessau; BHA Inv. 7671
134: Object BHA Inv. 10612; photo Atelier Schneider
135: Photographer unknown; Centre Pompidou, Paris
136: Object BHA Inv. 3257/1 and 2435 CB; photo Atelier Schneider
137: Object BHA Inv. 2435 (B); photo Atelier Schneider
138: Objects Staatsgalerie Stuttgart
139: Object BHA
140: Photographer unknown; BHA Inv. 3336/1
141: Photo Umbo; Collection The Josef Albers Foundation
142: Object BHA Inv. 1686; photo Atelier Schneider
143: Photographer unknown; BHA Inv. 6460
144 above: Object BHA Inv. 4669; photo Kiessling
144 below: Photo BHA
145 above: Object BHA Inv. 4671; photo Kiessling
146 above: Object BHA Inv. 580; photo Atelier Schneider
146 below: Object BHA Inv. 3243/13; photo Atelier Schneider
147: Object BHA Inv. 582; photo Lepkowski
148: Reproduced from: Offset. 1926.7
149 above: Object BHA Inv. 7425; photo Lepkowski
149 below: Reproduced from: Offset. 1926.7
150: Object BHA Inv. 1475; photo Lepkowski
151: Photo Lotte Stam-Beese; BHA Inv. 8082/36
152: Photos Erich Consemüller
153: Object Yamawaki estate; photo Knoll, Japan
154 left: Photo Lucia Moholy; BHA
154 right: Photo Lucia Moholy; BHA
155: Object BHA Inv. 1530; photo Lepkowski
156: Object BHA Inv. 578; photo Atelier Schneider
157: Photographers unknown; BHA
158: Photo Irene Bayer; BHA Inv. 8935
159 above: Photo Erich Consemüller; BHA Inv. 3252/20
159 below: Photo Erich Consemüller; copy in BHA
160: Photo Lux Feininger; private collection
162: Object BHA Inv. 2948/1; photo Atelier Schneider
163: Photo Hugo Erfurth; BHA Inv. 5244/1
164: Photographer unknown; Deutsches Architekturmuseum, Frankfurt
166: Object BHA Inv. 7529
167: Photo Hermann Bunzel (?); BHA
168/169: Redrawing of a copy from the Hochschule für Architektur und Bauwesen Weimar, GDR
170: Photo Judith Kárász; BHA
171: Photo Etel Fodor Mittag; BHA Inv. 10043/2-3
172: Photo Werner Zimmermann; BHA
173: Object in private collection; photo Lepkowski
174: Object in private collection; photo Lepkowski
175: Object Bauhaus Dessau, GDR; photo Lepkowski
176 left: Object BHA Inv. 3883; photo Lepkowski
176 right: Object BHA Inv. 3884; photo Lepkowski
177: Object Collection Liebetanz, Berlin; photo Lepkowski
178 left: Reproduced from: ReD special Bauhaus issue, 1930
178 and 179 below: Object BHA Inv. 3889/1-2; photo Lepkowski
179 above: Object BHA Inv. 2991; photo Atelier Schneider
180: Photographer unknown; BHA
181: Object BHA Inv. 7308; photo Lepkowski
182 above and 183: Photos in the Basel Kunsthalle
182 below: Photo in the Mannheim Kunsthalle
184: Kunstsammlung Nordrhein-Westfalen, Düsseldorf
185: Object BHA Inv. 8686/3; photo Lepkowski
186: Object BHA Inv. 10635; photo Atelier Schneider
187: Photographers unknown; BHA
188 left: Object BHA Inv. 7968; photo Atelier Schneider
188 right: Object BHA Inv. 4682; photo Hermann Kiessling
189: Object BHA Inv. 9755; photo Atelier Schneider
190: Photographer unknown; BHA
191 above: Reproduced from: bauhaus 2, 1928.4
191 below: Photographer unknown; BHA
192: Photo Arthur Redecker, Berlin; BHA Inv. F 3594
193: Photo Arthur Redecker; BHA Inv. F 3596
194 above and 195 above: Photos Walter Peterhans; BHA Inv. 8657/6
194 below: Photographer unknown; BHA
197 above: Photographer unknown; BHA Inv. 7680/1
197 below: Photo Eckhard Neumann; BHA
198 left: Photo Etel Fodor Mittag; BHA Inv. 10042/3
198 right: Photographer unknown; BHA
199: Object in BHA
200: Reproduced from: Baukunst, February 1930
201: Photo Lux Feininger; BHA Inv. 10044
202: Photo Etel Fodor Mittag; BHA Inv. 10043
205 left: Photo Werner Rohde; BHA Inv. F 6671
205 right: Object BHA Inv. 6229/1
206 and 207: Photographers unknown; BHA
208 and 209: Object BHA Inv. 7239
210: Photo Pius Pahl; BHA Inv. 2961-4
211: Object BHA Inv. 3487/2; photo Atelier Schneider
212: Object BHA
213: Object BHA Inv. 3488/2
214: Photographer unknown; BHA Inv. F 2319
215 above and below: Photos in BHA
216: Object BHA Inv. 3482/1
217: Object BHA
218: Object BHA Inv. 7299; photo Atelier Schneider
219: Object BHA Inv. 1640; photo Atelier Schneider
220: Object BHA Inv. 7837; photo Atelier Schneider
221: Object BHA Inv. 7453; photo Atelier Schneider
222: Photo Walter Peterhans; BHA Inv. 7216
223 above: Photographer unknown; BHA Inv. 3256/1
223 below: Photographer unknown; Yamawaki estate
224: Photographer unknown; Yamawaki estate
225: Object BHA Inv. 3987/1; photo Lepkowski
226: Object BHA Inv. 2961/2
229: Reproduced from: Berliner Tageblatt, autumn 1932
230: Photographer unknown; BHA
231: Object Yamawaki estate; photo Knoll, Japan
232: Reproduced from: Berliner Tageblatt, Oct. 1932
233: Photo Howard Dearstyne; BHA Inv. 8952
234 and 235: Photographs in BHA
236: Reproduced from: Berliner Lokalanzeiger, 12.4.1933
237: Photographer unknown; BHA
238 above: Object BHA
238 below: Photo Pius Pahl; BHA Inv. 2962/2
239: Photographer unknown; BHA Inv. 6546
242 left: Photo Ernst Louis Beck; BHA
242 right: Photographer unknown; BHA
243 left: Photo Irene Bayer; BHA
243 right: Photographer unknown; BHA
244 left: Photo Irene Bayer; BHA
244 right: Photographer unknown; BHA
245 left: Photo E.Bieber; BHA
245 right: Photographer unknown; BHA
246 left: Photo dephot; BHA
246 right: Photo Paula Stockmar; BHA
247 left: Photo Hugo Erfurth; BHA
247 right: Photo Hugo Erfurth; BHA
248 left: Photographer unknown; BHA
248 right: Photo Lotte Stam-Beese; BHA
249 left: Photographer unknown; BHA
249 right: Photo Lucia Moholy; BHA
250 left: Photo Lucia Moholy; BHA
250 right: Photo Grete Stern; BHA
251 left: Photo Ernst Louis Beck; BHA
251 right: Photo Lucia Moholy; BHA
252 left: Photo Casca Schlemmer; BHA
252 right: Photo Grete Reichardt; BHA
253 left: Photographer unknown; BHA
253 right: Photographer unknown; BHA